MULTILINGUAL MATTERS 96
Series Editor: Derrick Sharp

Language Education for Intercultural Communication

Edited by

Dennis Ager, George Muskens
and Sue Wright

MULTILINGUAL MATTERS LTD
Clevedon • Philadelphia • Adelaide

Library of Congress Cataloging in Publication Data

Language Education for Intercultural Communication/Edited by Dennis Ager, George Muskens and Sue Wright
p. cm. (Multilingual Matters: 96)
Based on conferences held in Dubrovnik in 1990 and in Pécs in 1991 as part of the Vienna Centre's program on multilingualism and ethnicity in Europe.
Includes bibliographical references.
1. Language and languages–Study and teaching–Europe–Congresses.
2. Multilingualism–Europe–Congresses. 3. Intercultural communication–Europe–Congresses. 4. Language policy–Europe–Congresses. I. Ager, D.E.
II. Muskens, George. III. Wright, Sue. IV. European Coordination Centre for Research and Documentation in Social Sciences. V. Series: Multilingual Matters (Series): 96.
P57.E9L36 1993
306.4'46'094–dc20

British Library Cataloguing in Publication Data

A CIP catalogue record for this book is available from the British Library.

ISBN 1-85359-190-4 (hbk)
ISBN 1-85359-204-8 (pbk)

Multilingual Matters Ltd

UK: Frankfurt Lodge, Clevedon Hall, Victoria Road, Clevedon, Avon BS21 7SJ.
USA: 1900 Frost Road, Suite 101, Bristol, PA 19007, USA.
Australia: P.O. Box 6025, 83 Gilles Street, Adelaide, SA 5000, Australia.

Printed and bound in Great Britain by the Longdunn Press, Bristol.

Language Ed[illegible]
for Intercultur[illegible]

Multilingual Matters

Attitudes and Language
COLIN BAKER
Breaking the Boundaries
EUAN REID and HANS H. REICH (eds)
Called unto Liberty
COLIN H. WILLIAMS
Cultural Studies and Language Learning
M. BYRAM, V. ESARTE-SARRIES and S. TAYLOR
Cultural Studies in Foreign Language Education
MICHAEL BYRAM
ESL: A Handbook for Teachers and Administrators in International Schools
EDNA MURPHY (ed.)
European Models of Bilingual Education
HUGO BAETENS BEARDSMORE (ed.)
Immigrant Languages in Europe
GUUS EXTRA and LUDO VERHOEVEN (eds)
Investigating Cultural Studies in Foreign Language Teaching
M. BYRAM and V. ESARTE-SARRIES
Life in Language Immersion Classrooms
ELIZABETH B. BERNHARDT (ed.)
Linguistic and Communicative Competence
CHRISTINA BRATT-PAULSTON
Linguistic Minorities, Society and Territory
COLIN H. WILLIAMS (ed.)
Multilingualism and Nation Building
GERDA MANSOUR
One Europe - 100 Nations
ROY N. PEDERSEN
Opportunity and Constraints of Community Language Teaching
SJAAK KROON
Second Language Acquisition and Language Pedagogy
ROD ELLIS
Sociolinguistic Perspectives on Bilingual Education
CHRISTINA BRATT PAULSTON
Tasks and Language Learning
GRAHAM CROOKES and SUSAN M. GASS (eds)
Tasks in a Pedagogical Context
GRAHAM CROOKES and SUSAN M. GASS (eds)
The World in a Classroom
V. EDWARDS and A. REDFERN

Please contact us for the latest book information:
Multilingual Matters Ltd,
Frankfurt Lodge, Clevedon Hall,
Victoria Road, Clevedon,
Avon BS21 7SJ, England

LANGUAGE EDUCATION FOR INTERCULTURAL COMMUNICATION

Contents

PREFACE

This book is about the language education situation in a number of European countries. It took its origin from conferences in Dubrovnik in 1990 and Pecs in 1991, held as part of the Vienna Centre's programme on Multilingualism and Ethnicity in Europe. By the time the conference participants came to deliver their papers for the first version of the book, Europe had changed again, even from the major developments of November and December 1989. And by the time revised versions of the chapters had been obtained in early 1992, Europe was dramatically different, yet again: some participants found themselves in different nations from those they lived in in 1990; others in situations where the tensions and loyalties they had been describing in a somewhat detached fashion as part of their research had become live, hot and in some cases deadly lines of division. To an extent, this book is a collection of reports from the front: a snapshot of policies and practices in the throes of change.

The history of mankind could well be written in terms of the history of languages in contact. For us in 1992, empires continue to fall, economic, political and social transformation is under way, and the identification and investigation of the relationships between unifying and divisive factors at the level of the nation, the community and the individual are of major importance. Some of the language-related issues and their causes, and the educational and other policies which are their consequence, are identified and analysed in the European studies presented here. But the policies and practices of States differ even when confronting very similar situations, and the present book also enables comparisons and evaluations of recent data. As editors, we have thought it appropriate to set the scene and to attempt to draw conclusions in this portrait of contemporary Europe at a moment of drastic change.

Birmingham and Vienna, June 1992.

ACKNOWLEDGEMENTS

The Editors' thanks go particularly to the Inter-University Centre, Dubrovnik and the ISSC, Vienna, which brought together many of the collaborators in this volume and which fostered the exchange of ideas and experience which is so essential to scholarship. Both are experiencing difficult times: the Vienna Centre is now superceded by new funding mechanisms for pan-European contact and the IUC bombed and partially destroyed in the course of the current war in the former Yugoslavia. We sincerely hope that the IUC will rise like a phoenix from its ashes and that the works of the Vienna Centre will survive.

INTRODUCTION

Effective communication has always been the cornerstone of human cooperation and endeavour. In late twentieth century Europe it is of fundamental importance for the success of the individual, of communities, and of nations. For individuals, it is important to be able to participate in democratic and cultural processes, and to gain access to the labour market, without suffering the drawbacks of illiteracy or inadequate knowledge of standardised languages. Language competence has become a matter of vital importance as communities realign, severing former alliances, and reform, creating new groupings. Nations interact on the international scene, and must ensure that their political and economic interests are helped by adequate communication skills on the part of their representatives. Each of these political acts entails a re-evaluation of language policy and practice, including the long-term question of language education.

It is generally agreed (Fasold, 1984; Fishman et al, 1968) that individuals base their identity as a community - in an ethnic group, a nationality, a nation, or a State - on factors such as language, culture, religion and the strength of intra-group ties. While Europe is a long way from any form of coherence, even within the European Community, its ethnic, religious, linguistic and cultural relationships are rooted in traditions, migrations, commerce and political arrangements which form the background to the present volume. In this introduction we consider first the nature of the contemporary European language environment, then assess the contributions the present volume makes to study in sociolinguistics, language planning and education.

Migration and Organisation

The mix of peoples, religions and political organisations through history, which gives us our current mental map of Europe, is usually dated from the birth of Christ (cf Sellier and Sellier, 1991). After the Mediterranean civilisations of Greece and Rome, and during the first millennium three main groups of migrations of peoples have created us: the westward move of peoples from the steppes of central Asia, through the Ukraine to the Danubian plains; the exodus of Germanic tribes from the lower Danube towards the Rhine and the Rhone, moving through the Alps and the Pyrenees to establish themselves throughout the West; and the expansion of the Slavs from western Ukraine to the North and Russia, South to the Balkans, and West to Poland. The movements of the Vikings throughout coastal Western Europe and the Mediterranean, of the Anglo-Saxons to the UK, and of the Norman French to the UK, were comparatively minor by contrast, although their consequences have been important. Parallel to this, the westward expansion of the Arabs, conquering Jerusalem, Alexandria, North Africa, Spain and much of France, formed a southern boundary to Europe, which has underlined the geographical with cultural, and in due course, religious and intellectual contrasts.

The second millennium has seen less mass migration. Nonetheless the military threats and movements of armies, bringing linguistic and identity problems in their train, have been striking: the Mongols occupying Poland and Hungary before returning east in 1241, the 'Moorish' domination of Spain which ended only in the late 15th century; the Ottoman Empire expanding from the South to attack Poland in 1498 before being defeated at Vienna - but not until 1683, and continuing to control the Balkans and many of the Arab countries of the Middle East until 1918; the Swedes dominating the Baltic in the 17th century before being defeated by the expansion of the Russians in the 18th; the French sweeping East under Napoleon in the early 19th; the Germans expanding west in 1870, and in many directions in the early and mid twentieth century. And the European diaspora world-wide, whether through colonial, imperial or commercial expansion, has made European approaches, whether to politics, economics or even linguistic research, internationally understood.

In political and organisational terms, the movement - not necessarily development - was in the first instance from small and mobile tribal communities to the Roman Empire, spreading a common form of governance throughout Western Europe. From the disappearance of the Roman Empire, in northern and western Europe feudalism and fragmentation contrasted with Mediterranean Arab civilisation. Changes continued from the creation of strong regions and provinces through late medieval times to kingdoms and eventually larger Empires, unifying on the political level but very rarely so on the cultural, social or linguistic; Empires resulted more from marriages of members of the great dynasties than from any cultural affinity of their peoples. After 1789, the Nation-State, based on a more coherent and deliberate approach to identity, started to replace previous regionally-based political organisations, leading to the unification of France, Italy, Germany and elsewhere, and with the successive defeat and decline of the continental empires of Turkey, Austria-Hungary, Germany and Russia/Soviet Union, to problematic Nation-State formation in Central and Eastern Europe.

Versailles in 1918, and Potsdam in 1945, have created political frontiers based on the westward movement of the influence of the then Soviet Union and of Poland, while the unification of the Balkans had until recent times submerged conflicting identities. Two millennia then to recognise the political reality of national identities? To move from the indeterminate mass of Peoples, through the unifying force of Empires, to the crisp realities of Nations, based on affective nationalities defined through language, religion, and ethnic origin? To believe this is to accept a simplistic and dangerous view of history. But it becomes even more dangerous when the view is adopted that this progression from one form of political organisation to another is progress, and that its next stage is Regions, based not on nationalities but on smaller and more unified ethnic groups.

Why dangerous? Simply because in the modern world no political organisation can encapsulate all the facets of group identity, isolate itself from other such political organisations, nor prevent the osmosis and migration of individuals and groups from affecting its 'purity'. To say this is hardly new; it is unfortunate that it appears necessary, and to rehearse the underlying facts, in the face of contemporary events and attitudes, which have tended to sharpen cultural distinctions and differences. How far, though, is it possible to discover any form of unity in Europe?

The Language Criterion

It is true enough that most European languages fall into one of the seventeen main language phyla (cf Ruhlen, 1987). But within the same phylum (Indo-Hittite) appears also the extinct Hittite language, and within the same Indo-European family 9 groups, each fairly remote from the others in terms of today's communication needs: Armenian, Tocharian, the Indo-Iranian languages (including for example Hindi, Urdu, Punjabi and Romany, and Farsi, Pashto and Kurdish), Albanian, Greek, Italic, Celtic, Germanic, and Balto-Slavic (including Latvian and Russian). Hungarian and Finnish are in another phylum altogether (Finno-Ugric subgroup of the Uralic family of the Uralic-Yukaghir phylum). Basque remains a language isolate. 'Nearby' languages such as Georgian, Turkish and Arabic are classified in completely different phyla (Caucasian, Altaic and Afro-Asiatic). So there is little room, even if one completely ignores immigration taking place more recently than a thousand years ago, for any language-determined special character for Europe: genetically, and even typologically, many European languages are not related to each other. If one were to attempt to pursue any kind of language-based territorial definition of a unified Europe, one would need to exclude such central communities as the Basque country, Hungary and a good part of Scandinavia, and cast the definition wide even then. Conversely, setting the geographical boundaries of Europe at the Urals, at Gibraltar, or half-way through the Balkans, makes little sense in language terms.

Even in terms of numbers of speakers this criterion is not helpful. The history of colonialism and empire means that European language speakers are everywhere. Estimates suggest (Crystal, 1987, 359) that there are more than 1.6 billion people in the world who can speak English, and that of these at least 316 million have English as their first language. Likewise, Spanish mother-tongue speakers number about 250 million, German 100 million and French 70 million, so the first-language speakers of European languages far outnumber the 400 million or so population of territorial (Western, including the former East Germany) Europe itself.

Table 1
Number of speakers in language phyla

Phylum	Number of languages	Number of speakers
1. KHOISAN	31	120,000
2. NIGER-KORDOFANIAN	1,064	181,000,000
3. NILO-SAHARAN	138	11,000,000
4. AFRO-ASIATIC	241	175,000,000
5. CAUCASIAN	38	5,000,000
6. INDO-HITTITE	144	2 ,000,000,000
7. URALIC-YUKAGHIR	24	22,000,000
8. ALTAIC	63	250,000,000
9. CHUKCHI-KAMCHATKAN	5	23,000
10. ESKIMO-ALEUT	9	85,000
11. ELAMO-DRAVIDIAN	28	145,000,000
12. SINO-TIBETAN	258	1 ,000,000,000
13. AUSTRIC	1,175	293,000,000
14. INDO-PACIFIC	731	2,735,000
15. AUSTRALIAN	170	30,000
16. NA-DENE	34	202,000
17. AMERIND	583	18,000,000

Source: Ruhlen, 1987, 286-9

It is just as true on the level of individual languages that national boundaries do not correlate with linguistic frontiers. Not merely does the phenomenon of the dialect continuum mean that each dialect shades into the next, and that contiguous languages often do likewise - for example from West to East, from Brittany to Strasbourg - but language minorities subsist - oh so painfully! - within neighbouring States, demonstrating the lack of correlation between language areas and political organisation. The Hungarian speakers in Romania, Swedish in Finland, Turkish in Ukraine, and the intimate mixture of Serbs, Croats and others in the former Yugoslavia, even the range of linguistic minorities in apparently monolingual countries such as the UK or France, indicate the difficulty of simple language-frontier correlations.

Language minorities, speakers of a language different from that of the majority of the population of a State, are caused by one of three processes: the first, usually political, as when a frontier is established or moved (Alsace), an original population retains its language after conquest (Wales), or a conqueror leaves behind a sufficiently large group when the conquest is over (Hungary); a second, often economic, as when colonies are systematically established in conquered lands or for purposes of trade (German speakers on the Volga); and a third, less systematic, through immigration, creating a 'non-territorial' minority: Jews, Gypsies, more recently Poles or Portuguese or Algerians in France, Pakistanis or Bengalis in the UK. Language minorities are hence usually classified as 'indigenous', 'regional' or 'territorial', on the one hand, and 'non-territorial' on the other. Almost inevitably, the existence of a minority becomes a problem, both for the minority itself and also for the majority. The minority 'problem' can be solved, sometimes dramatically, as for example by language expulsions or mass movements such as the exchange of over a million people between Greece and Turkey in 1920-22 (1,140,000 Greeks left Turkey in 1920-22), more normally by assimilation and integration, which means the death of the minority language. Inevitably, minority language speakers tend to be bi- and multi-lingual; if there is any surprising feature in the study of language minorities, it is the the extent of their survival!

European languages are not static, either. Quite apart from the normal process of language change through time (in French, '*cohabitation*' has acquired a new meaning since 1986-88), European languages are subject to interference from languages in contact. At one level all are subject to the influence of English. French has adopted '*le management*' and '*faxer*', but has managed by pure genius to avoid 'software' (*le logiciel*). This English-based international lingua franca is not quite 'real' English, of course: native English speakers have to get used to constructions like 'The obtained results show it is useful to distinguish' or 'they export in countries' (quoted by Kassis, 1991, 15). Interference comes also from a second level: the range of immigrant languages - *couscous*, *bled* and *toubib*, derived from Arabic, are now normal French words. And the third level of interference is from - and to - indigenous regional languages, well-established territorial minorities: the Basques, the Catalans, the Frisians. Languages change also from the need to name new products and encapsulate new ideas (*le baladeur, rapper*). Languages which don't move, die, and any linguist knows that attempts at preservation (as Breton or Welsh) or re-creation (as Cornish, or Hebrew) have to cope with coining new terms for new realities, as well as developments in pronunciation and grammar. Language creativity cannot be prevented if language itself is to form part of a group's living experience; all these forms of influence contribute to the dynamism of the language spectrum, and few of them are subject to change or control by planning.

The tenacious hold on life of many European languages, particularly those in a minority situation, has depended on strong functional differentiation, on strong feelings of group identity, and on limited migration. Contemporary events may well affect all: the example of new freedoms of movement in Eastern and Central Europe, combined with economic pressures; and tendencies towards greater coherence within the European Community, mean that intergroup communication, in and across the new Europe, will however have to be managed through deliberate language policies. If the European Community wishes to become a 'nation', in Fishman's sense (quoted in Fasold, 1984, 2), whether it does so after or before any coherent sense of 'nationality' evolves, a language policy will be essential. The most obvious contenders for the role of 'international' language are English, in the form of the international lingua franca already mentioned, and German, although the Community institutions have a history of French-based communication. Outside the European Community, Russian was at one time moving towards the status of international lingua franca, replacing German which had generally held the role since the time of Bismarck. Whether German will recapture the role, or whether English/American will take over, only time will tell. Certainly a considerable effort, both financial and diplomatic, is now being expended by different countries in order to establish their own languages within Eastern Europe, with a clear eye to the political and commercial advantages.

The Religious Criterion

If language does not uniquely identify a population, are there other cultural symbols that do? Christianity is the main religion of Europe, following progressive conversion starting in the fourth century and continuing to the fourteenth when the Lithuanians adopted this religion. But which form of Christianity? Catholics and Protestants have long divided Europe on a North-South basis, with some outposts of Protestantism in Eastern Hungary/Romania, in those parts of these countries cut off by the Ottoman advance. The viciousness of this religious division is still with us, whether in Northern Ireland or elsewhere. But division among Christian groups exists also in the East: Orthodox Christianity, originating in the Byzantine empire, converted Russians and Slavs, and the invasion of the Mongols split the Orthodox churches between Moscow and Kiev. Although those recognising Kiev eventually reunited with the Orthodox Church, a certain degree of split is still present.

Islam has always been present in Europe. It has been rooted mainly in Asia Minor, with two million believers (speakers of Serbo-Croat) in Bosnia-Herzegovinia and in Macedonia. As a religion and a military power, it was eradicated by the Inquisition in Spain. Recent immigration, particularly to the UK and France, has brought Islam to the status of the second religion in France, and to, admittedly extremist, calls for the UK to establish a parallel Islamic State. The liberation of Algeria in 1962 provoked a flood of emigration of North African Jews to France, with major effects on the Jewish population in

France, where communities were recreated and synagogues founded in towns where there had been no Jewish presence since the Middle Ages. The Algerian election results of December 1991, and the victory of Islamic Fundamentalists in the first round, may affect the French situation even more in the future, either by giving greater strength to Muslims currently in France, by provoking yet more emigration of non-Muslims from Algeria, or by providing fuel for anti-Islamic groups on the French political Right.

Political ideologies, Marxism in particular, have been found wanting, and are equally unlikely to offer an effective unifying cultural symbol. But one should not be unaware of pan-European ideologies and spiritual movements which may exercise considerable attraction as religions decline.

Ethnic Origin: Customs and Cultures

We have noted already the mix and flow of 'original' peoples which underlie the present European population. Within individual countries, of course, the diversity of ethnic mix varies greatly, as does the strength of attachment people feel to their origins, often measured by the degree of attachment they maintain to their original language. It is a well-documented fact, for example, at least in the USA, that language shift rapidly affects economic refugees - although the Chinese/Hong Kong diaspora tends not to fully support this - while those from low-prestige linguistic areas (as seen from the host environment) are also subject to language loss. But generally European countries are now ethnically diverse, as indeed the following chapters show.

The simplest model of a multi-ethnic state (Fasold, 1984) is that outlined with reference to bilingualism: where only two languages are involved, either one of the two languages is in some sense dominant or there is equality between the two. 'Dominance' is commonly reflected in political, economic, cultural and social institutions, implies a prestige difference and leads to the marginalisation and exclusion of the minority group from mainstream society, often against a background of conflict and instability. 'Diglossia' or functional differentiation, as now broadly understood, offers an alternative to dominance, in that each language is used for different purposes and stability is the norm. Here the 'superior' language is the official, public and solemn form, while the 'inferior' is used for private, domestic and intimate circumstances, without necessarily creating a marginalised minority group. The conceptual dimension for this model lies in the distinction between societal, as opposed to individual, bilingualism: in the former, two monolingual groups coexist, while in the latter, a large proportion of the population uses both languages.

Since diglossia is normally stable, the outcome is mutual accommodation - which may even lead in some circumstances to linguistic accommodation, each language 'lending' or 'borrowing' terms and concepts, so that essentially new languages are being created. An example would be the languages of urban youth in the UK, where Indian and various South Asian languages intermingle and interfere, or the adoption of new forms of 'verlan' by French urban youth. In nations with large populations, or in situations where the prestigious form becomes cut off from its base - English in India, Norman French in England - the eventual outcome may be a new language. Indeed the process is exactly that by which present European languages such as French or English have been formed.

A second possible outcome is that one group can lose its language (language loss or shift) and perhaps - but not necessarily - its separate identity, to be assimilated to the other (assimilation/integration, forming a monolingual and perhaps a monocultural State). This should logically be the outcome for a language perceived as 'inferior', and is indeed happening particularly among well-established immigrant groups in the USA. The 'inferior' language need not necessarily be the language of the minority, or that of the politically subject, as witness the disappearance of the Germanic tongues of those who conquered Gaul, or of the Norman French of those who conquered England in 1066.

In other circumstances, each group can maintain its separate identity (pluriculturalism), with mutual understanding and respect (interculturalism) or without it, and with or without a change from or to societal and individual bilingualism - pluricultural societies are not necessarily plurilingual. Finally, the groups can maintain and strengthen their separate identity, forming a federation, a multi-nation State or some other form of political association, as indeed happens in contemporary Belgium; or discarding this latter altogether to achieve full territorial independence.

Not surprisingly, different traditions, customs and habits have generated different outward forms of behaviour, and sometimes these behaviours can seem all-important indicators of identity. Dress styles, food, the appearance of the countryside - all can be observed, described and classified, noting factors of difference, the boundary markers; and also noting the opposite, the unifying or similarity factors. To establish a typology of cultures was a detailed process, similar to that involved in establishing a typology of languages: laborious and minute comparison and contrast of behavioural forms leading to a taxonomy.

Such approaches are not by any means discredited today, and an external observer's sketch of contemporary Europe is certainly possible. It would outline those aspects of the area which distinguish it from the USA, the Pacific rim, or Africa, and identify the political, economic, social and cultural institutions, processes and artefacts which define Europe. There are undoubtedly sufficient internal similarities to unite all the geographical area from the Atlantic to the Urals, and at least from the northernmost part of Scandinavia to the Mediterranean, and to differentiate it from the Indian sub-continent, from Africa, or from Asia.

A more common methodological approach today would be that of the ethnographer, noting Fishman's three 'Ps': paternity, or history and traditions; patrimony, or the learned cultural patterns of the group; and phenomenology, or the perceptions and reference groups of the individual citizen, his customs and habits, and the values these represent. With the spread of European values world-wide this would however make it much more difficult to establish what differentiates us from the African or the Japanese. Customs and habits are the outward symbols of social meanings, and not all national traits have disappeared or become indistinguishably European, despite our largely common history and our largely similar values, attitudes and beliefs. Even between two such very similar Western societies as France and Britain, cultural differences fundamentally affect business, for example:

> If we take ...France's Jacques Calvet, head of the Peugeot group...we see an embodiment of the 'French dream'...graduate of the Ecole Nationale d'Administration...head of the personal staff of former President Valéry Giscard d'Estaing while Giscard was Finance Minister, and later heading the Banque Nationale de Paris, the largest state-owned bank...Calvet has admitted to being...too Cartesian... 'I am too logical, not sufficiently directed by intuition'...he is representative of a tradition which puts a premium on educated cleverness and intellectual rigour. Contrast this with Britain's traditional emphasis on social skills and pragmatism. Is it any surprise that Britain's best-known industrialist is Sir John Harvey-Jones?...These differences are likely to persist beyond 1992.
> *Calori and Lawrence, 1991, 202*

Language Education for Intercultural Communication

The case studies on language education practice which follow seek to identify common problems, different approaches and different solutions; and through a process of comparison and evaluation, examine how far European policy makers and practitioners may find common ground. The approaches of the contributors are not uniform, and no single underlying attitude to the issues and concerns of relevant disciplines can be expected. We have deliberately chosen to offer a selection of valuable national contributions that fit together more as a patchwork than as a straight report of cross-national comparative research.

The latter, difficult enough when research is undertaken with a clear disciplinary, terminological and methodological focus, is doubly difficult when research comes from divergent disciplines like linguistics, education and the social sciences, when national institutions and discourse differ quite fundamentally among the countries involved and particularly when they are undergoing rapid processes of change. This is most obviously the case with the post-communist world. Here, we concentrate on the presentation of preliminary national reports on a wide spectrum of issues related to language education, multilingualism, national and minority identities as well as to cross-cultural communication, giving eyewitness accounts of practices, effects and policy concerns. The conclusions the Editors derive are more concerned with general, power-related aspects of national and regional arrangements for language education, the underlying attitudes of learning and using different languages, different educational policies in European countries and our views on further research policies and strategies.

Ludo Beheydt, of the Université Catholique of Louvain, studies Belgium, a trilingual country whose population is largely monolingual, and which has adopted legislation to manage conflict and introduced territorially defined language policies. The recent arrival of a significant number of immigrants further complicates the linguistic landscape. The author examines language attitudes to bilingualism, the relative success of different groups within the schools, and considers the requirements for a workable model of a multicultural, multilingual and multiethnic community.

In two chapters from the Bulgarian Academy of Sciences and the Agricultural Academy, Sofia, Madeleine Danova and colleagues first describe the language education situation obtaining in 1990 and 1991, and then note that the profound political changes over the past two years have meant a reversal in language education policies and a great desire for satisfactory theoretical underpinning. The opening of the educational system which was geared to the diffusion of Russian as first foreign language has instituted a change to Western European languages, in particular English; but also has affected cultural preferences and created a desire both to understand and to absorb different cultural models. The authors stress the importance in foreign language education of the cultural dimension, and underline the extent to which a whole society can develop a hunger for intercultural understanding through language.

Sue Wright, of Aston University, notes, in her study of England, the ways in which a traditionally monolingual country with a history of poor performance in language learning seeks to come to terms with its new linguistic minorities and its partnership in a multilingual economic community. She analyses a number of underlying dichotomies affecting language learning: between State and Independent schools, between girls and boys, and between languages chosen, and follows recent reforms of the educational system and their implications for language learning.

The question of Finnish and Swedish is investigated by Eero Laine, of the University of Jyväsklä. He notes that the problem is clouded by questions of prestige, and examines how perceptions of status, attitudes, choice and motivations cannot be ignored in questions of language policy. His analysis of affective factors: motivation, attitudes, stereotypes and self-notions, enables him to evaluate the nature of this filter to effective language learning.

In presenting France, Dennis Ager, of Aston University, observes that from 1789, French policy has been aimed at the creation of a coherent Nation State, accepting that this means the eradication of indigenous linguistic pluralism. This study focuses on how far this policy has also applied to contemporary regional and immigrant groups, and to Government policy in relation to the teaching of regional and immigrant languages as well as to that of French as a second language.

The 1977 EC directive on the language of education for linguistic minorities has been more rigorously applied by certain of the German Länder than in any other country, as Ingrid Gogolin of the University of Hamburg observes. The author examines the motives for this, looking at attitudes towards political and economic immigrants and the problems caused both by the continuing integration of the former DDR and of 'returning' Germans whose ancestors left Germany, in some cases in medieval times.

Szofia Radnai of the Institute of Linguistics in Budapest and Pécs University, studies the Hungarian linguistic situation, noting that Hungary is a special case in that the linguistic minorities with which it is most concerned are not within the country's borders: several million Hungarian mother tongue speakers live in neighbouring countries and must fight to safeguard their linguistic rights. Two foreign languages compete in popularity, while newly discovered mobility and freedom of trade influence the language-using situation as well.

Although relatively cohesive in terms of population with only two indigenous languages, the Dutch have not remained rigidly monolingual. The emphasis in this case study by Maria Oud-de Glas and colleagues, of the Institute for Applied Social Sciences of the University of Nijmegen, is on the motivations of a small trading country towards the languages of its trading partners, and on the identification of language need and language knowledge in the country.

In presenting the complex linguistic situation of the former USSR, Frances Knowles, of Aston University, notes the origin of language planning, its relationship with political ideology and practical politics, and the effects, both of domination by Russian speakers and of the drastic political events of the past two years. Using the census results from the last, 1989 census, he describes the ethno-linguistic swan song of the USSR, and poses a number of the questions which are fundamental, not merely to the future of the new Republics emerging from the USSR, but also to the whole of Eastern and Central Europe.

The Ukraine is another example of linguistic diversity and is witnessing a renascent movement for expression of national identity as central Soviet power weakens. Oleg Shamshur, of the Ukrainian Academy of Sciences, documents the demands for the restitution of linguistic rights and seeks to predict how far new language laws will enable a formerly repressed and dominated language to rediscover an official role, without itself adopting repressive solutions.

Ranko Bugarski, of the University, of Belgrade, first presents an overview of the situation in Yugoslavia as it was just before the recent problems erupted. The diversity of language and culture in Yugoslavia makes it a rich environment for research on language contact and conflict, and the mosaic of nations, nationalities, languages and educational practice has always provided fascination for the analyst. Bugarski then comments with sadness on the contemporary situation, and expresses the hope that present turbulence will nonetheless permit the survival of democracy and effective intercultural communication.

In studying Slovenia Albina Nećak Lük, of the University of Ljubljana, evaluates the current situation regarding Italian, Hungarian and Slovenian, and considers that existing and proposed legislation is making appropriate provision for language and identity maintenance among majorities and minorities in the new Republic.

Svenka Savić and Zlata Jukić of Novi Sad, discuss new trends in educational policy in Serbia from 1990 to the present. New language laws imposing requirements for learning Serbo-Croat where previously minority languages had been rather more freely available may lead to a number of possible outcomes: to conflict perhaps, although it is questioned whether previous multi-lingual policies contributed to reducing linguistic conflicts; to a different view of the practicalities of living in multilingual regions, although contrasts between the proposed policies and results from world-wide research on bilingualism are clearly indicated.

References

Clanet, C. 1990. *L'interculturel. Introduction aux approches interculturelles en Education et Sciences Humaines*. Toulouse: Presses Universitaires du Mirail

Crystal, D. 1987. *The Cambridge Encyclopedia of Language*. Cambridge: Cambridge University Press

Fasold, R. 1984. *The Sociolinguistics of Society*. Oxford: Basil Blackwell

Fishman, J., Ferguson, C. and Das Gupta, J. (eds.) 1968. *Language problems of developing nations*. New York: John Wiley

Kassis, J. H. 1991. European English - an emerging norm for native and non-native speakers. *La Tribune Internationale des Langues Vivantes*, 8: 15

Ruhlen, M. 1987. *A Guide to the World's Languages*. Stanford: Stanford University Press

Sellier, A. and Sellier, J. 1991. *Atlas des Peuples d'Europe Centrale*. Paris: La Découverte

Tollefson, J. W. 1991. *Planning language, planning inequality*. London: Longman

SECOND LANGUAGE LEARNING IN BELGIUM

L. Beheydt *Université Catholique de Louvain*

One of the major challenges for the future Europe will be the development of a workable model for a multicultural, multi-ethnic and multilingual community. Europe is a patch-work of languages and cultures and the continuing migration waves contribute to its kaleidoscopically changing pattern. As an illustration of the complexity of this challenge, Belgium is a textbook case. Officially Belgium is a trilingual country, where the three languages - French, Dutch and German - enjoy equality which is guaranteed by a series of language laws. This official trilingual situation is moreover affected by the presence of immigrant languages. Both the trilingual and the immigrant situation produce bilingual children, whose condition is however hardly comparable: the differences in their situation are closely related to socio-economic expectations and esteem factors, while school provision and particularly the bilingual approach in it does not adequately respond to these factors. This statement obviously requires some explanation.

The 10 million inhabitants of Belgium are made up of two main language groups: 40% French-speaking Walloons in the south and east of the country (Wallonia), and 60% Dutch-speaking Flemings in the north and west of the country (Flanders). The German-speaking minority, about 1% of the population, lives in a small eastern area. Then there is the capital city of Brussels, situated in Flanders, and an officially bilingual French-Dutch area but which is in reality majority French speaking.

To complicate the picture even more we have to add that in January 1989 almost 9% of the population had a foreign nationality although in Flanders this was only 4%. But these percentages are increasing.

The major groups of immigrants are Italians, Moroccans, French and Turks. Of the Italians almost three-quarters live in Wallonia, of the Moroccans 55% live in Brussels and almost half of the Turks live in Flanders. About half of the Belgian immigrant population was born in Belgium. The immigrant population is growing rapidly, due to dependants joining family members already settled, and a higher birth rate.

Within the immigrant groups there are great differences in linguistic attitudes. Italians learn either French or Dutch readily and seem to have no difficulty in integrating with the Flemish or Walloon population. The North African groups on the other hand seem to maintain their original language as much as possible.

The Inter Ministry Work Group for Migrants which was set up in 1988 under a Royal Commissioner for Migration Policy, has recently decided to oblige long term unemployed migrants to learn either Dutch or French.

This obligation is one more official language regulation which has to be accommodated with the two series of language laws (1932 and 1963) that have been enacted to settle the difficult language question in Belgium (cf Lindemans et al, 1981). The linguistic balance is maintained on the basis of the *personality principle* and the *territorial principle* (Grosjean, 1982, 12). The territorial principle is invoked to divide the country into three different monolingual areas, each with its own official language used by the administration and in the schools. The personality principle then is used to settle language use in the Brussels area. The personality principle states that bilingualism is the official policy in that area. Thus a speaker in the district of Brussels-Capital can use either French or Dutch to deal with the administration and can have his or her children educated in either of the two languages.

As far as education is concerned the Language Law of July 30th 1963 literally states that 'The language of education is Dutch in the Dutch-speaking area, French in the French-speaking area and German in the German-speaking area' (Article 4). For the district of Brussels-Capital, Article 5 of the same law states that 'the language of education is either Dutch or French according to the choice of the head of the family, if the latter lives in the district referred to'.

Further articles of that same law provide for the teaching of the official second language in the different areas. In the unilingual territories the second language may be taught in primary school from the 5th year on, for at most three hours a week (Article 9). In the bilingual district of Brussels-Capital the teaching of the second language is obligatory in the primary schools, for three hours a week in the second degree and for five hours a week in the third and the fourth degree (Article 10).

All these articles have created special forms of early bilingual education that do not fully coincide with the well known models of 'immersion' or 'submersion' (Ervin-Tripp, 1970; Grosjean, 1982, 208-20; Swain, 1981, 16-17). The territorial principle which has been invoked to allow each language group to protect its own language officially prevents education being given in the minority language. Thus the French-speaking minority is no longer allowed to have education in French in the Dutch-speaking territory. Neither does this regulation allow for the teaching of any other first language in primary school. Hence at the present time, no minority group can have its mother tongue taught in early school education. This legally regulated situation largely prevents the introduction of a *transition programme* (where the minority language is taught in the initial years of education) or of a *language maintenance programme* (where the minority language is taught throughout the school curriculum).

The consequence is that from kindergarten on, French-speaking children enter into Dutch language classrooms and Dutch-speaking children enter into French language classrooms and are mixed together with children who are native speakers of the target language. In this respect these children find themselves in a submersion position in that they are handicapped from the very start. Objectively, their position is the same as the submerged position of the Italian, the Moroccan or the Turkish immigrant children who cannot begin on an equal footing with native language speaking classmates either.

Yet there is generally a clear difference between the submerged position of the immigrant child and the position of the French-speaking child in Flanders or the Dutch-speaking child in Wallonia. Of course, their position is partly the same as their initial instruction is via the unknown majority language and as the programme aims at cultural assimilation. But due to esteem factors and socio-economic background, their position differs on a significant number of points.

The French-speaking or Dutch-speaking child is not dissociated from the indigenous culture which is very similar to that of the majority children. The Dutch-speaking majority children and the French-speaking children have the same religion, the same attitudes, beliefs and values. The immigrant child on the other hand is dissociated from its native culture. There is very often a culture clash in the child between the values, attitudes and life style of the majority group and those of the home community. Moreover, except for some lessons in religion there is no opportunity provided by the curriculum for lessons in the native language or culture of the immigrant children.

Secondly, the French-speaking or Dutch-speaking children belong to a prestigious and majority culture, whereas the culture and language of the immigrant minorities are not held in high regard. The parents of the French-speaking children belong to the upper or to the middle classes and as such they are well respected in the majority culture. The immigrant minorities on the other hand mostly belong to the lower socio-economic classes. They live in bad housing conditions and are often unemployed and poor.

The parents of the French-speaking or Dutch-speaking children are highly supportive of bilingual education. They believe that they must do everything possible to help their child become functionally bilingual. Their concern reflects the political and economic realities of their environment. The federal governmental policy leads to an increasing recognition and acceptance in both the French Community and the Flemish Community of the necessity of knowing 'the other country language'. This understanding is new among the

French-speaking Flemings. Only thirty years ago proficiency in Dutch was not a necessity, even in Flanders. A francophone could easily go to school in French and manage to do without Dutch even when dealing with local government and public services. Now the situation has changed. The parents of the French-speaking children in Flanders who belong to the leading socio-economic class, realise that becoming bilingual has become necessary to maintain their social and economic power in the monolingual situation that has been created by legal federalisation measures (State Reform 1971-1991) and political pressure. In the last twenty years Flanders has managed to create a unilingual Dutch-speaking community and the French-speaking minority elite in Flanders has very quickly adapted to this new situation. The middle-class French-speaking parents in Flanders have managed to raise their children bilingually, realising that their position depended on their success in learning the second language. The parents of immigrant children on the other hand are much less motivated to support their children's bilingualism. They feel the imposed bilingualism is an unavoidable nuisance rather than a socio-economic opportunity. Very often they experience the majority language and culture that are thrust on their children as threatening to their native language and culture.

For the French-speaking children who belong to a highly esteemed culture, learning Dutch as a second language does not pose a threat to their sense of cultural identity, nor to the maintenance of their mother tongue. Immigrant children on the other hand often feel that the majority look down on their culture and they hence turn their backs on their minority group in order to assimilate themselves to the majority. In that process they often lose their native language.

All this leads to different attitudes and behaviour on the part of the teachers towards French-speaking middle-class children and immigrant children. For French-speaking children, teachers have high expectations for the children's achievement, whereas in the case of immigrant children the expectations for the children's achievement are usually low and teachers are neither trained nor motivated to understand the specific problems of immigrant children. Moreover the teachers know or at least understand some French. And though they do not speak French in class, they are able to respond efficiently to the French-speaking child as they understand what the children say to them. With immigrant children the situation is different. As very few teachers understand Arabic or Turkish, the immigrant children are very often not understood or responded to in a way relevant to their situation. Consequently they feel insecure, lonely and rejected.

The respect for French, the official second language in Dutch-speaking territory, is also clear from the fact that French is taught as a second language from the fourth year of primary school on. So for the French-speaking child there is an element of mother tongue education. Moreover in addition to the regular French language component in the programme, parents very often provide extra courses to ensure the child acquires full literacy in French.

French remains, however, a second language; it is not the medium of instruction. For immigrant children their mother tongue (Turkish, Arabic, Italian, Greek) is never introduced in the course of education, either as a language of instruction or as a second language.

All in all, there seems to be 'real submersion' for immigrant children in the unilingual French- or Dutch speaking territory, whereas for the Dutch or French-speaking middle-class children the education is a mixed form of submersion and immersion. As in submersion the Dutch- or French-speaking children enter education together with the native language speaking majority children. On entrance they do not speak or understand the language used in the school, whereas for the other children the school language is their native language. This may of course slow down the initial learning of skills and of content. On the other hand the support of a highly motivated minority group, the general respect for their home language, the prestige of their background culture and the introduction of their home language in the course of the programme makes them comparable to children in monolingual immersion programmes. A very important difference between the immigrant ethnic minority children and the French-speaking middle-class children concerns the expectations of the teachers. Teachers have generally low expectations for the minority children, whereas they expect the French-speaking middle-class children to succeed. Such expectations tend to justify themselves in that the children adopt similar expectations for themselves. This phenomenon is known as 'the self-fulfilling prophecy syndrome' (Grosjean, 1982, 211).

On the whole this prophecy proves correct. French-speaking or Dutch-speaking middle-class minority children usually do better than ethnic minority children. Of the ethnic minority children, many fall behind in their school work and drop out of school; their bilingualism remains restricted.

The Dutch- or French-speaking minority children on the other hand develop a functional bilingualism without harming their home language development. And although their proficiency in Dutch or French is perhaps somewhat inferior to that of the native language speaking children, their academic achievement is not hampered.

Yet this apparent success of Dutch only, or French only, education must be interpreted with the utmost care. There is a tendency with policy-makers to cite this apparent success as evidence that monolingual education should work for *all* minority group children. A couple of fundamental aspects are overlooked if one adheres to such a tenuous generalisation. First of all this kind of submersion is only successful if all the special conditions that contribute to the success are present. This is not the case for the ethnic minority immigrant children and neither is it the case for *all* French- or Dutch-speaking middle-class children. What holds true for the group as a whole does not necessarily apply to all individuals in the group.

On the contrary, even the Ministry of Education recognises that there is an educational problem with a whole sub-group of French-speaking children. Teachers report that some of the French speaking children fail to adjust, that they fall behind when compared to monolingual children and that the initial handicap is becoming cumulative, so that bilingualism for some of them has obvious negative effects on their linguistic, cognitive and educational development. At this moment a project has been started to examine 'the lack of success and the educational failure of French-speaking children' in secondary schools in Flanders (Poel). The necessity for such a project is indicative of the existence of the problem and proves that obligatory submersion in the exclusively monolingual majority language education does not automatically lead to functional bilingualism. Up till now hardly anything has been published about this special group of bilingually educated children in Belgium. There is some literature on the acquisition of bilingual competence by immigrant children (Gailly and Leman, 1982) and there is a well-documented description of multilingual education in the European School of Brussels (Housen and Baetens Beardsmore, 1987) but research concerning French-speaking children acquiring Dutch through education has only just begun (De Schietere de Lophem, 1986; Beheydt, 1988) and the existing literature is either outdated or very general (François, 1967; Boileau, 1968; Bustamente, Van Overbeke and Verdoodt, 1978).

Of course, second language acquisition is a relatively new area of research and there is as yet no universally accepted research strategy. In a complex situation like the Belgian one, what we need first and foremost is a coherent and integrated model of second language learning that will permit the adequate description of the whole range of forms of bilingual education. A most promising model seems to me the *preference model* presented by Bernard Spolsky (1988). Basically, the preference model tries to capture the complex interaction of interlocking influences in second language learning. It is a comprehensive model in that it encompasses all the conditions relevant to second language learning and is flexible in that it attributes a differential value to each of the learning conditions, depending on its interaction with other conditions.

If the different forms of bilingual education can be described adequately by means of such a model, comparison of the forms becomes possible and variables that can be controlled may become apparent. In this sense 'criteria for finding more appropriate and so more efficient modes of intervention' may reveal themselves by using such a theoretical model and the development of a workable model for a multicultural, multi-ethnic and multilingual community may be facilitated.

References

Baetens Beardsmore, H. 1979. Bilingual education for highly mobile children. *Language Problems and Language Planning,* 3: 138-55

Baetens Beardsmore, H. 1980. Bilingual education in international schools, European schools and experimental schools: A comparative analysis. In: Lim Kiat Boey (ed.), *Bilingual Education.* Singapore, 3-19

Baetens Beardsmore, H., and Swain, M. 1985. Designing bilingual education. Aspects of immersion and 'European school' models. *Journal of Multilingual Development,* 6: 1-15

Beheydt, L. 1987. Het Certificaat Nederlands en Nederlands als Tweede Taal. *Voorzetten* 7. Groningen/Leuven

Beheydt, L. 1988. Early bilingualism in Belgium. *ABLA Papers,* 12: 207-27

Boileau, A. 1968. L'acquisition d'une langue seconde à l'age préscolaire. *Revue des Langues Vivantes,* 35, 6: 647-57

Bustamente, H. Van Overbeke, M. and Verdoodt, A. 1978. *Bilingual Education in Belgium.* Bruxelles: AIMAV

Cummins, J. 1979. Linguistic interdependence and the educational development of bilingual children. *Review of Educational Research,* 49: 222-51

Cummins, J. 1981. The role of primary language development in promoting educational success for language minority students. In: California State Department of Education. *Schooling and Language Minority Students,* 3-49

Cummins, J., and Swain, M. 1986. *Bilingualism in Education.* London and New York: Longman

De Schietere de Lophem, V. 1986. *Vroege tweetaligheid (Nederlands-Frans) in immersiesituaties. Een exemplarische studie van de taalvaardigheid vanfranstalige kleuters in het nederlandstalig onderwijs.* Master's thesis. Université Catholique de Louvain

Ervin-Tripp, S. 1970. Structure and process in language acquisition. *Monograph Series on Language and Linguistics,* 23: 313-44

François, F. 1967. L'apprentissage précoce d'une seconde langue. *Le Français dans le Monde,* 46: 26-8

Gailly, A., and Leman, J. (eds.) 1982. *Onderwijs, taal- en leermoeilijkheden in de immigratie.* Leuven: Acco

Gardner, R., and. Lambert, W. 1972. *Attitudes and motivation in second language learning.* Rowley, Mass.: Newbury House

Grosjean, F. 1982. *Life with Two Languages.* Cambridge, Mass: Harvard University Press

Housen, A., and Baetens Beardsmore, H. 1987. Curricular and extra-curricular factors in multilingual education. *Studies in Second Language Acquisition,* 9: 83-102

Kroon, S., and Vallen, T. (eds.) 1989. Etnische minderheden en Nederlands als tweede taal in Nederland en Vlaanderen. *Voorzetten* 23. 's-Gravenhage

Lambert, W.E. 1967. A social psychology for bilingualism. *Journal of Social Issues,* 23: 91-109

Lindemans, L., Renard, J., Vandevelde, J., and Vandezande, R. 1981. *De taalwetgeving in Belgie.* Leuven

Peol, J. van de, *Onderzoek naar de opvang van leerlingen uit Franstalige gezinnen in het vrij secundair onderwijs.* Research Project

Spolsky, B. 1988. Bridging the Gap: A General Theory of Second Language Learning. *Tesol Quarterly* 22, 3: 377-96

Schumann, J. 1978. The acculturation model for second language acquisition. In R. Gringas (ed.), *Second Language Acquisition for Foreign Language Teaching.* Washington: 27-50

Swain, M. 1981. Bilingual education for majority and minority languages children. *Studia Linguistica,* 35, 1-2: 15-32

FOREIGN LANGUAGE EDUCATION IN BULGARIA: PRESENT DAY SITUATION AND FUTURE TENDENCIES.

M. Danova, *Sofia University*, L. Krusteva-Bossakova, *Bulgarian Academy of Sciences*, and O. Stoitzov, *Agricultural Academy, Sofia*

The most characteristic feature of Foreign Language Education (FLE) in Bulgaria is the special place and the great importance it receives from the educational authorities. The demand for such an education is also great, especially in the big towns, but unfortunately the final results are not as good as they should be. Many reasons accounting for that can be listed but probably one of the most important is the constant change in educational policies.

At present FLE is quite diverse but for most children it starts with compulsory school education. There are, of course, preschool courses organised by certain institutions but they are neither compulsory nor wide-spread. Most schools have classes in a foreign language from the fifth form up to the seventh or eighth depending on the type of school, ie from the age of 10-11 up to 13-14. Russian at these schools is introduced one year earlier, in the fourth form. The classes are usually from 2 to 4 hours per week. There are certain schools where all foreign languages are introduced in the first form, including Russian, but their number is comparatively low mainly because of the lack of teachers. These schools are more common in the big towns. There are also several Russian schools where the education from the very start is entirely in Russian but their number is not so great.

After the age of 13-14 many of the children transfer to another school. Some choose the more technically oriented schools, some the more humanities oriented. In both, the pupils receive more or less the same share of FLE for the next two or three years - from 2-4 hours a week. There is a small group of pupils who, after passing entrance exams in Bulgarian literature and maths at age 14, enter special language schools. They study in their first year only one FL and they have 25 hours per week. The only other subjects that are taught are Bulgarian literature and maths. After this 'preparatory class' as it is called, they continue their education following the general curriculum for the next two years with most of the subjects taught in the corresponding FL. In the last two forms the subjects are taught in Bulgarian in order to prepare the pupils for their entrance exams at the University and other educational establishments. They still have 6-8 FL classes per week studying the literature, the culture and the language of the respective foreign country. Some of these schools are funded by UNESCO. There are Russian, English, German, French, Spanish, Italian and Latin and Greek schools that have such a curriculum. Usually the language proficiency of their alumni is very high and most of them continue their education at a higher level. There are other schools where the pupils, after the age of 14, study the FL as it is studied at the language schools, but do not study the other subjects in the respective FL. They have 6-8 hours per week and cover the material for the preparatory class. Usually the FL there is English but the number of such schools is not great.

There are other experimental schools where some new or quite untraditional methods are used not only in the teaching of the FL, but in the teaching of all the other subjects. One of the methods is Dr Losanov's suggestopaedia. It aims at the release of human capacity relying on the positive effect of the suggestion, the relaxation and the constant encouragement of the learner. Besides the school where the children start their education at the age of 6 and finish it at the age of 16 and where the entire education is based on this method, there are also courses for adults learners in FLs. They usually last for 25 days, 4 hours a day. Another such method is Professor Sendov's integrated cognitive approach but this is still in its experimental phase.

The pupils who continue their education at the universities and the other higher educational establishments after their secondary education has ended, also have classes in an FL. It is compulsory to study English and Russian at the technical and natural sciences faculties and departments, although Russian is losing ground nowadays and most of the departments will not include it in their curriculum for the academic year 1991-1992 as a compulsory subject. The students there have 120 hours of English for the first four terms plus one or two summer term courses of 150 hours in English each. It is not the same in the humanities, where students have from 180 hours (history, Slavonic philology, law - 240) up to 520 (political science, pedagogy - 480) of English, German and French. They have the opportunity to continue to study an FL in their third year as well as in their fourth one as a minor subject or as a language specialisation.

All the curricula are undergoing change, both at the universities and at the primary and secondary schools. The pupils can choose which language to study but this will not be a compulsory language. Obviously, English again will be the most popular language while Russian will not be taught on such a large scale since it also will not be obligatory. Turkish will also be introduced as an FL in some parts of the country and will be studied for 4 hours a week. FLE on the the higher levels will also be changed so that the students will have the opportunity to study a FL for 8-10 terms.

Graduates have different possibilities for continuing their FLE. Post-graduate students study two languages for two semesters: Russian and either English, German or French. This means in practice 12 hours per week for each of the languages. As a rule post-graduate students do these courses during the first year of their study. At the end of the year they sit for an exam in each of the languages. An advanced level of knowledge is required in order to pass that exam as well as good grades so they will be allowed to defend their dissertation papers.

Another form is the foreign language education of scholars at the Bulgarian Academy of Sciences which is done through different kinds of courses organised at the Institutes of the Academy. There are courses for beginners and for advanced learners. Usually the courses are in English, German and French with a priority interest in English. The courses are intensive, ie a 6 month period of study, 6 classes a day, 5 days a week, and extensive, ie 6 to 10 months study, 2 classes a day, 2 days a week. This education is done during the work time of the scholars and usually at their work place.

The so-called qualification language courses for specialists with higher education are organised by different institutions but one of the best is the Foreign Language Centre (FLC) at the Institute for Foreign Students. There they have several kinds of courses in English, French, German, Spanish, Portuguese and Arabic. The intensive courses last 3 months and 6 months with 6 classes a day, 5 days a week. Beginners and advanced learners are organised into groups of up to 10 learners, distributed according to the results of a language aptitude test designed by the scholars working at the Centre. The extensive courses, including evening ones, are only for advanced learners. Three classes a day are taught, 3 times a week for 3 months.

One of the interesting things that should be mentioned is that due to the economic and political changes in Bulgaria the interest in FLE has grown immensely, especially the interest in English: people wait for 2 or 3 years to get a place in English courses at the FLC. One of the major drawbacks, however, is the fact that there is practically no access to studying an FL in the native country even for teachers, which has quite a negative effect on the foreign language proficiency achievable.

The strengths which have led to increased interest in the Bulgarian situation are firstly, the type of education provided by the language schools; secondly, the emphasis that FLE receives through the Foreign Language Centre, particularly for postgraduates; thirdly, intensive courses enabling learners to achieve the threshold level and become autonomous learners. The weak points are mainly associated with general reliance on the model of language learning based on imitation and pattern drills instead of on creative and communicative approaches. A second weakness is the unrealistic expectations sometimes held for results from immersion techniques such as those described by Losanov 1979 or offered in intensive language school courses. A final weakness is that language education, until recently has been too ideologically biased.

Until 1990 all the references and context for language learning were exclusively Bulgarian. Now there are opportunities for contact and exchange which will affect motivation and performance and lead to greater effectiveness in FL learning in the future.

PORTRAIT OF A NATION AS A LANGUAGE LEARNER

I. Vitanova, J. Kristeva, M. Danova, and M. Ruski, *Department of Western Languages, Sofia University*

The aim of this paper is to outline the overwhelming changes in theory and approaches which have been under way in the field of foreign language learning and teaching in Bulgaria from the end of 1989 to early 1991. We believe that our attempt will profit from the adoption of a broader outlook, and propose to survey the situation in the wider context of socio-political and cultural life, along with the gradual evolution of new value judgements and patterns of behaviour, reflecting on the attitudes towards language learning and teaching which provide the conditions for a real discourse of cultures.

The radical changes which have swept over the whole of Eastern Europe have shattered the foundation of societies in those countries. The engine of reform is turning them from self-contained, non-communicable systems into avid seekers for contact at every level - cultural, economic, political, and social, the chief instrument of which is, naturally, language. Hence the renewed and so far unwitnessed interest towards foreign language learning and teaching in Bulgaria, which, it should be noted, has a long and fruitful tradition in this country, dating as far back as the late 19th century, when it was once again reintegrated into Europe as an independent state. The present situation, however, is peculiar in that it poses serious problems for the specialists engaged in teaching and organising foreign language education. The institutions so far in charge of providing FLT are in need of an early reassessment of their practices and the variety of demands society presses upon them, while the ever-increasing number of newly-established private firms (no less than 800), with the same purpose, lack sufficient numbers of well-trained and experienced teachers to meet the highly specific requirements of the public.

In any case, this welter of ever-changing conditions and factors, though rather confusing at first glance, is also a challenge to people who wish to search for trends, observe developments and find the underlying causes for the present situation.

We found Bernard Spolsky's graphic representation of a model of foreign language acquisition in *'Formulating a Theory of Second Language Learning'* (1985) a useful point of departure, as it is comprehensive and can accommodate a large body of facts and interpretations. It is precisely an interpretation of the main points that we would like to attempt in this paper, supporting it with observations from our current practice as teachers of English and French at Sofia University. The scheme is used as a general frame of reference only, and our notes in parentheses below suggest the specific treatment the main points have been given further on in the paper.

SOCIAL CONTEXT **leads to** **ATTITUDES of various kinds which appear in the learner as**

(the roots of change are found in the new cultural orientation of society, its rediscovery of the diversity and plurality of cultural traditions)

MOTIVATION, (a psychological portrait of the nation is attempted within the parameters making up the concept of motivation which are perceived as undergoing a definite change, unlike) **CAPABILITIES and PREVIOUS KNOWLEDGE of the learner,** (which we find to be difficult to relate to the all too obvious shift in the affective domain)

all of which explains the use the learner makes of the available SOCIAL CONTEXT which provides LEARNING SITUATIONS (FORMAL OR INFORMAL),
the interplay between learner and situation determining LINGUISTIC and NON-LINGUISTIC OUTCOMES for the LEARNER.

(The outcomes sought are novel means of communication, a constant striving to acquire a new communicative competence in the widest sense of the term, along with a revision of current classroom techniques and practices).

The first, and decisive change definitely affected *social context*. It might be interesting to note that the metaphor capturing the essence of the striving for reform during the first, and most turbulent period was 'the road to Europe'. This phrase, perceived by many as a paradox, since Bulgaria has never ceased to be part of the Old Continent, implicitly states the deeply felt, and regretted by most, forty-five year long alienation of the country from the mainstream of European culture, thought and tradition. Communication was obstructed not only on the interpersonal level, but on the level of traditional ties and widely-accepted human values. The thwarting of the spiritual life of the nation naturally affected the countenance of institutionalised language learning and teaching. It is a well-accepted fact that foreign language learning cannot be understood if it is not viewed as another form of communication. But all communication is culture specific and any language learning entails learning about culture or is one of the forms of cross-cultural communication. The dynamics of this process are determined both by the 'externals' of language - grammar, vocabulary, pronunciation, prosody, whose successful acquisition will lead to good linguistic competence - and the 'internals' - which are the underlying value systems at work and the way they affect understanding, response and communication, and consequently, the extent to which the exchange succeeds, falters, or fails (Garcia, O. et al, 1989) and whose successful acquisition will lead to cultural competence, the final aim of that process. We therefore consider that the present-day foreign language learning situation in Bulgaria cannot be fully grasped and explained in terms of the changes that are set in motion by the renewed contacts and re-appraisal - actually the rediscovery - of societies with different cultural traditions, ie, if it is not viewed as a specific acculturation process. The contact in this case is not direct, therefore the process cannot be equated to the processes of adjustment, adaptation, or assimilation, as is sometimes done.

The predominant factor will be the social context in which foreign language learning takes place. There will be socio-psychological conditions inhibiting or favouring it. Social context includes components such as the socio-linguistic situation, the general exposure of learners to other languages, the roles of the target language and other languages in the outside community and in the home; and the general perception of the value of the target language and of multilingualism. It is obvious that any change in these components will lead to a change in the actual nature of possibilities for social intercourse and other communicative transactions.

This is exactly what is happening in Bulgaria now. The radical change in the social context, and especially in the role of foreign languages and the general perception of their value is clearly expressed in the sudden boom of foreign language learning. According to a recent survey there is a dramatic shift in the emphasis put on the acceptance and evaluation of different cultures among the Bulgarian people: from the strongly marked preference for Russian culture in the near past to the clearly stated preference for French and American cultures, especially among young people, who are also the potential foreign language learners. This change in the 'internals', in the value systems of many people has actually produced a shift in the learners' attitudes towards the community speaking the target language and towards the learning situation. This change is so pronounced that it even overpowers the tendency, inherent in every culture, towards ethnocentrism, created by the inseparable relation of the self to the culture. As there is a collapse of the cultural models of behaviour, due to the collapse of communist ideology, the self is left without a real 'mental programme' to identify with, and in its search for a suitable one, it naturally starts identifying with a foreign one. To achieve that, however, it is necessary to accept the foreign categories of culture, its values and beliefs, all its elements.

According to Landis and Brislin cultural elements involve the following: patterns of dress, the use of particular technological innovations, methods of economic activity, patterns of social interaction, patterns of child rearing, patterns of educating the young, patterns of decision making and conflict resolution (politics), beliefs and behaviours, relevant to the regulation of the place of humans in the universe (religion), behaviours that produce aesthetic satisfaction, behaviours that increase understanding (philosophy), behaviours that are required in communication (language). It is clear that some of these elements are easily and readily accepted, like dress, technology and economic patterns, which are associated with progress. Others need longer time, like social interaction, child rearing and education, and still others are unlikely ever to be easily appropriated. It is possible, however, to learn language without this fact posing a threat to the personal or cultural ego identity. This explains why many people nowadays, while trying to free themselves from the old, both internally and socially rejected system of values, direct their efforts towards foreign language learning. Language, as one of the major tools for communication, is considered to be the easiest path towards the acquisition of the culture of the West, which is highly esteemed and identified with progress, democracy, and a return to the traditions of European civilisation.

Contemporary Bulgaria

Trying to outline the change of *attitudes* will inevitably involve a comparison of the psychological portrait of Bulgarian society as we know it from recent years, with the new countenance it is gradually taking on. It appears useful to attempt a psychological sketch within some parameters which are known to affect language learning. Despite the difficulties arising from the necessity of considering a multitude of variables, inherent to the emotional side of human behaviour, psychological terms and concepts such as empathy, aggression, extroversion, are extremely helpful in making our point. On the other hand, it appears that what could not be claimed to have undergone a radical change, are individual capabilities, and previous knowledge. Therefore, all the observations made will refer to a change in the psychological make up of society, reflecting on group behaviour and atmosphere, through the various components generally assumed to form the concept of motivation. The individual learner will only be implied as part of the larger whole.

Thus, at the highest level, that of society, it can be stated that a fundamental restructuring is under way, which has a significant effect on all five levels of affectivity, as outlined in Krathwool and Bloom, 1964. Society is willing to receive, to tolerate new stimuli, and to respond without coercion to those stimuli. A new system of values, unequivocal, and in unison with universal human values is once again revitalised, internalised and ordered within a hierarchy, where each individual can approach and find his own self. Though this taxonomy relates only indirectly to language learning, its relevance to more specific contexts is poignantly convincing to any person who carefully watches the course of events in a reforming society. Its other merit is that it can be applied on a lower level of social organisation, too: to the group as the natural medium of language learning, and to individual learners. If we envisage these three objects of study as concentric circles, we might contend that there will be a major trend towards social changes affecting group behaviour and individual learners, as part of groups, respectively. An interesting point, in our opinion, is that when examining our subject of study, most of the observations we made in class, concerning changes in group attitudes, were also true for society as a whole, and very frequently group behaviour could be predicted from changes in social values and motivation. Thus, factors which are traditionally considered as egocentric, such as self-esteem and inhibition, and whose relation to language learning has been studied and found to correlate with success in this task, can equally well be related to society as a whole. Now that Bulgarian society has initiated a search for its collective self and begun to explore its components, it is becoming increasingly evident that a crisis is tearing this inner self apart - the prevailing attitude is that of disapproval with itself, society is assailed with doubts, and global self-esteem is generally low. This will, in most cases, be reflected in situational, or specific self-esteem in group work, where both previously and at present, it is frequently doubted that the task of learning a foreign language is feasible at all, and especially that it is beyond the capabilities of a Bulgarian learner. Improved global national self-esteem, in our opinion, will ultimately reflect positively on the emotional well-being of language-learning groups.

In close unison with the concept of self-esteem is that of inhibition, which seems to be in inverse relation to the former. In a totalitarian society, made up of fragile egos, governed by weak self-esteem, individuals build walls of inhibition to protect themselves, to be able to withstand threats to their existence. Most teachers with longer professional experience, especially while working with adult specialists in various fields of science and technology, found themselves incapable of overcoming the mountain of inhibitions and taboos when attempting to develop their students' communicative competence, for the mere reason that the majority of the class promptly foresaw the unpredictable turn a discussion might take if they expressed their opinion freely. Thus, normal conversation was possible on just a few 'safe' topics, which, however, failed to keep the students' interest and were soon dropped. Inhibition seems to suppress not only the human ego in general, but the *language ego,* too. Some teachers often resorted to a 'change of identity' technique, students were encouraged to assume a new identity, a different nationality, and thus helped to come to grips with the demands of the learning situation, as this, in most cases, resulted in freer communication, unfettered by the defences they had built around their egos.

All these factors cannot be strictly separated from what would turn out to be the most encompassing, and maybe the easiest reason to resort to, when explaining the success or failure of any complex task - the change in motivation. Language learning has always been a great concern for Bulgarians, though until recently learners were meeting extrinsic needs and were largely instrumentally motivated to take up this time and effort-consuming enterprise. Most people acquired a foreign language as a means of furthering their career, reading technical or scientific material, for example, where language learning was an obligatory subject in a curriculum (schools, universities). The proper motivation was blatantly missing in most cases, thus turning classes into an endless drudgery. Teachers were facing the additional burden of providing the motivation for their groups since intrinsic motivation was lacking, except in the cases of learners (mostly adults, professionals or university students, approaching the end of their studies), who were aware of the necessity of acquiring one or two foreign languages. Motivation is generally interpreted as a fulfilment of needs, as an inner drive. For that drive to appear, though, an individual should perceive in his environment at least a minimum of choices, or degrees of freedom - he should be able to choose exploration, manipulation of the environment, and causing change. The inner realisation of the minimal chances for travelling and contacts with other cultures, seemed to sap many of the sources of intrinsic motivation. This fact sounds paradoxical to any person who is familiar with traditional Bulgarian attitudes towards foreign countries and culture. Bulgarians show a strong tendency for empathy on the cultural level. A desire is obvious for transcending the national ego boundaries and being permeated with the traditionally accepted values of European and North American societies. Until recently, this empathetic urge was restricted to the cognitive phase, rather than the affective one. At the present time, new possibilities are emerging for real-life, unfettered, direct communication. Learners and teachers, alike, are seeking to fill the gaps in the learning-teaching situation. Efforts seem ultimately directed towards acquiring a better communicative competence, with its several components.

The economic, political and cultural isolation of the country in the last forty-five years has unfavourably affected the language teaching situation, in that its aim - communication in a foreign language - was reduced to repeating and memorising artificial models of communication, and attempts were made at fitting the target language into a different situation - all too unfavourable in the socio-economic and cultural respect. Thus, a certain 'distance' appeared between the target language and the version taught. In other words, the learner's communicative competence was restricted to certain aspects only, and incapable of performing a variety of functions.

The components of communicative competence follow a definite hierarchy within the general framework, which largely determines the stages of teaching and acquiring communicative competence and the process of communication in general.

Linguistic competence implies the knowledge and usage of phonetic, lexical, grammatical and text models of the target language. It is relatively easy to acquire in the initial stages of the learning process, as it is least dependent on the situation. Teaching has changed least in this aspect. Good linguistic competence was acquired even before the changes discussed were initiated, owing to a fruitful tradition dating far back into the years, and the new forms of institutionalising the process - language schools. The learning of a relatively large number of lexical items, grammatical and syntactic rules, phonetic norms could not go further however than a passive mastery of the target language. The efforts are now directed towards the activation of this knowledge.

Discourse competence implies the knowledge and use of the various types of speech, and their organisation along the parameters of the communicative situation, where they have been produced and interpreted. Teaching has not been very satisfactory in this respect, as the tasks set so far were minimal and did not go beyond learning to make elementary everyday contacts - acquaintances, introductions, supplying information, etc. A more general, though rather undifferentiated, and hence mediocre level of discourse competence was achieved, which frequently amounted to drab linguistic performance. Present day beginner courses seem to aspire towards the acquisition of understanding and oral communication, ie, they aim at communicative and discourse goals.

Referential competence presupposes knowledge of the spheres of human activity, our reality and the ties among its components. Foreign language teaching at universities largely centres around specialised scientific texts, authentic documents and materials, employed by both beginners and advanced learners. Scientific discourse has its own specifics, despite the language it has been written in. Modern scientific competence is an international phenomenon, and a researcher should be able to recognise and employ the typical scientific and discourse strategies used in that language, so as to obtain the information necessary for his work. Attention is now focused on mastering the organisation of discourse in specialised texts, eliciting the traits characteristic for text competence in each type of discourse a language possesses.

The knowledge and use of the social rules and norms of interaction among individuals and institutions, the knowledge of cultural history and the relationships among social subjects make up *socio-cultural competence*. A language class is not always an exercise in intercultural communication. It is most often intra-cultural, as teacher and learner alike share the same language and culture. Communication is performed in the target language, but is based on the common culture. A higher degree of intercultural communication is achieved when authentic texts are employed. Present Bulgarian learners attempt to acquire better socio-cultural competence. Beginners even have the ambition of plunging into a mass of contextualised data concerning the foreign language/culture, which are totally unfamiliar, and even alien in the beginning. Contacts with foreign culture gradually teach learners to specify, correct, reformulate initial hypotheses, and later realise their increased linguistic and socio-cultural competence. The 'shuttle' between the two languages/cultures accompanied with numerous attempts at assimilation and distancing, reveals to the learners their specific 'way of thinking', which is both similar to, and different from that of other nations. Beginners are, naturally, in no position to judge the truthfulness of socio-cultural phenomena, but they do learn to correlate linguistic traits to the more comprehensive cultural background. The very recognition of cultural aspects is the initial stage in the acquisition of cultural communicative competence.

Various competences participate to a different degree in the production and interpreting of discourse. The lack of one element might be supposed to be compensated for by the presence of another. The explanation of these phenomena may be sought in individual communicative strategies, which interact with the various aspects of communicative competence.

It is becoming increasingly obvious that the new demands require adjustments to the qualitative parameters of the learning-teaching process. Both sides participating in the process are in need of reassessing their roles.

The old model of FLT seems to have exhausted its capabilities and pertinence. Even though in recent years an attempt was made to transcend traditional approaches, it rarely went beyond the framework of the lexico-grammatical and structural model. The language - civilisation dichotomy was not given proper elicitation in language classes. One of the most serious insufficiencies of the old teaching approach, in our opinion, is the lack of reference towards the respective socio-cultural realities, and its firm reliance on local ones. This yielded sterile knowledge, well-structured morpho-syntactically, but completely inadequate in its psychological, social and cultural aspects. Thus, for example, a simple dialogue in an everyday situation was deprived of its contact-establishing, sociative (phatic) elements; the articulators, realising the transition between utterances; even information relating to a concrete communicative situation, ie, the elements, pertaining to the purely communicative competence, such as empirical knowledge of the linguistic, psychological and socio-cultural rules underlying the processes of speech production and interpretation within a given communicative group. A new model of the language class is emerging, with new tasks and new ways to accomplish them. Though it is not radically different from familiar practices, described in literature, it is perceived as such when compared to the new communicative demands of the learners.

Present-Day Foreign Language Learning and Teaching in Bulgaria

What are the present-day goals of foreign language learning and teaching in Bulgaria? The pragmatic role of language in human behaviour seems to come to the fore. 'Structure' is gradually dethroned by the 'speech act', which appears as the new basic unit, around which linguistic and thematic content is organised.

Pragmatisation of FL learning and teaching emerges as the most radical change in this discipline in Bulgaria. It has been brought about by the realisation of the learner as a potential subject of communication in the target language, in unison with socio-cultural norms, and not only with linguistic ones.

Each instance of linguistic usage is regarded as satisfying three main demands: *pertinence, adequacy* and *competence.*

Pertinence implies the presence or absence of a certain communicative element. A 'yes or no' question is constantly asked: 'Shall I speak or not?', 'Shall I take leave or start without saying a word?', 'Shall I express gratitude at the end of a letter or not?'

Adequacy bears on the correlation between the utterance and the communicative situation. The main issue is the presence of elements which violate the socio-cultural norms adhered to by the participants in the speech act, and related to the referent and the time and space coordinates.

Competence relates to the means employed, like the quantity of speech necessary, the choice of direct or indirect expression, the adequacy of the phrase in a specific situation, the rhetoric pertinent to various circumstances, etc.

The new communicative orientation of foreign language classes is trying to provide an answer to these questions and offer some rules for the production of utterances, adapted to the specific set of communicative norms existing in society. These norms are comprised of the following elements:

- participant in the speech act: the norms, pertaining to speech act participants vary in different societies, and even in a given community. Hence, foreigners' difficulties with mastering discriminatory, honorific address forms, and the vocative forms, which are much more complicated than the simple opposition between second person singular and second person plural it is usually reduced to;

- place of the speech act - human behaviour differs in a cafe, the cemetery, at home, at a friends' place or with strangers;

- time of speech - certain problems are not touched upon at certain times of the day, phone calls are not made after 9pm;

- type of communication - each type of communication presupposes a certain number of strategies: for taking the floor, joining, maintaining and finishing a conversation, addressing the partner in a conversation, changing partners or topic. There is sufficient evidence to show that these strategies vary with culture.

It is while teaching these specific elements of communicative competence that the greatest difficulties arise, in just the same way as using them in actual intercultural communication sometimes proves to be a stumbling block. Concrete practices involved in the classroom might be: paraphrase, role-play games in specific communicative situations (telephone conversations, the epistolary genre), comments on some gestures, silences, body language, styles of dress, misunderstandings due to socio-cultural differences, comparison of communicative prototypes stemming from different cultural sources, work with authentic documents, especially audio-visual ones showing native speakers in various communicative situations.

The new role of the foreign language teacher is not merely that of the instructor, or tourist guide, but rather the conveyor of skills for communicating in a foreign language and fostering a specific communicative culture.

We would finally wish to express our hope that the tremendous change in attitudes towards language learning and teaching, triggered by social conditions, will ultimately sway the pendulum in the opposite direction, and exert positive influence on the nation's strife towards a new identity.

References

Besse, A. 1984. Eduquer la perception interculturelle. *Le Français dans le monde*

Cortillon, J. 1984. La notion de progression appliquée à l'enseignement de la civilization

Hofstede, G. 1980. *Culture's Consequences*

Ferdman, B. 1990. Literacy and Cultural Identity. *Harvard Educational Review,* 60, 2

Garcia, O., and Otheguy, R. (eds.) 1989. *English Across Cultures, Cultures Across English. A Reader in Cross-Cultural Communication.* New York

Gardner, R., and Lambert, W. 1972. *Attitudes and Motivation in Second Language Learning*. Rowley, Mass: Newbury House
Guiora, A. Z. et al. Empathy and Second Language Learning. *Language Learning*, 22: 111-30
Krathwool, D., and Bloom, B. 1964. *Taxonomy of Educational Objectives. Handbook: Affective Domain*. New York
Hymes, D. 1984. *Vers la compétence de communication*. Paris
Landis, O. and Brislin, R. (eds.) *Handbook of Intercultural Training*. v. 1
Morand, S. 1982. *Enseigner à communiquer en langue étrangère*. Paris
Oller, J. and Richards, J. (eds.) 1973. *Focus on the Learner: Pragmatic Aspects for the Language Teacher*. Rowley, Mass. Newbury House
Spolsky, B. 1985. *Formulating a theory of second language learning*

LANGUAGE LEARNING IN ENGLAND AND WALES: POLICIES AND ATTITUDES IN FLUX

S. Wright *Aston University*

The English have a reputation, perhaps not ill-deserved, for being poor linguists. The reasons for this reside in a number of political, geographical, social and educational factors which together have moulded English attitudes towards foreign language learning. It may now be an appropriate moment to re-examine and re-evaluate the relationship of the English to foreign language learning, since there are indications that for the first time in decades, perhaps centuries, attitudes and practices in this area are in flux.

Diversity in the Education System of England and Wales

Until 1988 the education system in England and Wales was organised at national level by the Department of Education and Science, based in London, and implemented at local level by individual local education authorities (LEAs) situated in each major city or region. Scotland and Northern Ireland have different systems which will not be described here. Organisation at local level in England and Wales has caused educational provision and organisation to differ according to area and thus it is not possible to speak of the education system even in England and Wales as a cohesive whole. To confuse the picture further, alongside state (or 'maintained school') provision exists a thriving private (or 'independent') school system, including some of the most prestigious schools in the country and called, misleadingly, the public school system.

State schools are organised according to decisions made largely at LEA level and this produces diversity at each stage of education and a situation where individual initiatives proliferate. At three years of age the country's children attend either private playschool, private nursery or state-run nursery or they remain at home. The State has no reliable statistics for this since much of the sector is organized by voluntary organizations, and, typically, run by mothers in church halls. By five, all children are attending primary school, some having started at the age of four and the rest at five. Most children remain in the primary sector, which is coeducational, until the age of eleven, although in some areas children go at the age of nine to middle schools, which have features of both primary and secondary provision. Such children progress at the age of twelve or thirteen to high schools, to complete their secondary education. In those areas which do not have this system, children progress at the age of eleven to secondary education. According to the system prevailing in their district they may attend an all ability coeducational comprehensive, an all ability single sex comprehensive, a selective coeducational grammar school, a single sex grammar school or a school called comprehensive but because of selection in the catchment area catering only for the lower ability range. At sixteen, compulsory education finishes and students may elect to remain at their secondary school, if it has a sixth form; to move to a sixth form college, to a tertiary college or to a college of further education; or to leave school and enter the job market. They may study full or part-time, and follow academic or vocational courses. At eighteen, students may continue to study at a university, polytechnic or college of higher education.

Further choice and diversity is introduced by the presence of church schools as part of the state sector. Generous funding is available for Christian schools of all denominations and for Jewish schools, although Muslims, Buddhists and Sikhs have sought but not obtained state funding, which has led to debate on equality for all sectors of the population.

In Wales there is another element of choice since some schools offer Welsh medium education rather than English. A Welsh speaking school is defined as one in which core subjects, including religious instruction, are taught wholly or partly in Welsh (Welsh Office, 1991). Parents can choose whether their children attend such a school; in areas of the country which are mainly anglophone there are some Welsh units attached to English speaking schools. Welsh is not at present a compulsory subject in all schools on Welsh territory but will become so in 1992, when all English speaking children entering a primary or secondary school for the first time will be required to learn Welsh.

This short description of the complexity of education provision explains why it is no easy task to describe the foreign language education experience of a typical English or Welsh child. Bearing in mind that these are only two amongst the many possible scenarios, the following examples show what has commonly been the case in language education in the recent past:

Child A, who has followed the primary/secondary school pattern, has no opportunity to study a foreign language before secondary school. At secondary school he studies a foreign language for the first three years. At fourteen a degree of specialization is allowed, commonly known as ‘choosing options’, and the child chooses a programme that excludes a modern language. Thus such a child will have studied a modern language for only three years at a period of schooling when the curriculum is very broad and each subject area is allotted a restricted time, typically two to three hours a week for the modern foreign language. Such a pupil has, therefore, only reached a very basic level of competence in the foreign language and is likely to forget the little that he does know.

Child B, who has followed the primary/middle/secondary pattern, will probably begin study of the foreign language at the age of nine, although classes may be with a non-specialist teacher. At twelve she is offered the possibility of studying a second foreign language which she accepts and at fourteen chooses to continue to study both foreign languages to GCSE (General Certificate of Secondary Education) level, the 16+ examination. After GCSE the two languages are two of the three subjects that child B chooses to study for Advanced Level (AL), the 18+ examination. Thus, such a child will have studied one foreign language for nine years and the other for six years.

One cannot surmise from this that child A is more or less educationally able than child B; members from each group can and do progress to higher education. The system has simply provided flexibility and variety of choice and the opportunity to continue the study of a foreign language is not linked to ability. In fact it has been widely noted (NCLE, 1984) that a good many able linguists opted out of learning a language in order to specialize in other areas. This very early specialization has resulted in a large number of highly educated English adults leaving the education system at 18+ or 21+ with the barest acquaintance with a modern foreign language.

The advantages of the English and Welsh education system have been seen to be its flexibility which allowed for a degree of individual choice of subjects from 14+ and for the option of part-time study from the age of 16+, and its freedom which gave rise to syllabus design by individual teachers and schools and to some very creative and excellent teaching. This flexibility and freedom also cause some of the problems endemic in the system: in many cases pupils choose subjects they like and find easy and shy away from more difficult subjects, mastery of which may prove to be necessary for them personally in later careers and for the economy as a whole; too many young people leave full-time education at 16+ giving England and Wales a work force that appears to have had less formal education than that of other Western European countries; control of their own curriculum has also led in some schools to a lack of central direction and to a fall in standards. All this has been a cause of some concern and has prompted recent government legislation on education, which attempts to address some of the problems.

Languages - a Minority Subject and a Subject for the Minority

At 16+ only a minority of the nation's children are still studying a modern foreign language. Typically, in the school year 1986 - 1987, 33.88% of 16 year olds attempted an exam at 16+ in French, the most commonly studied modern foreign language, and 14.45% were awarded an O (Ordinary) Level or a CSE (Certificate of Secondary Education) Grade 1 (the 16+ examinations which have since been replaced by GCSE). This was considered to be the minimum requirement for progress to a higher level in the subject. In the same year only 2.29% of those taking examinations at 18+ attempted the Advanced Level examination in French (DES 1990a). The figures for German, the second most popular language, were 9.29%, 4.42% and 0.88% respectively, and it must be remembered that, since many specializing in languages study two languages, a candidate taking German may also have taken French and thus may appear twice in the statistics.

The low numbers of linguists coming through the school system had implications for the universities and polytechnics which experienced difficulty in recruiting and competed for the most able linguists. In 1986 - 1987 only 1.17% of those still studying at 18+ achieved a grade C in French at Advanced Level, normally considered the bench mark for those who wish to study the subject in higher education. It was noted that standards of entry dropped at this time and those with D and E passes were able to find university and polytechnic places.

If we consider the reasons for the lack of pupils choosing to study a modern language we find that there are a number of causes: firstly, considerations of class, always of interest in Britain, are one of the background issues here; secondly perceptions that languages are 'female' subjects play a role; thirdly, there is undoubted influence from the world of industry and commerce which did not appreciate the utility of foreign language skills until comparatively recently; finally, there is the question of which foreign language will be most useful for an English mother tongue speaker.

Foreign languages have been treated as and have commonly been seen to be the province of the elite. In the 1950s and 1960s the study of a modern foreign language was the prerogative of pupils in the public school system (private schools) and in the grammar schools (state selective schools) but was not considered appropriate for most pupils in secondary modern schools. In the 1970s the school system underwent a period of fundamental change as many local education authorities began to reorganize state schooling on comprehensive lines; pupils were no longer to be selected for a two tier system but were to be educated as a whole year group in one institution. Comprehensivisation brought the study of a modern foreign language to a wider ability range and almost all pupils had some language tuition in the first three years of secondary school. However, the divide still remained since comprehensive pupils were less likely to continue to examination level in languages than pupils in the private sector or in the grammar schools which survived.

This is illustrated by the following statistics which show pupils who attempted an examination in French or German as a percentage of all leavers from that sector.

Table 1
Percentage of all leavers who attempted examinations: maintained and independent schools

FRENCH	1983	1984	1985	1986	1987
Maintained schools (state comprehensive and grammar)	35%	36%	36%	36%	39%
Independent schools (public)	78%	76%	76%	77%	78%
GERMAN	1983	1984	1985	1986	1987
Maintained schools (state comprehensive and grammar)	10%	10%	10%	10%	10%
Independent schools (public)	20%	20%	20%	19%	18%

Source: Department of Education and Science, Statistics branch. Examination attainments in Modern Languages.

Examining the reasons for these statistics may lead us to suggest that the majority of state educated children rejected languages because they could not see the relevance of studying French, the first foreign language in most schools in England and Wales. To the average school child it was not clear why he should need competence in this language. Despite France's position as Britain's closest neighbour, it is not a country which the majority of British children is likely to visit. In broad terms the pattern of foreign travel for leisure purposes in Britain is closely allied to class and income: members of the working class who are economically buoyant, holiday in Spain, Greece, North Africa and the United States on package holidays; members of the working class who are not in well paid employment do not travel; members of ethnic minority groups whose families have recently immigrated to Britain have close ties with their country of origin and if they travel tend to visit family and friends in that country. France appears to be a holiday destination for affluent middle class professionals who rent houses, camp and tour or ski in winter.

France is, therefore, not a destination for a large proportion of the British school population and often the only experience that a British school child has of France is the exchange trip arranged by the school or local education authority so that the language may be practised. Motivation is thus stronger in some social groups than in others, which may be one of the elements which explains the class divide in language learning.

The class bias in language education is also to be noted at the primary level. An attempt to introduce the subject into primary education was dropped in the mid

1980s when educational budgets were restricted and local education authorities were searching for areas in which to make cuts. The scheme had never been very successful since it had been introduced piecemeal, with the result that some pupils entered the secondary system with a foundation in the subject whilst others did not. The secondary school language teacher was forced to teach a heterogeneous group and often solved the situation by treating the whole group as beginners - which had implications for motivation and enjoyment of the subject both for those who had studied a language before and for those who had not. Private preparatory schools continued, however, to teach their pupils a language.

The second reason for the low numbers choosing to study languages may reside in sexual prejudice. The personal pronouns, he and she, in the examples given above were chosen advisedly; it is far more common for girls to choose to study a foreign language at 14+ and at 16+ than boys. As an illustration of this we may consider the French GCSE and AL examination results of all school leavers of all ages in 1987 - 1988 in England.

Table 2
Percentage of school leavers with GCSE in A level French

	GCSE grades A-C (As a % of all leavers)	GCSE grades D-G	Leavers with AL (as % of all 17yr olds)
Boys	12%	14.8%	1%
Girls	20.4%	21.95%	2.7%

Source: House of Commons. Reply by Angela Rumbold to parliamentary question 5th March 1990. Published in Education 4/5/1990

The perception that languages are a 'girls' subject' may have caused foreign languages to have lower status amongst some young male groups and contributed to the lower numbers studying the subject from this section of the population. The high proportion of girls taking the subject produced proportionately larger numbers of female graduates and female teachers, thus reinforcing the perception. Both the inspectorate and individual local authorities were aware of the problem and tried to redress it, usually together with a campaign to persuade young women that Science and Technology were not just male preserves. The inclusion, albeit belatedly, of languages in the Technical and Vocational Education Initiatives from 1986 onwards, (e.g. in Birmingham) gave opportunities for schools and colleges to demonstrate the use and value of a modern foreign language within the context of future work in commerce and industry, and also funded the provision of computers for Modern Languages departments. Both actions were likely to have some effect on male recruitment.

The third cause of the traditional unpopularity of language learning may be traced to perceptions of utility which used to be prevalent amongst certain sections of the population. The linguistic legacy of the British Empire and the indisputable excellence of the United States in many technological areas has led to the use of English as a lingua franca in many commercial and industrial situations, with the consequence that the need for foreign language competence has not always been perceived or rewarded in British commerce and industry. Some key people in these sectors simply could not 'see the point' of learning a foreign language and this opinion expressed in private conversation and in the media had consequences for language learning, depriving pupils and students of powerful extrinsic motivation. Lord Young, Secretary of State for Trade and Industry, was typical of continuing British complacency when he said in 1988:

> I'm not sure that it's language that's important (in the European market) because English is becoming more and more the commercial language for most of Europe (Quoted in Wyburd 1990).

This was given wide media coverage at the time and prompted attacks both at home and abroad. Subsequently Lord Young retracted his remarks and in a more diplomatic mood made it clear that:

> The message to the British must be clear. We must overcome the arrogance (or laziness) which leads to the attitude that shouting louder in English will do (Letter to the International Chamber of Commerce UK 1989, quoted in Wyburd 1990).

There was undoubtedly a lack of regard for language competence in British industry and commerce. Research carried out in the early eighties discovered entrenched prejudice against professional qualifications which had 'been watered down' by the inclusion of the study of a foreign language (Wright, 1986). Where graduate linguists were employed, their position was ambiguous. Most were principally linguists with little training in a specialism, since the majority of universities and polytechnics had not developed a range of applied language courses. These linguists found themselves regarded as part of the secretarial service and were paid and treated accordingly. It did not help that, as we have seen, Modern Languages had traditionally been a female subject with larger numbers of girls and young women choosing to study it at every level.

Finally, there is the difficult problem of which language should be offered in schools and colleges. In the late twentieth century a form of international English is perhaps the closest the world comes to possessing a lingua franca and thus for speakers of languages other than English, the choice of language, if there is no other motivation, is often English. A learner investing time and effort into acquiring English is learning both the language of British and

American culture and a language of communication which he may well use with another non-native English speaker. The reasons for learning the language are twofold: entry into a culture and access to a lingua franca. When the native English speaker starts to learn a foreign languge, he can only be motivated by his desire to have access to a certain culture and not by his desire to acquire a lingua franca (although it could be argued that English mother tongue speakers need to learn the rules and practices of international English (Henderson Kassis 1991). This makes the decision on which languages to offer within an English medium education system problematic and has implications for the motivation of learners.

It has been mentioned that French is the most frequently taught language at all levels of the English education system[1]. The reasons for this are mainly historical and self perpetuating; since French has been the main foreign language there are graduates in that language who enter the teaching profession and can teach it to the next generation. Many attempts at diversification have foundered: pilot schemes have often been set up by peripatetic staff to encourage a range of languages, raise interest and develop the methodology and when the team moves on to do the same elsewhere in the local education authority, the schemes collapse because schools have not been able to appoint staff to continue them (Birmingham L.E.A., 1991; *Education*, 1990). Despite an awareness of the need to diversify, examination entries for some minority languages plummeted in the early 1980s.

Table 3
Examination entries for Russian

Entries for Russian	CSE	O level	A level
1975	359	2290	619
1985	188	1388	309
% change	-47.6	-39.4	-50.1

Source: CILT Information sheet 8, January 1987.

Other languages, such as Hungarian, had so few entries that the examination boards, who must function in Britain as profitmaking companies, withdrew them completely.

A Growing Awareness of the Need for and Utility of Foreign Languages - a Cause for Cautious Optimism

Advances in language teaching theory and course design

The low numbers of students and pupils opting for modern languages in schools and colleges in the early and mid-1980s eventually forced teachers and lecturers to reassess their methods and to take action to make language learning a more successful and enjoyable activity. Since foreign languages were not obligatory and since pupils and students were 'voting with their feet', modern languages teachers had to woo them back; the eighties had seen a number of government cost-cutting exercises and language classes with small numbers had been particularly vulnerable. The language teachers were fighting for their jobs and this proved a strong motivation to re-examine the theoretical basis of their teaching. Theories of language acquisition and learning were questioned and methodology (delivery and course and material design) reassessed [2]. A number of groups, influenced by the work of the American theorist, Krashen, and by the developmental work on threshold levels carried out by Jan van Ek and a team under the aegis of the Council of Europe (van Ek, 1976), turned to the concepts of comprehensible input and communicative competence. Learners were to be motivated by using authentic material collected from countries where the target language was in use. This material would deal with topic areas of evident use to travellers and of clear interest to adolescent learners. There would be tests at regular intervals so that there could be constant feedback and recognition of achievement. Local education authorities set up groups to work on certification for the early stages of language learning in the hope that recognised achievement would also motivate learners and influence them to continue to study the language; the Oxford (OCEA) group's Graded Objectives in Modern Languages proved to be most influential.

An overall improvement in language teaching was noted by the inspectorate. [3] Her Majesty's Inspectorate had carried out a survey of 10% of all comprehensives in the years 1975 and 1976 to ascertain what happened when a language was offered to all. From this cross section of schools the inspectors had to conclude that most practising foreign language teachers were not equipped to deal with low ability groups and that there were serious methodological problems which needed to be addressed. The reflection and reassessment of language learning and acquisition and the research in methodology which then took place seemed to have some beneficial effects, since, when HMI returned ten years later to see how language teaching was progressing in comprehensive schools, they were able to report that:

> There is enough evidence to suggest that a foreign language experience for all pupils up to the age of 16 can be both feasible and beneficial. (DES, 1985, 33)

Language learning in English and Welsh schools and colleges has continued to improve in terms of numbers studying the subject and in terms of effort and reflection on methodology. There is, nevertheless, still a great deal yet to be done before we could consider that a satisfactory benchmark had been reached. Three HMI reports from the late 1980s show the advances that have been made and the enormous work that is still to be accomplished. They also reflect the class divide that still exists within the language area. The least encouraging of the three was the survey of the teaching and learning of modern languages in a sample of inner city and urban schools carried out in 1989. The inspectors found that:

> Nearly half the lessons were less than satisfactory and showed some or many shortcomings in important areas. (DES, 1989a)

However, HMI inspectors looking at 200 separate language classes in higher education and twenty-three departments of modern languages in large further education colleges throughout 1989 and 1990 found that standards of both teaching and learning were mostly satisfactory and that there were many examples of good practice (1989b; 1990b).

Successful Language Diversification: the Languages of Immigrant Communities

In one area language diversification was successful. From the early 1980s onwards there had been pressure from linguistic minority communities in Britain to include languages such as Arabic, Bengali, Chinese, Greek, Gujarati, Hindi, Italian, Panjabi, Turkish and Urdu in the school curriculum (Frith, 1991, Reeves and Wright, 1992). In some local education authorities there were large numbers of speakers of these languages and where classes were offered there was often an enthusiastic response. Two major problems had to be overcome before these languages could take their place in the mainstream curriculum. Firstly, the attitude of central government was far less enthusiastic towards this diversification than individual local authorities; secondly, for many of these languages there were no appropriate materials, no ready made courses, no relevant examinations, and most importantly few qualified teachers whom the Department of Education and Science would recognize and employ.

The Swann report in 1985 recommended that the prime responsibility for the maintenance of the languages of the minority linguistic communities lay with the communities themselves:

> Mainstream schools should not seek to assume the role of community providers for maintaining ethnic minority community languages (DES, 1985b, 771)

The committee did concede, however, that language diversity could also be seen as a positive asset for a country and that where there was sufficient demand languages of the linguistic minorities could be offered as a language option.

Others saw the resource that the presence of these speakers represented and the Parker report (1986) pointed out the needs of diplomacy and commerce for Asian and African languages and cultural expertise.

The late 1980s saw a number of advances in this area: the GCSE boards developed examinations in many of the languages of the linguistic minorities; modern language departments in areas where there were linguistic minority communities began to offer these languages alongside or in place of French and German; most universities and polytechnics accepted the languages of the linguistic minorities as having equal status to all other subjects for matriculation purposes (Wright, 1991). The struggle to have these languages accepted as fully equal to French, German and Spanish has been a long one and the outcome is not yet assured since both GCSE and the National Curriculum pose problems that have yet to be resolved.

The Education Reform Act 1988

In order to address some of the problems inherent in the system and which we have discussed above, the Conservative government introduced legislation in 1988, to carry through far-reaching reforms throughout the education system.The Education Reform Act was to bring about some control by central government through the provision of a core curriculum, standardisation of assessment techniques, a raising of standards through the introduction of attainment targets for each age group and a broader curriculum which would halt early specialization. There was also a large hidden agenda which included the dilution of local authority power.

The relationship between the Conservative government and the teachers, seen as traditionally more sympathetic to the centre and to Labour, was not good. The government had fought the teachers' unions earlier in the decade over the question of pay and negotiating rights and had defeated them. Conservative treasury policy had enforced a series of financial measures which had cut funding for the day to day management of education and caused teacher redundancies. The fabric of school buildings had been neglected, capitation for text books and equipment had not kept pace with inflation. In such a climate the majority of teachers were not in a receptive mood for government reform. They complained bitterly that they were being asked to implement educational change that had been decided by politicians not educationalists and that the funding and the time scales for change were inadequate. The teachers saw their power further eroded by the government's proposal to increase the power of school governors. Governing boards composed of local politicians, local businessmen and industrialists together with parents would now exercise extensive rights over the organization of schools, including delivery of the curriculum. The appointment and promotion of teachers, which had always been the province of the local education authority and the senior management team in schools also passed to this governing body.

The Cultural Hegemony of the Educational Reform Act

Despite attempts to halt it, by the end of 1988 the bill had been passed and reform was under way. Working parties were constituted for each subject area to advise on syllabus content, forms of assessment and the constituent role of the subject in the whole curriculum. As they reported it became clear that the ethos of the legislation was the promotion of the Western European cultural legacy. The attempts that had been made in some local education authorities over the past years to provide a non-European dimension to children's education were dismissed. It became clear that part of the hidden agenda was an attack on attempts by individual local education authorities with large numbers of children from families of recent immigration to diversify the curriculum to encompass culture, history, language, geography specifically relevant to these groups (Macey, 1990, Tomlinson, 1990). Some of these authorities had promoted a multicultural approach within all their schools for pupils from both immigrant and indigenous families as discussed above. To a lesser extent, some authorities had instigated the teaching of the languages of minority linguistic communities who had settled in Britain.

The first report from the Modern Languages working party took little account of these recent developments and the first draft suggested that languages in schools were to be taken to mean first and foremost the languages of the European Community. This was in part a result of pressure from the Community for legislation within each constituent member on the linguistic question. It provoked intense lobbying from local authorities, schools, educationalists and representatives from linguistic minority language groups who wished to see Arabic, the languages of the Indian sub-continent and Chinese as part of the list of languages permissible as foundation subjects. When the first draft of the bill appeared concessions had been made; the languages of the linguistic minorities had been included. Nevertheless, there was still to be a two tier system, in which all pupils had a statutory right to learn a European Community language. Other languages could only be offered as an alternative not as a substitute.

A Modern Foreign Language as Part of the Core Curriculum

The most important recommendation in the Education Reform Act concerning modern languages was the inclusion of languages in the core curriculum. This would have the effect of making the subject compulsory for all but a tiny minority from 11 - 16, although the 16+ examination, GCSE, would not be obligatory. The tiny minority absolved from study of a foreign language were to be those pupils who were 'statemented', in other words those of restricted ability who needed extra support to achieve bench marks in the other core subjects. This philosophy of 'languages for all' was a fundamental change in English education and bore witness to great changes of attitude not just within the Department of Education and Science but within the country as a whole and showed that the traditionally monolingual and monocultural British were bowing to economic and political pressure. However, the point to which all pupils are obliged to progress remains at a very basic level. For Britain to acquire a work force in which a significant number have language competence, it is clear that the nation's sixteen year olds will have to progress to further study either within the education system or within commerce and industry.

1992 the Open Market - British Business Thinks Belatedly of Language Training.

The economic recession of the early eighties forced many companies to seek new or larger overseas markets. The individual experiences of companies that selling must be done in the target language were discussed and publicized in both higher education and industry and commerce (RSA, 1979, Liston and Reeves, 1985). However, change towards in-house language training and the employment of linguists was uneven and depended largely on the insight of individual managers and their heightened awareness of the languages question.

Nevertheless, attitudes were changing enough for there to be a response from higher education to the demand for linguistically competent lawyers, economists and scientists and the number of combined and integrated degree courses offering a language expanded. Further education also responded with courses for full-time students on vocational courses and with courses designed for local industry and commerce.

In 1993 Britain, together with the other eleven countries of the European Community, faces an economic situation without historical precedent: the Single Market will mean that there will be free movement of goods and services, free movement of capital and free movement of people. The advent of this huge market of 320,000,000 consumers, 260,000,000 of whom are not English speakers, seems to have succeeded in focusing the attention of commerce and industry on the question of language competence and the gaps that need to be plugged. British business seems to be motivated equally by an awareness of opportunity and apprehension of the threat the market poses (Embleton and Hagen, 1992).

Medium sized manufacturing industry selling mainly in the domestic market has realized that this domestic market will henceforth be the whole multilingual European market and if they are to survive, they must adopt less parochial strategies. The free movement of services such as banking, insurance, and financial services seems to offer opportunities of expansion and substantial gain to British business. The competitive advantage of this sector will, however, be jeopardized if British companies remain unrepentantly monolingual and thus unable to exploit the full potential of the new market.

Transnational mergers are increasingly possible and probable and have implications for British business in terms of language and of management style. With the Single European Market comes the management issue: 'how to manage a multi- or, better, a transcultural concern that is now not only selling across borders but owned and directed across borders' (Reeves, 1990, 65). Those who will be able to exploit the free movement of labour are those with marketable skills and language competence. The monolingual is not likely to be on the move either geographically or heirarchically. The personnel consultancy company, Saxton Bampfylde International, defined the ideal manager post 1993 as the person who 'is able to operate with equal confidence anywhere in Europe' (quoted Reeves, 1990, 67). Reeves suggests that those who have a mother tongue which is a minority language in the community and who are thus propelled into multilingualism and multiculturalism at an early stage of their education acquire linguistic competence and cultural sensitivity. There is a creeping awareness that in Britain we may have to acquire this interculturality and linguistic prowess or be marginalised (Embleton and Hagen, 1992).

There are signs that the message has been heard both in the education system and in commerce and industry. Statistics from the Department of Education and Science show that there has been an increase in the numbers taking foreign languages (Table 4, page 53).

These figures will rise steadily in the next few years as the National Curriculum is implemented throughout the age range and language learning becomes compulsory for all until the age of 16 +.

The Department of Trade and Industry launched a campaign in 1990 to heighten awareness in industry and commerce of the linguistic implications of the Single European Market. There are already indications that some sectors of industry and commerce are responding: language audits, and language and cultural awareness training programmes have a high profile.

Table 4
Entry Figures for Modern Languages Examinations 1988 -1990

A Level	Number 1988	Number 1989	Number 1990
French	20422	22334	27359
German	7084	7639	9619
Spanish	2478	3277	3896
Modern Greek	231	279	257
Urdu	326	394	503
GCSE	Number 1988	Number 1989	Number 1990
French	265317	270416	279081
German	75795	69051	84827
Spanish	19073	22226	25870
Modern Greek	390	690	812
Bengali	602	986	1330

Source: Schools Examination and Assessment Council statistics division.

This is not to say, however, that the battle is won. The complacency of English speakers is profound. Since 1945 Britain's position has changed from that of a colonial power, exporting massively to anglophone countries, to that of a member, 'inter pares', of a twelve nation trading group probably heading towards federation. Attitudes towards foreign language learning have failed to keep pace with these changes and recent initiatives may perhaps be too little too late. Complacency and resolute monolingualism may be further shaken if the economic and political influence of the new Germany in Central and Eastern Europe causes German to become increasingly important as an alternative lingua franca.

Notes

1 In Wales the situation is slightly different in that for Welsh medium education English is the first second language and for many English medium education Welsh is the first second language.

2 The traditional method of teaching languages in the public and grammar school system had been the grammar/translation/composition method. At 16+ examples of literature in the foreign language were read and then literary criticism taught through English. Traditional university degree courses continued in the same vein.
Developing teaching strategies which could be used with the whole ability range became a priority. Adoption of the audio-lingual method derived from behaviourist psychology led to the development of courses based on pattern drills and repetition. The use of the language laboratory was seen as a solution. It soon became clear, however, that this approach could be stultifying and did not appear to produce competent language users any more readily than the abandoned grammar translation method.

3 Standards in education in England and Wales are protected by Her Majesty's Inspectorate of Schools who visit schools and colleges, English and Welsh, to assess the quality of teaching and to monitor the success of courses.

References

Advertised vacancy rates in English maintained secondary schools by subject 1985 -1990. 20/7/1990. *Education*, 47

Birmingham LEA. 1991. Advisory teacher and leader of Russian diversification programme in conversation April 1991

Department of Education and Science, Inspectorate of Schools and Colleges. 1977. *Matters for Discussion: Modern languages in comprehensive schools.* HMI Report. London: HMSO

Department of Education and Science, Inspectorate of Schools and Colleges. 1985a. *Inquiry into practice in 22 comprehensives where a foreign language forms part of the curriculum for all or almost all pupils up to the age of 16+.* HMI Report. London: HMSO

Department of Educaiton and Science. 1985b. Report of the committee of inquiry into the education of children from ethnic minority groups, under the chairmanship of Lord Swann. London: HMSO

Department of Education and Science and Welsh Office. 1988. *Modern languages in the school curriculum: a statement of policy. Towards a national capability.* London: HMSO

Department of Education and Science, Inspectorate of Schools. 1989a. *A survey of the teaching and learning of modern foreign languages in a sample of inner city and urban schools.* HMI Report. London: HMSO

Department of Education and Science, Inspectorate of Schools and Colleges. 1989b. *Modern Languages in Polytechnics and Colleges: a survey of good practice.* HMI Report. London: HMSO

Department of Education and Science. 1990a. *School Examination Survey.* London: HMSO

Department of Education and Science, Inspectorate of Schools and Colleges. 1990b. *Modern language courses in business and management courses in further education.* London: HMSO

Department of Education and Science, Inspectorate of Schools and Colleges. *Boys and Modern Languages.* HMI Report. London: HMSO

Embleton, D. and Hagen, S. 1992. *Language in International Business.* London: CILT

Frith, A. 1991. *Rationale for improved community languages provision in schools.* Unpublished paper given at CILT conference 2nd July 1991

Gwent County Council. February 1990. *General circular: information for primary and secondary schools*

Henderson Kassis, J. 1991. European English - an emerging norm for native and non-native speakers, *La Tribune Internationale des Langues Vivantes,* 8: 15

Liston, D., and Reeves, N. 1985. *Business Studies, Languages and Overseas Trade: a study of education and training.* London: Macdonald and Evans with the Institute of Export

Macey, M. 1990. *Education, Racism and Ideology in Britain: the implications of 1988 Educational Reform Act.* Paper given at One Europe Research Group, Cracow, Poland, 21-27 October, 1990

NCLE. 1984. *Language and Languages 16-19.* Papers given at the National Congress on Languages in Education, 4th Assembly

National Curriculum Modern Foreign Languages Working Group. 1990. *Initial advice*, under the chairmanship of Professor Martin Harris. DES and Welsh Office

National Curriculum Council. 1991. Consultation Report, under the chairmanship of Duncan Graham. DES and Welsh Office

Parker, Sir Peter. 1986. *Speaking for the future: a review of the requirements of diplomacy and commerce for Asian and African languages and area studies.* London, University Grants Committee

Reeves, N. 1990. The Foreign Language Needs of UK based Corporations. *Annals, AAPS*: 511

Reeves, N., and Wright, S. 1992. Languages and Pluralism in Britain *The Challenge of Multi-culturalism.* The Linguist. 31: 65-5

Royal Society of Arts. 1979. *Languages and Export Performance: the BETRO report.* London: Royal Society for Arts

Schools Council Modern Languages Committee. 1982. *The second foreign language in secondary schools: a question of survival*

Tomlinson, S. 1990. *Multicultural Education in White Schools.* London. Batsford.

van Ek, J. A. 1976. *The Threshold Level for Modern Language Learning in Schools.* Strasbourg: Council of Europe

Welsh Office Education Department. 1991. *The School Curriculum: briefing booklet 1 for school governors*

Wright, S. 1986. *Language Training Audit of companies in the GKN and Lucas groups*, for company circulation only

Wright, S. 1991. The currency of community language qualifications. *Language Learning Journal*, 4: 39-41

Wyburd, G. 1990. Why bother: the changing view of the DTI. *Language Matters*, 6: 3

SECOND NATIONAL LANGUAGE LEARNING IN FINLAND

A REVIEW OF SECOND NATIONAL LANGUAGE EDUCATION, WITH PARTICULAR REFERENCE TO INTERGROUP LANGUAGE ATTITUDES

E. J. Laine *University of Jyväsklä*

What are the factors that determine which languages are taught and learnt, and to what degree, in the schools of a country? Obviously, such factors fall into two broad categories, namely, those pertaining to society, and those affecting the individual. The size, geopolitical status, cultural and commercial needs of a community largely determine the content of the foreign language (FL) teaching programme. Within the community, two (or more) indigenous linguistic groups may need to communicate with each other, while the presence of various minority groups, immigrants, and so on, often further complicates the situation. As a result of the official school curricula, the individual may be left with comparatively few choices, if the list of languages offered is short. The scope may be further narrowed by 'obligatory choices', if one or more languages on the list is compulsory. In his choice of language(s) to be learnt, the individual may be influenced by material or other reasons, by attitudes, beliefs and stereotypes prevailing in that society. Furthermore, the learner about to embark on language learning is influenced by his notions about himself in general, and as a language learner in particular. Such factors, together with the student's experiences in the course of second/foreign language learning, will eventually be largely responsible in determining the outcome of his study. Taken together, the factors listed above determine the efficiency of the country's language education programme.

The discussion which follows examines these factors in relation to the situation in Finland. After a presentation of the factual context, the question will be examined from an affective point of view. That is, we shall look at the role of affective factors in national and individual programmes of language education. The discussion will focus in particular on intergroup relations as determiners of second national language (SNL) learning.

An Outline of Community Factors

In order to set the context, Finnish community factors are described here in rough outline. The features discussed are those which are of central relevance to the theme. The main issues are firstly, the development and present state of the linguistic situation, and secondly, the state of school language instruction, with regard to SNL learning.

The linguistic situation in Finland

Within the context of modern history, Finland is linguistically perhaps best defined as a monolingual Finnish-speaking country, which in the early centuries of the Modern Age received a strong injection of Swedish. This general statement calls for some elucidation. In the days of Swedish dominion - which started in the 12th century and ended in 1808 - Swedish came to be the language of administration, education, and culture. 'Appointments to public office ... followed no official 'nationality' line' in the single state formed by Sweden and Finland (Wuorinen, 1965, 123), but the Finnish language had no part to play in public affairs: knowing Swedish, then, was a precondition of upward mobility in society. Altogether Swedish enjoyed for centuries an unquestioned superior status over Finnish. It has been pointed out that 'as late as the second half of the nineteenth century, the most important towns in Finland were mainly Swedish' (Fishman, 1989, 124). Even after this situation had changed radically, Swedish remained the language of distinction, an 'upper-class language', in some people's minds. It was probably only after the Second World War that full emotional equilibrium was achieved: only then was the time ripe for linguistic as well as political peace.

Finnish was established as a literary language in the 16th century, and although badly neglected in the centuries that followed, remained the vernacular of the vast majority of the population. It was only in the latter half of the 19th century that Finnish, with the strengthening of nationalist thinking, became the object of energetic revival and development. In this period, educated people, many of whom had Swedish roots, worked to 'reverse the process which had made the upper classes increasingly Swedish', by promoting Finnish as the mother tongue of the nation (Wuorinen, 1931; see also Fishman, 1989, 320). 'Reversing the process', in the words of a well-known slogan, meant 'one nation - one language' (that is Finnish) to many, long into the 20th century. Ancient folk poetry and new national poems were celebrated as language-tied symbols of nationhood. Here, then, a national process of 'self-identification via language' is seen in a pure form. (For a discussion, see Fishman, 1989, 276-84). Here, Fishman's views on nationalism apply with great precision; for a criticism of such nationalistic views, see Edwards, 1984, 1985. Complete equality of the two languages as official languages of the country was established in 1902 (Wuorinen, 1965, 45). Although somewhat slow in coming, as I have suggested in dating full emotional equilibrium to after the Second World War, equality in terms of value status is thus seen to have its roots in the early 20th century.

In our day, Finnish has become the prevailing means of communication in all fields of life, while Swedish has the official status of second national language. The rights of those for whom the 'second national language' is in fact their first language, are extremely well secured, stipulated in the Constitution of 1919 and further developed to protect the minority's interests. The Islands of Ahvenanmaa/Aland, which have a population of some 24,500, have semi-independent status, and language laws do not apply there. The local language is Swedish, and the islands have taken strong measures to protect it, to the exclusion of Finnish.

External pressure is a factor to be noted in an attempt to understand how the present balance has been achieved. In the 1800s, Finnish citizens were united against growing 'Russification' pressures from Tzarist Russia, Finland at this time enjoying autonomous Grand Duchy status. This promoted the growth of nationalism, and had its effect on the language balance. In 1939-44, the two wars against Russia united the nation in an unforeseen manner, healing the wounds left by the Civil War (1917-18), but undoubtedly also levelling the differences between the two linguistic groups. (Cf. Fishman, 1989, 127 ff, and see Wuorinen, 1931; Lindman, 1963; Juva in Ringbom, 1987, 22.)

Some further remarks concerning the Swedish-speaking minority group are in order. Strictly speaking, Swedish has age-old roots in Finland along a narrow strip of south-western coast. Yet, even in the heyday of Swedish dominion, the number of Swedish-speaking people was fairly low: the estimates put the figure at about 17.5% in the early 1700s (about 70,000 people), and the population register gives 14.3% as the share of Swedish speakers in 1880 when Finnish had started its rise (Allardt and Starck, 1981, 120). Today, speakers of Swedish form a minority of barely 6% of the population. This means that their number is about 300,000 in the country's population of 5 million.

A fair number, nearly 50%, of the Swedish-speaking minority are fully bilingual, and taken together with the non-bilinguals, 75-80%, perhaps even more, have at least a working knowledge of Finnish. As regards the Finnish-speaking majority, most of its members have at best some working knowledge of Swedish, having learnt it in school as if it were a foreign language; under 10% consider themselves bilingual to some degree (Ringbom, 1987, 9; see also Laurén, 1988).

On language teaching in Finland

In the context of the present discussion, it may be relevant to consider briefly the last few decades of FL teaching in Finland. It was in the 1940s and 50s that modern teaching ideas grew stronger in the country, and voices were heard demanding FL instruction for every student who 'was interested and had the aptitude'. In the late 40s, fewer than 15% of school-aged young people studied FLs. The FLs were Swedish, which, psychologically, has the status of an FL to most monolingual Finnish speakers, and German. It was only after the Second World War that English started its rise, and finally took the position which by tradition had belonged to German (see, e.g., Laine, 1984).

Today, English is chosen as the first FL by about 85% of school-aged children, who start it in Grade 3, while Swedish is obligatory for all, starting in Grade 7. Thus, the learning of languages has increased enormously, but the situation is basically the same: one 'obligatory' and one 'favourite' language dominate the scene. However, the language programme is of course much wider, as we shall see below. But the question is, how much can the students take in, and under what conditions?

Since the 1940s, in fact, even earlier, official instructions concerning methodology have recommended using the target language widely for true communication, for example, as the medium of instruction in FL lessons, not simply as an object to be analysed (Laine, 1984). With the influx of communicative methods in the last decade, this recommendation has been keenly observed, with the aim of providing optimum conditions for successful language adoption and acquisition in the classroom. Attaining these goals, however, depends on teacher competence and on linguistic attitudes. (A very different line is taken if it is decreed that a 'second national' language is to be taught just as another school subject - possibly as a means towards separatism; consider Swing, 1982; Laine, 1990.)

The two linguistic groups learn the other's language as compulsory subjects in the comprehensive (basic) school, and in the upper forms of secondary school. Owing to the different starting points, the results of study also differ for each group. For the Swedish speakers within Finland, natural learning of the second national language is supported by the overwhelmingly Finnish-speaking environment while most members of the majority have very little experience of speaking Swedish. By and large, SNL instruction, for the majority, is a 'must' while for the minority it is a 'need' (see Ringbom, 1987, 13).

The present SNL/FL teaching programme

In the comprehensive school, all students take two languages. Of these, 'Language A' starts in Grade 3 and 'Language B' in Grade 7. In theory, there is a free choice between Swedish, English, German, French, and Russian, if the commune is large enough to offer them all, as long as the SNL is one of them. In practice, however, in the mid-80s over 85% chose English as Language A, 6% chose Swedish, and 5% (Swedish speakers) chose Finnish. Thus, under 3% was left over for other languages as Language A. These can, however, be studied as optional languages, 'Language C', in the comprehensive school, starting in Grade 8, and almost 40% of the pupils take an optional language (Nikki, 1989).

In the upper secondary school, the choice is widened further by the possibility of taking another optional language, 'Language D'. The optional languages compete with all the other optional subjects, and recently, choosing optional languages has been on the wane (Nikki, 1989).

The above figures reveal that the game is largely played between the two 'big' languages on the programme. It is feasible to maintain that in the study of Swedish and English, the level of linguistic competence attained will depend not simply on the time allocated and other 'frame' factors, but more decisively on language attitudes. The very choice of an optional language at all may be at stake where negative affects are present.

Language needs in the country

For a small linguistic area like Finland, foreign languages are all-important for international communication. English as a world language might very well top the list of languages considered necessary. Yet, the first place goes to Swedish (Bergren, 1982, Mehtäläinen, 1987). The explanation probably lies in the fact that a knowledge of Swedish is a prerequisite, decreed by law, for entry to the professions, for civil servants, and others.

The need for more German is currently felt acutely; for commercial reasons, much more Russian is required; Spanish-speaking countries are significant commercially, but extremely little Spanish is taught; only the beginnings of Japanese teaching are appearing in some high schools... the list could be continued.

In sum, the need for many FLs has been shown, and the language programme allows an enrichment. What is more, the communes have been required to teach more German, French and Russian, but the results have been meagre (Nikki, 1989). At the cognitive level, then, the readiness to meet the needs is there but the present economic depression, for its part, is also militating significantly against the desired change.

Individual Factors: Language Attitudes

An individual's attitudes, beliefs, stereotypes, values and norms are formed in the society that he lives in, and thus 'community' and 'individual' are interdependent concepts. Consider here the theory and model of L2 learning by Gardner et al, 1974; Gardner, 1979, 1985; the intergroup theory of Tajfel and Turner, 1979; and Hall and Gudykunst's work, 1986, on the intergroup theory of second language ability; a good review of recent research into the problem of ethnic identity is provided in Gudykunst and Schmidt, 1987. In the following discussion these points will be kept in mind, although the focus of attention will lie on the individual.

For convenience, 'language attitudes' is used here as a blanket term for factors operative within the affective domain of language learning: motivation, attitudes, and notions of the self.

Finnish-Swedish relations in Finland

As was noted above, Swedish was considered superior in terms of status during Swedish dominion in Finland, and it may have remained the language of distinction to some people up to the first half of the present century. Likewise, reactions against it, growing with the rise of Finnish nationalism in the 19th century, continued to be commonplace long after the turn of the century. A period of language strife, culminating in the 1920s and 30s, disturbed inter-group relations considerably. Yet, there have never been actual riots over linguistic problems. Covert negative attitudes die hard, however: even today, many school-learners of Swedish may just feel unwilling to make a serious study of the language, although frequently they are probably no longer aware of the historical reasons for this resistance. The nationalist slogan, 'One country, one people, one nation' (cf. Edwards, 1984, 1985) may also still exert its influence in some parents' minds. On the other hand, many members of the Swedish-speaking minority, although on the defensive psychologically, seem to have developed quite open attitudes towards learning Finnish (Ringbom, 1987, 9; see also below).

Over the past few years, voices of resentment have been heard ever more strongly in the mass media concerning the alleged privileges of the Swedish-speaking minority. The main causes seem to be the fact that the youth of the minority have easier access to institutes of higher education, and the general obligation for the youth of the majority to learn Swedish. The latter, as was pointed out above, is a real problem: what can be done to make the school second language programme lighter, and more flexible? Towards the end of 1990, debates concerning 'obligatory Swedish' sharpened, and there was a motion before parliament to reduce, or remove, the hours of obligatory Swedish in schools. However, the motion was not carried. The latest (early 1992) proposal is to make Swedish an optional language in the comprehensive school, while affect-loaded discussion concerning the position of SNL/Swedish as a school subject at large continues.

Face-to-face contacts between members of the two linguistic groups are infrequent, except in the narrow band along the coast where the minority is concentrated. When they do meet, the language most used is Finnish: most members of the minority know Finnish much better than members of the majority know Swedish. To be more exact: a growing fraction of the minority, composed largely of educated younger people in the cities, mixes readily with Finnish speakers and uses Finnish fully competently to communicate. A monolingual fraction, consisting largely of 'common people' in the islands and along the coastline, is unable to do so, while some members of the old elite are perhaps not overly keen to use Finnish either (see Ringbom, 1987). It would seem that most Finnish speakers lag behind the 'enlightened' group of Swedish speakers in their readiness to communicate with members of the other linguistic group in either language.

To sum up, language strife between the two linguistic groups, which grew in the latter half of the 19th century and became accentuated in the period between the two World Wars, has calmed down and been replaced by language harmony. The linguistic minority shows an attitude of growing openness, and the majority has adopted a policy of live and let live. Expressions of resentment are, after all, only superficial phenomena, or based on minor grievances: where intergroup relations are concerned, they do not seem irreparable. By international standards, language strife in Finland has never been very significant.

Popularity of FLs

Reference was made earlier to the fact that learning the second national language in schools is obligatory, but not necessarily very popular. English, again, is among the more popular school subjects: research data allow us to conclude that, given the choice, the majority of learners would like to have more English at the cost of Swedish (Laine, 1978, 1988; Mustila, 1990; Nikki, 1989). In fact, it has become a common joke to call English the 'third national language' in Finland, although a student vote would give it second place (for a discussion, see Ringbom, 1987, 13-14).

It has also become clear (see above) that the rest of the school FL programme is suffering because of 'obligatory Swedish' and the popularity of English: as the figures showed, German, French, and Russian are all but 'exotic' languages in Finnish schools. Of these, Russian may still suffer some unpopularity for historical reasons. Yet, quite recently new interest has been shown towards it in the eastern areas of the country, close to the Russian border. In some schools in this area, a change from Swedish to Russian was suggested as an experiment, but this was not considered possible.

Before the Second World War, German used to be by far the commonest FL in secondary schools; it was the most commonly taught FL in exactly the way English is now. With the rise of Germany in recent years, and especially since reunification, there has been a fresh interest in the language, although this has not, so far, been reflected in the official figures.

With the growth and expansion of the European Community/European Union, and with discussions concerning it in Finland, learning a larger variety of European languages has become a topical issue. At the time of writing, the impact has been attitude-forming more than anything else. In the near future, however, it is likely to be reflected at community level in the form of more diverse school FL programmes.

On affective factors: motivation, attitudes, stereotypes, self-notions

Why should a young person learn a second, or foreign, language, or perhaps several languages? What kind of lures can make such a goal attractive? What turns him away from such activity? The community around him may offer a number of sound reasons for language learning, and many of them are adopted, nominally. Yet, full commitment can only follow if the reasons for study are internalized personally.

Among the reasons that a community may have for promoting the study of second or foreign languages, those which best guarantee survival and prosperity seem the most prominent, not least in our day, but cultural reasons also have an important role to play. An individual's mind will reflect, often to a high degree, the values and attitudes prevalent in his community. When a learner in a school setting is faced with a language-learning task, questions relevant to that learner, on a more or less conscious level, might include, 'What is to be gained from this?', 'Will this help me to get on with people speaking language X?', 'Will this make me a more knowledgeable/civilized/enlightened person?' In other words, his motivation to learn language X may be instrumental, integrative, or cognitive (consider Gardner and Lambert, 1972; Clément et al, 1976; Gardner, 1985; Laine, 1978, 1988).

Consequently, the identity of the group whose language is to be studied is an important determinant of motivation. If the outgroup is considered unimportant, or inferior in some way, learning its language will hardly prosper

- for an eye-opening case, see Nida, 1957; and consider the theory and results of Giles et al., e.g., Giles and Johnson, 1987. If the outgroup is superior, the learning activity will lead to fairly good results for instrumental reasons, for example, upward mobility. The prospects for good learning are best when the in- and outgroup are experienced as equal, and as in many ways resembling each other. This means that the perceived distance between the two groups and cultures is minimal (see, e.g., Schumann, 1978).

In Finland today, the two linguistic groups do not differ from each other significantly in any essential respect (Allardt and Starck, 1981; Ringbom, 1987, 8, 21-22). This means that the starting point for successful SNL study exists: if given good grounds, most members of the two groups 'do not mind' learning the other group's language, to say the least. Many bilinguals of the Swedish-speaking minority have clearly had such grounds: the prevailing language of the environment is Finnish. Thus if, for some reason, one must speak in public, using Finnish will guarantee a wider audience. Members of the Finnish-speaking majority, however, largely fail to see such advantages of SNL learning. Swedish for them is not a necessity: in the monolingual Finnish areas - by far the largest part of the country - they seldom even encounter Swedish speakers. It is therefore hard for them to see the need for SNL study. Ignorance of the other group, its life and culture, even its existence, hardly promotes meaningful learning.

Tourism and Scandinavian co-operation are further reasons, officially, for Finnish speakers to learn Swedish. However, as many Scandinavians are willing and able to make use of English in 'Scandinavian' communication, this particular integrative motive hardly comes fully into play. In sum, for many learners of SNL/Swedish in Finland the main, if not only, motive is purely instrumental: a working knowledge of Swedish is required in professions (by law) and in business.

With regard to intergroup attitudes, a recent survey showed an outstanding asymmetry between Finnish and Swedo-Finnish attitudes. Speakers of Finnish - especially males - rated their Swedish-speaking co-nationals remarkably lower than did the 'Swedes' when rating Finnish speakers (McRae et al, 1988). 'Finns' also rated the importance of Swedish (in comparison with other languages) much lower than Swedish speakers did; the latter, naturally, rank their own mother tongue high. Both groups, while rating Finnish high, rank English as the most important foreign language in the country (McRae et al, 1988, 28). Such findings indicate a readiness to learn less SNL/Swedish in school, and a general willingness to have a maximal dose of FL/English in the school curricula.

The general attitudes of Finnish learners towards other languages seem positive: in a small country with a language not related to that of any of its neighbours, the need for FLs is apparent. Among FLs, English stands in first position, and in fact takes the lion's share, to the exclusion of other languages, as we can see in the figures already quoted above. The obvious instrumental motivation is complemented by the Finns' positive attitude to, and stereotypes of, these outgroups, both British and American (Laine, 1978).

As regards the attractions of the other FLs on offer at school, the learners' motives for choosing Russian seem predominantly instrumental, even though there are old cultural connections; for choosing French, cultural; and for choosing German, instrumental and cultural, as there are age-old commercial and cultural ties between the two countries.

In his choices and learning activities, the individual is guided largely by the notions he has of himself in general, and as a (FL) learner in particular (Laine, 1988). It would seem that many Finnish FL learners are still slightly hampered by notions of their inferiority in comparison with members of various outgroups. This would seem to be the case in the countryside in particular (Laine, 1978, 1988).

Affective factors in school SNL study may be negative and prevent efficient learning (on this 'filter', see Laine, 1988). But although intergroup relations in Finland in our day do not seem a great obstacle to SNL learning, much more could be done in research to pave the way for such activities.

Suggestions for Further Research in the Area

The basic problem underlying the present discussion is how affective factors, both societal and individual, may determine human goal-directed activity. An individual's choices and preferences must be seen against his societal background; the prevailing values and attitudes of the community are a synthesis of individual values and attitudes. Consequently, doing adequate research into the area is a complex task.

Naturally, the question of a country's language policy can be approached from a purely sociological point of view. On the other hand, language choices and the ensuing learning activity may be approached as a purely psychological problem. It is not very difficult to find examples of these approaches. Interesting as the results often are, their coverage may be narrow, if not fragmentary.

Social-psychological theories of second/foreign language acquisition today, such as Gardner's, offer quite a broad approach; and are being yet further developed. But these theories are not without their critics (see e.g. Giles and others in the late 80s). Further points of criticism are likely to be made, perhaps faster than the old ones have been met with satisfactorily. Even so, the confrontation of various theories with each other seems fruitful, though here a sound eclectism is needed.

A broad theory must take into account a vast numbers of factors. To test a complex model, adequate research methodology is needed. Multivariate analyses, such as those made possible by the Lisrel technique, today are a must (see Gardner et al, 1983; Laine and Malin, 1990). Modern techniques make possible the testing of vast models and the verification of latent variables formerly only approached indirectly and/or by inference. 'Perceptions' of various things - status, prestige, and others - gained in earlier research may be a starting point for further investigation using such sophisticated methods as these.

A brief glance at the new independent countries in Europe, with their various linguistic groups, necessarily continuing a life of coexistence, is an eloquent example. Learning national languages is internationally a growing problem.

The difficulties encountered are often of an affective nature. In these days of great change, one does not need to look far to find 'hot' examples. The cool, matter-of-fact approach provided by research, with its paradigms, techniques, and instruments developed and tested in less strained environments, may here offer invaluable aid and services.

References

Allardt, E. and Starck, C. 1981. *Språkgränser och samhällsstruktur*. Stockholm: Almqvist and Wiksell

Bergren, O. 1982. *Vieraiden kielten käyttö ia tarve teollisuuden insinööritehtävissë teknillisten korkeakouluien kieltenopetuksen tavoitteiden ohiaaiana*. Lappeenrannan teknillinen korkeakoulu. Kielikeskuksen julkaisuja 3

Clément, R., Gardner, R.C., and Smythe, P.C. 1976. *Motivational Variables in Second Language Acquisition: a Study of Francophones learning English*. Research Bulletin No 351. Department of Psychology, University of Western Ontario, London, Canada

Edwards, J. (ed.) 1984. *Linguistic minorities, policies and pluralism*. London: Academic Press

Edwards, J. 1985. *Language, society and identity*. Oxford: Basil Blackwell

Fishman, J.A. 1989. *Language and ethnicity in minority sociolinguistic perspective*. Clevedon: Multilingual Matters

Gardner, R.C. 1979. Social psychological aspects of second language acquisition. In Giles, H. and St Clair, R. (eds.), *Language and Social Psychology*. Oxford: Basil Blackwell

Gardner, R.C. 1983. Learning another language: a true social psychological experiment. *Journal of Language and Social Psychology*, 2: 219-39

Gardner, R.C. 1985. *Social Psychology and second language learning: the role of attitudes and motivation.* London: Edward Arnold

Gardner, R.C., Lalonde, R.N. and Pierson, R. 1983. The socioeducational model of second language acquisition: an investigation using LISREL causal modelling. *Journal of Language and Social Psychology*, 2, 1: 1-15

Gardner, R.C., and Lambert, W.E. 1972. *Attitudes and motivation in second language learning.* Rowley, Mass.: Newbury House

Gardner, RC Smythe, P.C., Kirby, D.M., and Bramwell, J.R. 1974. *Second language acquisition: a social psychological approach.* Final report. London, Ontario: Ontario Ministry of Education

Giles, H., and Johnson, P. 1987. Ethnolinguistic identity theory: a social psychological approach to language maintenance. *International Journal of the Sociology of Language*, 68: 69-99

Gudykunst, W.B., and Schmidt, K.L. 1987. Language and ethnic identity: an overview and prologue. *Journal of Language and Social Psychology,* 6, 3-4: 157-69

Hall, B.J., and Gudykunst, W.B. 1986. The intergroup theory of second language ability. *Journal of Language and Social Psychology*, 5, 4: 291-301

Laine, E. 1978. *Foreign language learning motivation in Finland II.* Turku: Suomen sovelletun kielitieteen yhdistyksen (AFinLA) julkaisuja 21

Laine, E. 1984. Methodische Tendenzen und neusprachliche Unterrrichtspraxis in Finnland in den letzten Jahrzehnten. *Informationen Deutsch als Fremdsprache*, 2: 3-9

Laine, E.J. 1988. The affective filter in foreign language learning and teaching. *Jyväskylä Cross-Language Studies 15*, University of Jyväskylä

Laine, E.J. 1990. *Learning a second national language: a comparative inspection of milieu factors in two countries.* Paper presented at the AILA World Congress, Greece

Laine, E.J., and Malin, A. 1990. *Investigation of the affective domain in FL learning: from description to causal explanation.* Unpublished manuscript.

Laurén, U. 1988. *Sprakfel och interferens hos tvasprakiga skolelever.* Licenciate thesis, University of Helsinki

Lindman, K. 1963. Finland's Swedes: an introduction and a bibliography. *Scandinavian Studies,* 35: 123-31

McRae, K.D., Bennett, S.E., and Miljan, T. 1988. *Intergroup sympathies and language patterns in Finland: results from a survey.* Helsinki: Suomen Gallup

Mehtäläinen, J. 1987. *Teollisuuden toimihenkilöiden kielitaidon tarvetutkimus.* Teollisuuden koulutusvaliokunta. Monistesarja 8

Mustila, E. 1990. *Finska qymnasieelevers motivation för, attitYder till och intresse för svenska.* Helsingin yliopiston kasvatustieteen laitos. Tutkimuksia 125. University of Helsinki

Nida, E.A. 1957. Some psychological problems in second language learning. *Language Learning*, 8, 1-2: 7-15

Nikki, M.-L. 1989. *Suomalaisen koulutusiariestelmän kielikoulutus ia sen relevanssi.* Osa 1. Kasvatustieteiden tutkimuslaitoksen julkaisusarja A, Tutkimuksia 33. University of Jyväskylä

Ringbom, H. 1987. *The role of the first language in foreign language learning.* Clevedon: Multilingual Matters

Schumann, J. 1978. Social and psychological factors in second language acquisition. In Richards, J.C. (ed.), *Understanding second and foreign language learning.* Rowley, Mass.: Newbury House

Swing, E.S. 1982. Education for separatism: The Belgian experience. In Hartford et al. (eds), *Issues in International Bilingual Education*, 265-90

Tajfel, H., and Turner, J.C. 1979. An integrative theory of intergroup conflict. In Austin, W.C. and Worchel, S. (eds.), *The Social Psychology of Intergroup Relations*. Monterey, CA: Brooks, Cole

Wuorinen, J.H. 1931. *Nationalism in modern Finland*. New York: Columbia University Press

Wuorinen, J.H. 1965. *Scandinavia*. Englewood Cliffs: Prentice Hall

IDENTITY, COMMUNITY AND LANGUAGE POLICIES IN CONTEMPORARY FRANCE

D. Ager *Aston University*

Introduction

French language policy is well established, supported by all the main political groupings, and slow to change. It reflects a coherent approach to the creation and maintenance of a national identity, followed since the sixteenth century. It has affected territorial minorities like the Basques or the Bretons, who have been integrated and almost completely assimilated through language and educational policies inside France - the 'Hexagon'; while, outside, the 'civilising mission' of France has imposed French educational systems and priorities on many countries of Africa and Asia. Nonetheless, French, even within France, is still confronting the surviving regional languages and, now, the languages of recent immigration. The present chapter attempts to assess how far existing language policy and educational practice respond to changing problems of identity and community in a France facing a European, but also a world, future.

Regional Languages

Throughout the 1970s pressure from France's indigenous minorities was maintained on French governments for action to improve the status of the regional languages. Basque, Breton, Catalan, Corsican, and Occitan had been recognised in the Deixonne law of 1951, but other languages or dialects such as those of Alsace, Moselle or the gallo-speaking area near Brittany had not. Full implementation of the Deixonne provisions for language teaching, and recognition by the central government of any official role for regional languages, was lacking, and the growth of regional feeling was met mainly by indifference. Each of the main regional languages has a different relationship to Parisian French, the accepted standard for education and official usage, and each has suffered in different ways from the long history of oppression, marginalisation and exclusion, dating particularly from the French Revolution of 1789, which has nonetheless had the effect of creating the French nation.

Alsace and Lorraine, together with the Moselle region, are basically German-speaking border areas. Alsace joined France around 1648, although the process was not complete until 1781, was interrupted by two periods of German occupation from 1870 to 1918 and again from 1940 to 1945, and there remain a number of special characteristics such as a different social security system. The language laws introduced at the time of the French Revolution led to a reign of linguistic terror, and inhabitants of Alsace have suffered since - under the Germans when French was banned, and under the returning French when

German similarly disappeared. Autonomy movements were violently suppressed during the 1920s and again in the 1970s, and it has been difficult for the education system in particular to come to terms with the underlying multilingualism of standard written French and standard written German, at least three German-based spoken dialects and spoken popular regional French.

Today the German-based dialects are still understood by at least 60% (1962: 87%, 1975: 75%) of the local population, more than a million people. They are used in primary schools as a means of education, at least for part of the time. Language shift towards French is, however, strong and increasing; there is marked French-dialect diglossia, and the strength of religion, a potent force for maintaining the dialect, is declining. Yet the prestige of German is high, cross-frontier working is common, (standard) German is pervasive in the media, regional French is strongly marked and regionalism is by no means a spent force. Alsace, particularly Strasbourg, is regarded by both the 'French of the interior' and by native-born Alsaciens as the centre of the new Franco-German Europe, and the region where French ambitions for housing central European and particularly European Community organisations have the best chance of success.

The *Basque* region has special ties to the Spanish Basques: three of the seven Basque provinces are located north of the Pyrenees, have been part of France since 1598 and retained their own laws and customs until 1789. In more recent times the region has had strong autonomy movements, matching anti-Madrid with anti-Paris attitudes and apparently supporting terrorist actions against police and official property: it is often in France that ETA leaders have been arrested.

The strong Basque identity of the Spanish provinces is undoubtedly a factor in the survival of Basque in France. As with German and Catalan, the existence of the language in standardised form and in public usages in a nearby political entity - Province or Nation - retains prestige for the local form and prevents marked diglossia. But although kindergarten schools are fairly well supported, and the language is taught through to University level, it is only spoken by about 40% of the local population, mainly in rural areas, in one *Département*, and has a fairly uncertain future in France, where its formal public use is rare.

Brittany, independent from 938 although formally held in feudal relationship to the kings of France, retained considerable practical independence until 1532, and only lost the economic and political privileges of its nobility in 1790. In recognition of its opposition to Paris the region was not occupied in 1815, and from 1940 to 1944 a Breton batallion fought alongside German troops - with a fairly bloody subsequent revenge by the returning French in 1944. Brittany has always regarded itself as economically subservient to Paris: 30% of Paris cleaners were Bretons in the 1950's, and the profits of the massive agro-industries, particularly pig and chicken production, traditionally go to Paris-based financiers or feedstock producers rather than locals. So economic and demographic problems have led to political violence, and minor terrorist actions continue today to register local opposition to the French state.

Bretons are fond of contrasting their situation with that of Wales, where Welsh is accepted in many aspects of contemporary life. The prestige of Breton is low, it is little used, if at all, in official public situations, and its preservation seems to be generally regarded as quaint and folkloric rather than associated with an active economic, educational or cultural life. Nonetheless, it is still understood by about 600,000 people and used by half that number; there are active kindergarten (Diwan) groups, and a strong Breton movement actively fosters language rights and seeks common ground with other European minority cultures.

3% of *Catalan* speakers are located in France, and like the Basques, take comfort from the strong sense of regional identity displayed by the Spanish provinces, where the language is standardised, proudly used in official and public functions, and independence from Madrid in most aspects of life is now well-established. Barcelona forms a natural regional metropolis, but the wealth of industrial 'Spanish' Catalonia presents a problem for the generally rural northern Catalonians: if they exchanged their Paris masters for Barcelona-based political control, would they be any better off?

About 200,000 inhabitants use the language in France; there is a strong Catalan-language kindergarten movement and the codified, widely used and respected language of the Spanish Catalans offers a prestige model of considerable attraction. So the linguistic future for the region is not so clear-cut, or so negative, as elsewhere: it could well be that the pride and power of the Catalans could raise the linguistic profile considerably.

Corsica, until 1982, was regarded as merely a more or less normal French region - one of the 26 - divided into two Départments. A history of dependence - on the kings of Aragon, on the Genoese, on the French after 1768 - was interrupted by a short period of autonomy from 1793 to 1796 under the Corsican hero Paoli. The island's poverty, together with political and administrative structures based on a close-knit, clan-based family structure similar to that of Sicily, has led to massive emigration, with about 400,000 people claiming Corsican connections living world-wide (Marseille has about 200,000). It has also led to massive immigration, particularly of State workers - bureaucrats, teachers, civil servants - with the result that the present population has only about 50% 'native' Corsicans; only about 80,000 speakers of Corsican (a dialect of Italian) in the population of about 294,000.

A continuing history of electoral fraud, political violence, corruption and a continuing struggle for local identity led to a new, and hopefully longer-term structural solution in 1991, although the French Constitutional Council decreed that any mention of a 'Corsican people' was illegal, since the French Constitution only recognises the French people, 'composed of all French citizens without distinction of origin, race or religion' (Olivesi and Pastorel, 1991). Corsica has rights in relation to language teaching - particularly of Corsican dialect, and within normal school hours - but cannot remove the rights open to other pupils in the French system, so dialect teaching is rudimentary, particularly as the centralised educational system regards Italian as the educational form of the regional language.

Occitan is the name commonly given to the language also known as *Provençal*, or the '*langue d'oc*'. After the crushing defeat of the 'Albigensian heresy' in 1228 by the northern French kings, southern France has gradually lost its linguistic identity, with the result that although about 12 million of the total French population of 55 million could call themselves 'Occitans', few do. There is nonetheless an identity problem, many native speakers, and a healthy recruitment for classes in the five recognised dialects of this particular regional language - about half the 21,662 enrolments (ages 10-18) for the study of regional languages in 1991-2 are for Occitan.

Many of the identity problems of southern France are closely linked to economics. Until 1945, southern France was arid, dedicated to wine-growing, poor and politically unimportant. Since then, tourism, irrigation and immigration have fundamentally changed the situation, so that nowadays the native Occitan speaker is 'rural, old, poor and male' (Ager, 1990), but the region is wealthy, a Mecca for the old and for Mediterranean refugees, and politically significant, for example in the growth of Right-wing politics.

In northern France the '*langue d'oïl*' (so named to contrast with the '*langue d'oc*' of southern France) is divided into a number of dialects: eleven are normally recognised. Of these, '*francien*', the dialect of the Paris area, has produced standard French, and it was thought that the others had more or less died out in the early years of this century. Recent surveys have however shown continuing traces of sufficient differences from standard French to continue to justify the label 'dialect' rather than that of 'accent', reserved for the more widespread regional variants on standard spoken French.

A language policy for regional languages

The Giordan report on language policy of 1982 reflected the position of the Socialist Government coming newly to power. Following the pledges given by Mitterrand as presidential candidate in 1981, it was intended to 'repair the historical damage and remedy the affront to human dignity' created by over-centralisation since the French Revolution of 1789 by accepting local identities, decentralising administration and devolving power. One part of this process was to enable wider teaching of regional languages than had been allowed by the 1951 Deixonne law.

To a certain extent this has been done: it is now possible to study recognised regional languages within the official educational system. There is provision for State help for kindergarten schools teaching through the regional language, although these are mainly funded by parental and regional contributions. In secondary schools, although the overall recruitment for regional languages in the formal system in 1991-2 - 21,662 of the 8,105,971 total enrolments in secondary education for all languages, whether for first, second or third language - hardly indicates a major level of interest (Enquête 16, 1992), it is possible to offer a language as an optional subject for any Baccalauréat stream, and as a compulsory or optional subject within particular ones, and small numbers of students in the second, first and terminal classes do so: 1,341 as their second language, 8,636 as their third (all languages, public and private education) (Ministère, 1992). In order to make this possible, some changes were made to the qualifications allowed in the teacher training system from 1983 and 1984, and teachers can now qualify in (some) regional languages provided they also take another language or French as a main subject.

Not much change has taken place regarding which regional languages are recognised, however: the only changes from the approved Deixonne list now include gallo (the only '*francien*' dialect recognised), the Alsace and the Moselle 'languages', and (soon) the Melanesian languages spoken in New Caledonia. Of these, only the Melanesian languages can be offered as compulsory subjects, the others only being available as options.

The regional and decentralisation reforms which accompanied these cultural reforms increased to some degree the local political and economic autonomy which is essential to enable cultural and language policy to flourish, although the 26 French political regions do not necessarily coincide with language areas. But despite local taxation and spending powers, local elections and political Assemblies with their own President, the French regions are not fully autonomous and the traditional French fear of fragmentation in language as well as in power is as strong as ever, as evidenced by the ferocity of the Parliamentary debate on the notion of a Corsican 'people' in 1989 and 1990.

Linguistically, regionalised forms of standard French have in most cases replaced both the regional language and standard (spoken) French itself. These forms are often strongly marked, both in pronunciation and indeed in vocabulary and syntax, and show no signs of dying out, although the written language is everywhere codified and uniform - indeed, the curriculum is so centralised that even handwriting styles are absolutely the same everywhere. Other influences reinforcing the use of a single official language, apart from the history of the creation of the Nation State since 1789, are the prestige of a literary culture and the power and influence of the television services, State-run until recently; the written Press is mainly regional. The reputation of France as a, if not the, prime example of the uniform European monoglottal State, is understandable.

The future for regional languages may therefore be one of decline and eventual disappearance, although the situation is by no means static and there are very active pressure groups, usually of militant teachers or local historians, who campaign strongly for official status. Already some languages are in danger of becoming just one more aspect of folklore, no longer used in the economic or public life of the region, part of a diglossic situation and the object of scholarly attempts at revival. Educational policy has to recognise the efforts of the pressure groups, but, in the classroom, studying a regional language may be regarded as an easy way out for wayward or backward pupils. The future of some languages may be more successful, particularly if a neighbouring State or Region has a lively linguistic life and belief in identity and autonomy - the case particularly with Basque and Catalan in the South. But Wales is too far from Brittany to be of much help, and Occitan is different from other Romance languages. For Alsace and Corsica, the standard German and Italian of the educational system may indeed be a negative influence on survival, by ensuring the teaching of the prestige form and hence increasing negative attitudes towards the local dialect.

Non-Territorial Minorities

Nowadays, with increasing immigration to metropolitan France, both territorial and non-territorial minorities find themselves faced with similar pressures: rules for citizenship and nationality bear as hard on those who would retain their own separate identity and yet wish to participate in the French State, as the Revolution and nineteenth century educational practice did on the regions. According to the Giordan report of 1982, three long-established communities retain their own identity to an extent which should be supported in any democratic State: the Armenians, the Jews and the Gypsies. All these communities are however bilingual in French and their original language, or indeed monolingual in French; most of them have adopted French nationality.

Approximately 300,000 *Armenians* form the second largest community, after that in the United States, outside the Armenian regions. Many retain contacts with the region of origin, to the extent of continuing political action against Turkey or the former Soviet Union, and there is a well-developed community life, organising its own schools, hospitals, churches, radio stations and Press, and naturally retaining its own language. Nonetheless, as a community whose main entry to France took place in the 1920s, most members are nowadays well integrated. Armenian is little taught in the French educational system, although it is possible to take it in the Baccalauréat.

The nomadic way of life of Western *Gypsies* continues, with approximately 200,000 in France, faced with the classic problem: if members settle for long and follow the educational norms of the host community, assimilation and integration inevitably follows within a generation, while rejection by the host community, and classification as 'antisocial' is the fate of those insistent on retaining traditional customs. The range of Gypsy communities and the associated languages (see Ager, 1990) is unknown to the formal educational system, although the communities themselves offer a degree of support, tuition and information exchange. The future for Gypsies as separate communities in France is bleak.

Jews in Western Europe have a long tradition of retaining their religious, linguistic and social character within hostile States. After its near destruction during the 1939-45 war, the French community of at least 660,000 has been to a large measure restored to pre-war levels, particularly by recent immigration from the Maghreb into southern France, although these are mainly Sephardim, contrasting with the traditional Ashkenazim communities of Alsace-Lorraine and Paris.

Linguistically, Jews have often assimilated completely to the host community. Nonetheless, because of the history of migrations, some French Jews retain languages which have been used in previous settlement: Yiddish is thought to have some 60-80,000 speakers, while Ladino and of course Arabic have been imported from north Africa. Hebrew is taught in the French educational system, as a foreign language, although with only 4,797 students in 1991-2 at the secondary level.

More recent immigrant communities

Limits on immigration were imposed from 1974, and offical immigrants since then have entered the country for family reunification or because of political asylum. Nonetheless the last five years have seen for example an increase of 8% in children with foreign nationality in the colleges, of whom about 23% come from other European Community countries, and about 53% from the Maghreb countries. The proportion of immigrants from the Maghreb, from the Near East (particularly Turkey) and from Africa, is increasing rapidly.

France's *Arabic-speaking* community is large - about two million, although legal immigrants number less than this. The majority come from the three countries of the Maghreb (Algeria, Morocco and Tunisia), and are Muslim. Recent problems with the Gulf war of 1991, during which many immigrants supported Sadam Hussein, created perceptions of tensions and fears which offered rich grounds for political extremists. So did the Creil affair of 1989, in which three young Muslim girls caused offence to some by insisting on wearing headscarves as a sign of religious belief while studying in that monument to lay Republicanism which French public education represents. There are continuing problems both with Muslim assertiveness and 'French', usually Right-wing, direct action against immigrant communities.

The *Portuguese* however form the largest single nationality among 'European' - and indeed among all - immigrants to France. Originally, and still to a large extent, Portuguese immigrants were seasonal workers, both in the agricultural areas of the South and also in domestic and industrial work elsewhere. Many, however, have become established, and brought in their families and children who make major contributions to youth culture, particularly in urban centres. As European immigrants, the Portuguese seem to integrate well with local communities and have little difficulty in adapting to social and economic conditions.

Table 1
Immigrants in France

Portuguese	845,000
Algerians	710,000
Moroccans	575,000
Italians	370,000
Spanish	340,000
Tunisians	230,000
Turks	159,000
Yugoslavia	66,000
Belgians	64,000
Poland	59,000
Other countries	1,035,000

Source: Mermet, 1991 and INSEE, 1989

Language and education policy for immigrant languages

Called 'original languages and cultures', Arabic (Moroccan, Algerian and Tunisian), Italian, Portuguese, Spanish, Turkish and the languages of the former Yugoslavia are taught in the public education system at the first cycle, by arrangements with the countries 'of origin', and on an optional basis. Teaching takes place during (54.3% of the 112,147 pupils in 1989-90) or outside (45.7%) school hours, and is carried out by 1,429 teachers, principally in the first level, up to age 10 (Note 90-27). These classes take place only in certain approved schools, schools in which only 21.6% of the 520,157 'foreign' children (ie those without French nationality) in French schools are enrolled.

Less than 15% of such 'foreign' children from the Maghreb countries participate in these language learning programmes, while the figures are 28% of Spanish, 31.7% of Portuguese, 34.6% of Turkish and 23.2% of 'Yugoslav' children. The Italian figure, of 146.4 %, indicates the continuing liveliness of the Italian-speaking community, many of whom now have French nationality yet wish to ensure their children retain close linguistic contact. Within the figures, the numbers of Moroccan (up 18% over 1989-90) and Italian (stable since 1988-89) children have increased since 1984, while Spanish and Portuguese have decreased slightly, and 'Yugoslav' children have decreased by 23% since 1989-90.

Importantly, this teaching is paid for by the countries concerned, is carried out by teachers who come from the relevant countries, and the curriculum and its delivery are not under the control of the French educational authorities. These simple facts have a number of consequences: for France, immigration has been thought to be exclusively economic, based on the idea of a temporary stay in France by people who will shortly return 'home'. The teaching affects less than a quarter of all children with foreign nationality - in itself less than the total number of immigrant children who might have language problems, as the figures for Italian enrolments show. In the case of such teaching taking place during normal school hours - about half - the children lose general cultural activities like drawing or music. Necessarily, since the teachers are not part of the normal French system, the assessment of the children's ability is not taken into account, in addition to the quality of teaching being subject to variation according to the resources and plans of the sending countries. In some cases (particularly with Arabic - cf Galtier and Ballard, 1992) the teaching is less concerned with language skills than with religious or cultural teaching, and this seems to apply to children from 'Black' Africa, who often gravitate to the Arabic - and Islamic - teaching if their own languages are not on offer.

French as Second Language

657,947 children of foreign nationality were studying in French schools in 1989-90, some 9.8% of the total school population and up from 7.7% in 1975-6. The proportions are 9.5% of children in Colleges and 10.2% in primary education, however, and only about 6,500 enter the second level direct. Children born in France of foreign parents do not of course appear in these statistics, as they would have French nationality at birth.

Table 2
Schoolchildren of foreign nationality

Algerian	162,157
Moroccans	162,860
Tunisians	51,119
Other African:	
Francophone	43,924
non-Francophone	11,093
Portuguese	84,832
Turkish	48,130
South-east Asia	33,916
Spanish	10,925
Italians	9,159
Yugoslavia	6,345
Other EC	7,709
Other	25,778
Total	657,947

Source: Repères, 1991, 65

The current general policy for foreign and immigrant children, based on a number of recent reports - by Berque in 1985; Hussenet, in 1990 (Ministère, 1992) - aims at a global integration approach, involving other Ministries such as those specifically concerned with 'integration', Urban Affairs, Social Affairs etc. The intention is to ensure integration - 'knowledge and respect for French cultural values by young foreigners as well as knowledge and respect of foreign cultures by French youth; not assimilation aimed at denying the original culture' - as rapidly as possible, with academic success for children of diverse social and cultural backgrounds being one of the objectives of the 1989 Education Law, and to do so through deliberate 'intercultural education' whose aims are 'to make foreign cultural values known, to examine other civilisations, to use the notion of cultural support and to cause reflection on phenomena which present problems'. The need for teaching material on foreign cultures is recognised and pilot projects are under way.

Despite the best intentions, it is too often the case that immigrant children are relegated to inferior streams and levels because of their poor control of written French. Despite the creation of classes for initiation (Classes d'initiation expérimentales - CLIN) and adaptation (Classes d'adaptation dans l'enseignement du second degré - CLAD) in the early 1970s, language research, particularly by CREDIF, pilot projects on a European basis (a recent one on the learning of French by Turkish or Portuguese children is cited), and surveys of potential solutions, there is a recognition of a serious lack of appropriate material, teachers and training for teachers. The relationship of academic failure with the poor status of the teaching of French as a foreign language, the poor resource level for classes, poor training for the teachers, and the lack of specific research into teaching methods, is nonetheless clear to recent observers (Hannoun, 1987).

French is taught, in the first level, to immigrant children in integrated classes and also in special groups withdrawn from normal programmes, either as reception ('initiation') or as learning support ('adaptation'). In the second level, the number of special classes for new foreign children has risen from 151 (2,575 children) in 1981-2 to 346 (5,595 children) in 1990-1 (Ministère, 1992).

The main problem with these approaches is clearly that of segregation and of the fairly recent policy change from assimilation to intercultural education. Segregation, paradoxically, is often reinforced by the provision made for the teaching of immigrant languages, when the children are again withdrawn from 'ordinary' classes. Unfortunately, too, the extensive provision made in France for parental involvement often bypasses the parents of immigrant children, who are often inarticulate, unaware of the system and unable to influence it. Conversely, parental pressure to leave school is particularly high on Turkish daughters.

Generally speaking, immigrant children do not succeed well as a group: 19.1% of them were in the Sections d'Education Spécialisée (SES) and the Groupes de Classes-Ateliers (GCA), where those with learning difficulties are 'relegated', although they were only 7.4% of the total secondary school population in 1989-90 (Repères, 1991, 128). Likewise, immigrant children have been proportionately more present in vocational education, and do not stay on at school in large numbers after compulsory education finishes at age 14.

Children with foreign nationality may be educationally 'at risk' in a number of social factors (Table 3), although comparably disadvantaged 'French' children showed similar 'failure' rates.

Table 3
Children of foreign nationality: risk factors

Factor	Foreign children	Other children
Father of low socio-economic category	90%	40%
Father illiterate or only primary education	90%	not known
Four or more children in the family	50%	20%
Had attended kindergarten	'fewer'	'most'

Source: Repères, 1990, 165

The situation is not unknown to the Ministry, and a recent Circular (89-036 of 6.2.1989) reminded the local authorities that Special Education was not intended for those with language difficulties. There is some improvement, too, in the movement of foreign children towards the 'lycée' (second cycle of second level) after the completion of compulsory education - over six years a tripling of Turkish children, a doubling of Tunisians and Moroccans, and a 50% improvement for the Portuguese. There is some movement also away from the vocational streams, but immigrant families do not in general encourage their children to enter the long cycles of post-compulsory education.

The Teaching of Foreign Languages

The teaching of foreign languages has achieved a high profile in recent years in France. Every child must study one foreign language from entry to the sixth class, may take a second from the fourth, with a second chance in the second; and a third foreign language is possible from the second as an option or as a compulsory subject in the A2 streams for the Baccalauréat (Note 92-10). Lionel Jospin, Minister of Education until April 1992, had introduced in February 1992 even more ambitious plans for languages, based on making the second language compulsory from the fourth class (87% of pupils currently choose this anyway); increasing class time devoted to languages; and establishing language resource centres in partnership with industry and aimed at supporting language teaching to adults as well as to the schools. One of the major reforms for 1989 had already been to generalise the teaching of a second foreign language throughout the secondary level, and to introduce, experimentally but more systematically, that of a first foreign language in the primary level. These reforms seem likely to survive the new Minister, Jack Lang, Minister of Education and Culture from April 1992.

In secondary education, in theory at any rate, parents tell the College which foreign language they want; if a minimum recruitment (8-15 pupils) is obtained, the College tells the Rectorat (local office of the Ministry) and this provides either the teaching post, or resources for part-time teaching (although there is a degree of local management by the College itself; and children can follow a correspondence course if local teachers are not available). The role of the central government is hence to respond to local demand, although in practice it decides the languages the country can offer: currently, 13 are widely available (Arabic, Chinese, Dutch, English, German, Modern Greek, Modern Hebrew, Italian, Japanese, Polish, Portuguese, Russian and Spanish), in addition to the regional languages and the languages specifically provided for immigrants. Since 1970, Governments have aimed at providing continuity of teaching within school districts together with a real choice for parents, and have thus intended diversification of language choice.

The choice of language hence depends on parental preference, what the College and Rectorat can provide and what central government agrees to. In practice, the choice of language depends mainly on College size, location (region and urban/rural contrasts), and the social background of parents. Evidently, bigger urban Colleges with a preponderance of middle-class parents will provide more choice than small rural ones; the languages of nearby countries may influence choice in the border areas; but it is also worth noting that the Centre and the East offer more choice than other regions, and that some Rectorats have a tradition of wide choice anyway (Paris, Dijon, Reims) (see Oeuvrard, 1987).

Enrolments in order of popularity of the language in 1991-2 were as follows:

Table 4
Secondary school enrolments in foreign languages

English	5,150,702
Spanish	1,444,906
German	1,387,411
Italian	177,337
Russian	29,388
Portuguese	14,388
Arabic	13,226
Modern Hebrew	4,545
Chinese	2,732
Japanese	1,403
Dutch	570
Polish	297
All others	4,121
Languages by correspondence	5,232
Regional languages	22,129
Total number of children:	5,519,964

(France including overseas Departments - Antilles, Guyane, Réunion; but not overseas territories - St Pierre et Miquelon, Wallis et Futuna, New Caledonia, French Polynesia, Mayotte and French Antarctica. All language choices - first, second, third and optional courses - included. Both public and private secondary schools are included. Some professional and preparatory courses excluded).

Source: Note 92-10

There are regional and other differences. In Alsace particularly, the early teaching of German is well established, with 80% of children following four half-hour classes weekly in Middle Course first year; even so, German only just beats English, with 105,510 secondary enrolments as against 103,581 for English - although choices of English are increasing. Similarly, Spanish with 99,211 far exceeds German, with 33,892 in Bordeaux, although English has 223,314 there. In Corsica, 5,658 choose Italian as against 4,871 Spanish - and 18,319 English; but the regional language has 4,008 choices there. The next region with high regional language choice is Toulouse, with 3,345, followed closely by Strasbourg with 2,984, Bordeaux, with 2,788, Rennes, with 2,558 and Montpellier with 2,357.

English is the overall winner across the country, with 93% of children studying it (82% in 1980-1). English is chosen usually as the first foreign language; Spanish and Italian mainly as second or third. German is stabilising at about 12% of all choices, but becoming more popular, particularly in private education. The overwhelming preponderance of English in foreign language learning at all levels is obvious, and coping with its consequences has led to a number of strategies in diversification. Nonetheless, the language learning problem remains, and the accepted solution is to generalise the teaching of the second foreign language, as has now been accepted by the government at least in principle.

For the Ministry, there is concern at this domination by English and despair at what to do about the 'minor' languages. Diversification has not worked, and some languages - Italian is a case in point - have practically collapsed except in certain regions and among certain groups. Language choices made by parents are often made for all the wrong reasons: German is used as an indicator of academic brilliance - only the bright ones choose it; regional, and even more, 'immigrant' languages as the opposite. With no official policy of imposing diversification and prioritisation of languages, France's capabilities in foreign trade may well be affected in the future: the contrast between the popularity of Spanish and the miserable showing of Portuguese is a case in point when one looks at South America as a trading partner.

And there are specific problems for individual languages: for Japanese, whether to limit teaching to the spoken skill, in view of the difficulties of the writing system; for Arabic and Portuguese, the phenomenon of social rejection and hence low recruitment. For all languages, the aims remain educational, however, rather than social or commercial; and France's overall aims in the curriculum are ambitious, perhaps indeed too ambitious. It might be better to aim for greater communicative competence in situations in which French youth may expect to experience real communication, rather than to concentrate on the higher literary forms and formal discourse, where much foreign language teaching still sees its role (Gauthier, 1992).

Traditionally languages have indeed been an elitist subject, with the two- and three-language streams generally considered superior to most others. The importance of the European Community in French policies in all domains, and the general awareness of new relationships with Eastern and central Europe are two main factors in their continuing popularity. For the contemporary situation, the 1992 reform proposes a shift in the aims and objectives of teaching: towards teaching languages for communication; to the study of civilisation (rather than just high culture) along with language; and towards increasing study of languages for professional purposes (Langues Plus, 1992). How far these reforms will be implemented remains to be seen.

In primary schools, however, a major experiment in the early teaching of foreign languages has been conducted recently. 245,763 children and 7,168 schools in the Middle Course, approximately 20% of the total, took part, and classes were run mainly in collaboration with the secondary Colleges in the languages already taught in the 6th class there. 80% of children took English, 15% German, with some Spanish, Portuguese, Dutch, Arabic and Russian. The schemes will be evaluated again during 1992, but will not lead to more generalised provision for ten years. On the negative side, the national Inspectors noticed in 1991 five types of problem: lack of precise aims and objectives; failure to achieve diversification, with excessive reliance on English; lack of follow-up in the Colleges; poor training and inadequate recruitment of teachers; and transport problems for rural schools. On the positive side, the Inspectors noted favourable public opinion; the undoubted enthusiasm of primary school teachers and their openness to exchange programmes; good liaison between primary and secondary sectors; and methodological advantages for the Colleges in teaching foreign languages more effectively (see La Blache, 1991; Inspection, 1991; Note 90-42).

Conclusion

France stands out among European countries as a prime example of a Nation-State with a high level of awareness of its own identity, of the importance of language, and of the sense of community in the creation and maintenance of that identity. In recent years it has had cause to re-examine its educational, and some aspects of its social, policies in the context of changes in international communication, its internal demography and its desire to protect and further national aims.

The strong historical sense of nationalism in the creation of the present-day French nation has been seen as a priority by successive governments for centuries, and recent history, particularly attacks on territorial integrity most recently in 1939-45, has done nothing to weaken negative attitudes towards any movements for autonomy or separatism on the part of territorial or non-territorial minorities. A number of sociolinguistic processes are clearly at work here: prestige, linguistic insecurity, the elevation of language as a community symbol, and when these are combined with the role of economic forces, for example in the characterisation of immigrants as causative agents in unemployment, they serve to reinforce prejudice and unreasoning defence of the past. Political debate in France often seems to concern itself with the 'defence' of French, particularly 'against' English, on the world scene; or with the coherence of French identity in the face of immigration within France. In education, the role of language teaching, whether for foreign, second or mother tongues, is often problematic.

But there is also a close relationship between language use and socio-economic category. The prestige factor in language teaching, based on the concept of language skills as marking the socially successful, spills over into language attitudes towards socially marked varieties such as youth language of course, but also into attitudes towards foreign languages. Belief in France's 'civilising mission' and in the innate superiority of Parisian culture easily leads to arrogance and protectionism, as well as to a powerful sense of fright at the loss of France's international role and fear of the increasing power of English/American. And similar fear of social fragmentation following support of minorities sometimes prevents rational educational planning.

What then will be the linguistic future for France? Will she remain monolingual, or move more towards a multilingual, multicultural and multiethnic future? On one hand, the growth of nationalism and of extremist nationalist political movements, the long history of conservatism and chauvinism, offer signs of strengthening the concept of identity and community. For some, this can be stressful: increasing suicide rates, sales of sleeping pills, racist and xenophobic incidents mean for some commentators that the French are perhaps losing self-confidence (Mermet, 1991, 205). As many as two thirds of the French support a stop to further immigration. They think they see, and are afraid of, a demographic decline of 'native' French and hence a possible dilution of their traditional identity. On the other hand, if immigration is now no longer a temporary phenomenon associated with economic need for additional labour, but a permanent feature of French demography, France will need to develop educational policies according value to minority languages and cultures and move to multiculturalism, or plan for rapid or gradual assimilation as is happening with policy shifts towards intercultural education; and probably, at least as an interim measure, accept policy distinctions between European languages such as Spanish or Portuguese, and Arabic, for France the main 'problem' language of immigration.

One must say, however, that Islam is now the second religion in France, and that there is plenty of space to absorb refugees and a long French tradition of refuge and asylum. Immigrants, measured as those with foreign nationality, are no more numerous now at 8% of the population than they were in the 1930s. Assimilation has worked well with major communities, as with the Armenians for example. Added to this, is France's political and diplomatic awareness of the need for friends, and hence the support for the development of a vibrant international Francophone community. Africa is central to France's plan for her future, and certainly for some, is as important as Europe. The future looks good therefore for a greater degree of interculturality, more tolerance and understanding.

French identity and community attitudes hence have features, at one and the same time, of a confident, monolingual world power; a world power facing potential weakening of its influence through the fragmentation of its language into differing varieties representing different societies - Quebec, Africa; a world power facing potential domination by an even more powerful monolingual world power, the USA, and hence finding itself forced into the position of a linguistic minority on the world stage; and a concerned society facing possible fragmentation whether from internal or immigrant linguistic minorities. All these features combine to explain recent developments in educational attitudes and policies.

Dabène (1990) describes these policy shifts as aimed at assimilation, up to 1970-75, and from then on at recognition of difference and of interculturality. But she identifies the dangers of the latter: ghettoisation, limiting the outlets available for minority children, on the one hand, and preventing majority children having access to their languages and cultures; and ossification, leading to teaching foreign languages and cultures in France as though minority groups were still part of their society of origin and had not developed special ways of communication, and indeed of being, precisely because of their presence in a different country.

References

Ager, D. E. 1990. *Sociolinguistics and Contemporary French*. Cambridge: Cambridge University Press

Bouvier, J.-C. and Martel, C. 1991. *Les Français et leurs langues*. Aix-en-Provence: Publications de l'Université de Provence

Capul, J-Y. 1991. Le Système Educatif. *Cahiers français*, 249

Dabène, L. (ed.) 1990. Les Langues et cultures des populations migrantes: un défi à l'école française. *LIDIL*, 2

Enquête 16. 1992. *Effectifs des élèves répartis par langue vivante étudiée*. Paris: Direction de l'Evaluation et de la Prospective, Ministère de l'Education et de la Culture (private communication)

Galtier, G and Ballard, M. 1992. Pour une école laïque et interculturelle. *La Tribune Internationale des Langues Vivantes*, 10: 6-7

Giordan, H. 1982. *Démocratie culturelle et droit à la différence*. Paris: La Documentation Française

Hannoun, M. 1987. *L'homme est l'espérance de l'homme*. Paris: La Documentation Française

Hargreaves, A. 1991. Islam in France. *Modern and Contemporary France*, 45: 3-47

INSEE. 1989. *Tableaux de l'Economie Française*. Paris: INSEE

Inspection. 1991. *Rapport de l'Inspection Générale de l'Education Nationale: 1991*. Paris: La Documentation Française

La Blache, V. 1991. Les Langues Vivantes à l'Ecole Elémentaire. *Le Monde de l'Education*, juin 1991: 56-8

Langues Plus. 1992. Langues Plus: un nouveau programme pour les écoles, collèges, lycées. *La Lettre TGV*, 89. Paris: Ministère de l'Education Nationale
Mermet, G. 1991. *Francoscopie 1991*. Paris: Larousse
Ministère. 1992. *Les langues régionales; et la scolarisation des élèves étrangers en collège*. Paris: Ministère de l'Education Nationale et de la Culture (private communication)
Note 90-27. 1990. *L'enseignement des langues et cultures d'origine*. Note d'Information. Paris: Ministère de l'Education Nationale, de la Jeunesse et des Sports
Note 90-42. 1990. *Les langues vivantes à l'école*. Note d'Information. Paris: Ministère de l'Education Nationale, de la Jeunesse et des Sports
Note 92-10. 1992. *Les langues vivantes dans le second degré en 1990-91*. Note d'Information. Paris: Ministère de l'Education Nationale, de la Jeunesse et des Sports
Oeuvrard, F. 1987. L'offre d'enseignement d'une langue vivante dans les collèges. *Education et Formations*, 13: 8-23
Olivesi, C. and Pastorel, J.-P. 1991. La nouvelle collectivité territoriale de Corse. *Regards sur l'Actualité*, 173: 33-43
Repères, 1991. *Repères et Références Statistiques sur les Enseignements et la Formation*. 1991. Paris: Ministère de l'Education Nationale

Appendix
The French Educational System

The French educational system is a centralised structure from the training, appointment and employment of staff to the content of the curriculum; and from the establishment of examination systems to the content of the tests, and to the approval of the success of individuals taking them. The arguments for and against this approach are easily summarised:

> (it) contributes to establishing national unity by a uniformisation process, for example by eliminating local dialects and languages or by integrating the children of immigrants; it participates in the formation of the French citizen. Centralisation allows egalitarian treatment of different parts of the country unless geographical disparities arise through lack of political will or administrative incompetence. It also allows, through a single political initiative, the entire educational system to follow individual new measures.
> The system also has risks: excessive size, inertia, conservatism, slow reactions, inability to recognise problems.
> Capul, J-Y. 1991. 6

The Ministry of Education operates through regional offices (Rectorat) which administer all levels of the system from kindergarten to University, but work in close conjunction with decentralised administrations at Regional, Departmental, and Commune level. Parental opinion is sought at school level, although not in the management of schools, and pressure groups can be very effective in instituting change.

Figure 1
The French Educational System

Higher Education (Third level) in

Universities (Medical)	Universities			Specialised Schools	*Grandes écoles*
Third University cycle:					
Diploma Medical education 11,919	Doctorate 7,683				Diploma
Second University cycle:					
	Masters 41,296 ---4 years--				
	Degree 54,743 -- 3 years--			Diploma	
		IUT	*STS*		
First University cycle:	----------------2-year qualifications------------				
	DEUG 69,855	*DUT* 40,107	*BTS*		*CPGE*

Secondary education (Second level)
Second cycle in *Lycées* or in ---------Vocational *Lycées*------

Age at entry			
18	Baccalaureate 210,451	Technical Bac. 101,163	Professional Bac. 7,555
17	Terminal class		
16	First class		
15	Second class		
			BEP *CAP* *CAP* *CAP* (2 yrs) (2 yrs) (3 yrs) 139,275 -- 278,556--

First cycle in Colleges

15	*Brevet* 546,437			
14	Third class	Technical third	*CEP*	3rd prep *CPA*
13	Fourth class	Technical fourth		4th prep *CPPN*
12	Fifth class			
11	Sixth class			

Primary education (First level)
Elementary education in primary schools

10 Middle Course second year
9 Middle Course first year
8 Elementary Course second year
7 Elementary Course first year
6 Preparatory Course

Pre-elementary education
Kindergarten (2-5 years; 36% of 2-year olds, 100% of 3, 4 and 5-year olds in 1988-89)

Notes to Figure 1

1 Each line of the Table represents one normal study year, from age 6 to age 18 (compulsory education finishes at age 14). However progression is not by age, but by achievement, so in 1988-9:
- 30.3% of children in Middle Course second year had 'redoubled' (repeated a year) by at least one year, and were up to 3 years older than the 'normal' age of 10;
- 25% of children who had entered the sixth class in 1986 had not reached the third class;
- 18% of students in Terminal had 'redoubled'.

2 44% of the age group achieved the Baccalaureate (of all types); about 12% leave education with no qualification.

3 Of those going on to University, 33% leave after one year, about 40% enter the final year for a 'licence' (3-year course) or 'masters' (4-year course).

4 The numbers indicate numbers achieving this award in 1988.

5 IUT: Institut Universitaire de Technologie - University-level technical institutes
STS: Sections de Technicien supérieur - postsecondary education in Lycées
DEUG: Diplôme d'Etudes Universitaires Générales - normal first University qualification, taken after two years study
DUT: Diplôme Universitaire de Technologie - equivalent of DEUG for technology
BTS: Brevet de Technicien Supérieur
CPGE: Classes Préparatoires aux Grandes Ecoles - Postsecondary courses (in Lycées) for entry to Grandes Ecoles (professional schools)
BEP: Brevet d'Etudes Professionnelles - vocational qualification
CAP: Certificat d'Aptitude Professionnelle - vocational qualification
CEP: Certificat d'Education Professionnelle - vocational qualification
CPA: Classes Préparatoires à l'Apprentissage - classes leading to apprenticeships
CPPN: Classes PréProfessionnelles de Niveau - classes leading to vocational education
Sources: Capul, J-Y. 1991; and Repères, 1991.

MULTILINGUALISM IN THE GERMAN SCHOOL

I. Gogolin *Gesamthochschule Kassel and University of Hamburg*

Translated by J. Stagg *Aston University*

For nearly 40 years now, the Federal Republic of Germany has been facing large scale immigration. Approximately 10% of the population have passports other than German ones, and nearly 15% of school children belong to immigrant families. Immigrant children are the least successful in the German school system. In 1991 for example, about 70% of German pupils gained good results in a school-leaving examination equivalent to the former British 'O' level, but only 36% of immigrant children did so (for the example of the Federal State of Hesse, see Ausländerreport 1991). Still today, about 25% of immigrant children in Hesse leave school without any certificate, which very few German pupils do. There are many reasons which might be factors in the failure of the German school system to meet the needs of so many immigrant children; one of these is the marginal status of their mother tongue in the German state school system.

In this chapter, as far as is possible in a short space, I present first of all a picture of present-day societal reality in the Federal Republic of Germany, where people of many linguistic backgrounds and cultures live and where immigrant and indigenous children usually attend the schools together. In the second section I give some information about the regulations which the FRG has established for the teaching of minority languages.[1]

Demographic and Legal Situation: Immigration in Germany

'The Federal Republic of Germany is not a country of immigration' - this is one of the most frequently heard slogans, to be heard from the mouths of politicians as well as from lawyers, administrators and from the 'the man and woman on the street'. This opinion is both correct and completely wrong.

It is correct that the Federal Republic, according to the letter of its constitution and its legal status, is not a country of immigration. It has a 'Foreigners Law' (Ausländerrecht), which is not an immigration law. This Ausländerrecht regulates legal sojourn for foreigners on Federal German soil. In addition to this regulation, the constitution contains a paragraph which guarantees the right of political asylum. At least for the time being and at least according to the letter of the law, the right of asylum is considered a very liberal rule for granting protection from political persecution.

In recent years however, this rule has been increasingly criticised and restricted through bureaucratic regulations, not least as a reaction to the enormous success of extreme right-wing political parties in recent elections. It must be apprehended that the guaranteed right of political asylum is falling victim to the revival of nationalism in the new and greater Germany.

The law relating to foreigners, originally a law of 1965, has just been revised; the new law is valid from January 1991. This law regulates the different conditions under which the right of sojourn is granted to foreigners in the Federal Republic of Germany. It determines the presuppositions for a foreigner's stay in Germany with regard to the potential length of sojourn, as well as the freedom to settle according to one's own choice, and to enter legally into an occupational relationship. For several groups of foreigners, above all for asylum seekers, taking up gainful employment is illegal; offences against this prescription can be taken as a reason for expulsion. The law relating to foreigners determines also those circumstances under which a foreigner may lose his or her right to stay in the Federal Republic. The spectrum of rules includes for example,

1. the regulation that evidence must be forthcoming of adequate living quarters, i.e. the size of the dwelling. In the case of families the number of square metres per head are laid down. If proof of this cannot be furnished then, under certain conditions, expulsion can be enforced;

2. the condition that a regular income or property must be assured. The payment of social security, as for instance in the case of unemployment or sickness of long duration, can, under certain circumstances, serve as a cause for expulsion;

3. the regulation that a criminal offence or suspected punishable acts can serve as a cause for deportation, in which case some offences against the Ausländerrecht itself can likewise represent indictable actions.

The intentions of the Ausländerrecht are explicitly expressed in its preamble as well as in several official comments: to protect through prescriptions in law the 'affairs of the Federal Republic of Germany', for they merit a higher status than the affairs of foreigners in this country (see the discussion of the new law and its consequences: ISS, 1990, Iranbomy, 1991).

Consequently, the sentence, 'The Federal Republic is not a country of immigration' is correct on the formal level of rules and regulations. But it is completely false on the empirical level. There has been a de facto immigration into the FRG since the day of its foundation. The number of immigrants living in Germany is still rising, not as steeply as in the sixties and seventies, yet nevertheless constantly.

Table 1
Foreigners in West Germany 1960 - 1989

Year	Total (000's)	Percentage of total population	In employment and paying Social Security tax (000's)
1960	686.2	1.2	279.0
1968	1 924.2	3.2	1 089.9
1969	2 381.1	3.9	1 372.1
1970	2 976.5	4.9	1 948.9
1971	3 438.7	5.6	2 240.7
1972	3 526.6	5.7	2 352.3
1973	3 966.2	6.4	2 595.0
1974	4 127.4	6.7	2 286.6
1975	4 089.6	6.6	2 038.7
1976	3 948.3	6.4	1 920.8
1977	3 948.3	6.4	1 869.4
1978	3 981.1	6.5	1 864.1
1979	4 146.8	6.7	1 937.4
1980	4 453.3	7.2	2 013.4
1981	4 629.8	7.5	1 900.3
1982	4 666.9	7.6	1 771.9
1983	4 534.9	7.4	1 709.1
1984	4 146.8	7.1	1 608.1
1985	4 378.9	7.1	1 536.0
1986	4 512.7	7.4	1 544.7
1987	4 630.2	7.4	1 624.1
1988	4 489.1	7.3	1 607.1
1989	4 845.8		1 689.3

Source: German Statistical Office
1989 figure includes the former East Germany

Following the legal situation already indicated, three main groups of people from abroad living on the territory of the Federal Republic of Germany must be distinguished.[2]

Firstly, those who, from the moment they cross the German frontiers are supplied with a German passport: the so-called *Aussiedler* (the resettlers). This group of people from Eastern European countries can, at some point or other in their ancestral chain, demonstrate the existence of 'German blood'. They come predominantly from Poland, the former Soviet Union, Rumania and the former Yugoslavia.[3] Many of the *Aussiedler* of today are descendants of German-speaking peasants who were sent to eastern Europe as colonial settlers in the middle ages or in the ages of absolutism (e.g. the '*Banater Schwaben*' or the '*Wolgadeutschen*'). Emigration of settlers from Germany to eastern Europe carried on until the Second World War (Auernheimer, 1990, 57ff).

Notwithstanding their legal status the members of this group are to be categorized as immigrants. Their cultural background is determined by life in other countries, even though they were regarded as a 'German minority' there. Many of them, and in particular their children do not speak German or only in a very limited way. The primary linguistic experiences of the *Aussiedler*-children are determined by a language other than German, and almost none of them have had schooling in German in their country of origin.

Compared with the other groups of immigrants, the *Aussiedler* enjoy special privileges because they count as Germans. Their stay in Germany is not put into question; under no circumstances can they be threatened with expulsion, and they receive special social and psychological support that is intended to guarantee their rapid integration into the society of the Federal Republic. Nevertheless, they very often face hostility or racist attacks, just as the other groups of immigrants do.

The second group we have to deal with are people who, as a result of bilateral recruitment agreements between Germany and altogether eight, mostly Mediterranean States, in the sixties and seventies, immigrated to Germany in large numbers. These immigrants were described by the term '*Gastarbeiter*' for a time, a term which is rarely used now. They represent the largest group among the approximately five million immigrants in Germany.

Like all the other western European immigration countries in the 1970s, the Federal Republic of Germany prohibited the recruitment of workers from abroad. The stop to recruitment was announced in 1973. But for several reasons the end of recruitment did not bring about an end to immigration. Different forms of legal immigration continued to be possible, above all the so called 'family reunification'. This label indicates the change of perspective in the employment of workers from abroad. At first, employment of foreign workers followed the principle of rotation, which meant the recruitment of the workforce and their return to the country of origin after a few years. It was not humanitarian considerations alone, but in fact economic considerations in the early 1970s, that led to the replacement of the 'rotation paradigm' by the 'integration paradigm'. The employers noticed that it was much more profitable to continuously employ reliable people who adapted well to their work, instead of investing again and again in making newly immigrated people acquainted with their duties. It is not surprising that employers belonged to the first groups who vigorously demanded the promotion of 'family reunification' by the State.

Today, the former *Gastarbeiter* and their families make up the largest group of immigrants in the FRG. Most of the families have lived more than 15 years in Germany; most of their children were born here. They are considered as 'new ethnic minorities' (or 'settlers', cf. Castles, 1987), because they do not intend or practice remigration. Meanwhile, these groups have developed ethnic networks comparable to those in classical immigration countries.

The third group of immigrants, the one with least rights, is represented by the so-called asylum seekers; I term them refugees, in common with many colleagues. Refugees come from all regions of the world in which life is being threatened by war and torture, hunger and natural catastrophes.

Only very few of these people seeking help get the help they are looking for. Less than 10% of applications for political asylum per year receive a positive answer, usually after long and time-consuming court cases. A considerable number of refugees receive 'leave to remain', mostly on account of previous court cases which have sometimes lasted years. The rest are deported to their country of origin.

According to recent regulations, asylum seekers are not allowed to earn their living by themselves but receive social welfare. They are also not allowed to choose their place of lodging, but are allotted to the place where they may attend for their court case; according to the regulations, they are to be lodged in camps, if possible. These regulations are meant on the one hand to keep them under control, and to ensure, on the other hand, that they do not integrate into German society before their application is given a positive judgement. In political terms, the integration of asylum seekers into German society is not wished for (cf. Auernheimer, 1990, 53; see for the very complicated German debate on political asylum Cohn-Bendit et al, 1991; in the context of EEC regulations: Lutz, 1992).

Due to this fundamental idea in the official policy for asylum, the children of asylum seekers in the FRG have no right to education. Although in practice many of these children do attend schools, by law they are excluded from access to the state school system.[4] The regulation of the state school system (a private school system does exist, but is in fact of no importance) contains an 'obligation to attend school' that holds good as the legal basis for access to schooling for the individual child. This obligation affects every child that has his or her permanent residence on German territory - therefore it does not apply to those children whose residence status is not clarified. For the children of immigrant workers exceptional rulings were created in the 1970s. As yet, these do not apply to the children of asylum seekers. In practice, many children of asylum seekers, in spite of this, do attend German schools. In some regions, e.g. in the Federal State of Hamburg, they are given special coaching. But the consequence of the legal position is that they have no individual right to schooling - we possess several reports concerning principals of schools who have refused to allow the attendance of refugee children at their schools, and according to the letter of the regulation they had every right to act so. For whoever in Germany does not have an obligation has no rights either...

Table 2 gives a survey of the demographic situation in the FRG (incl. ex-GDR) at the end of 1989 and shows the composition of the domiciled population.

Table 2
Foreigners in Germany (percentages) as at 31 December, 1989

West Germany		East Germany	
Turkey	33	Vietnam	31
Yugoslavia	13	Poland	27
Italy	11	Mozambique	8
Greece	6	Russia	8
Poland	5	Hungary	7
Austria	4	Cuba	4
Total Numbers	4,850,000	Total Numbers	190,000

It is clear then that the FRG, despite any public assertions of a political nature is de facto an immigration country. At present, the immigration figures are increasing every year; to give an impression of the most recent situation, see Table 3.

Table 3
Immigrants in 1991

Total	414,070
of these:	
political refugees, 'Aussiedler':	389,000
from Eastern Europe:	340,675
of these: political refugees:	221,995
Aussiedler refugees from Yugoslavia:	74,854
from Asian countries:	30,000
from African countries:	8,358

Not least as a consequence of the migration of workers and refugees German society is multicultural and multilingual in its composition, and the signs are that this will be intensified in the future rather than reduced. One only needs to mention the key phrase 'Europe 1992' - when the treaties on European freedom of movement come into force - in order to indicate that international migratory movements will inevitably affect all the European industrial nations in the future. According to a model projection of the Federal Office of Statistics[5], the share of the foreign population domiciled in the FRG will at least double in the next 40 years. In the same period of time, the indigenous population will reduce by more than 10 million, so that the proportion of foreigners in the domiciled population will rise from about 7% now to about 14% then (Geiss, 1990, 139).

The schools in the Federal Republic present roughly the following picture at the moment.

Nearly 15% of the boys and girls in the state school system do not have German nationality. There is a regional variation in these figures; in urban schools there are more immigrant children than in rural schools. In the Federal State of Hamburg, for example, in 1991 there was an average of 20% of immigrant children in state schools, whereas in the State of Hesse there was an average of 14% (Ausländerreport, 1991). Also the figures vary according to the type of schooling. Primary schools and a few types of schools in the vocational sphere have the highest proportions of foreign pupils. On the other hand the representation of children of immigrant families in the section of the school system awarding higher qualifications is slight. These children are hardly represented in grammar schools, the type of school that awards the highest educational school-leaving qualification, the Abitur (leaving certificate), which is the precondition for taking up university study. As I mentioned already, the German educational system is far from granting 'equality of opportunity' for children from immigrant families.

A vivid picture of the linguistic and cultural variety in the FRG can hardly be obtained using only these dry figures. In addition to this, the figures are limited in this respect: statistics from official government sources do not reproduce the numerous nationalities, let alone the number of languages which we have to deal with. The official statisticians include only a limited number of selected national groups, primarily those coming from countries with which official recruitment agreements at state level have been concluded. Another limitation derives from the fact that only nations are counted; the official demographic observations follow the principle that one country equals one language. Therefore, only those languages which are the official national languages of the countries of their origin are statistically considered as the languages of immigrants.

Table 4
Foreign pupils in State schools and Private schools in Hamburg

Type of school	State School			Private School			Totals		
	Male	Female	All	Male	Female	All	Male	Female	All
Primary Schools	4,841	4,537	9,378	481	417	898	5,322	4,954	10,276
Class 5-6 in Primary Schools	1,297	1,110	2,407	136	100	236	1,433	1,210	2,643
Class 5-6 in other Schools	88	102	190	0	0	0	88	102	190
				Secondary Schools					
Hauptschule	1,521	1,152	2,673	122	86	208	1,643	1,238	2,881
Realschule	1,242	1,104	2,346	130	137	267	1,372	1,241	2,613
				Grammar Schools					
Gymnasium	2,027	1,966	3,993	191	194	385	2,218	2,160	4,378
Samtschule**	1,633	1,533	3,166	12	11	23	1,645	1,544	3,189
Förderschule*	482	352	834	1	2	3	483	354	837
Spezielle Sonderschulen*	393	231	624	4	4	8	397	235	632
Totals	13,524	12,087	25,611	1,077	951	2,028	14,601	13,038	27,639
Preschools	855	665	1,530	54	73	127	919	738	1,657
Schulkindergarten in special education	18	9	27	0	0	0	18	9	27
Overall totals	14,600	12,848	27,448	1,131	1,024	2,155	15,731	13,872	29,603

* Special education (two types)
** Comprehensive schools

Table 4 attempts to illustrate the situation by the example of the Federal State of Hamburg, where I myself live and work. As already mentioned, in the urban centres of the FRG, of which the Federal State of Hamburg is an example, the proportion of foreigners in the population and correspondingly in the schools is higher than on average in Germany. In 1990, 11% of the Hamburg population had passports other than German ones. The school population in Hamburg schools was composed as in Table 4.

In order to give an idea of what this means in everyday life in schools tables 5 and 6 show the composition of two average inner-city schools.

Table 5
Distribution of nationalities in Arnkielstrasse School, March 1989

545 children from 23 Countries			Percentage
221	from Turkey		40.6
193	from Germany		35.5
54	from Yugoslavia		9.9
19	from Portugal		3.5
9	from Pakistan		1.7
7	from Ghana	Others	8.8
5	from Spain		
4	from Greece		
4	from Italy		
4	from Netherlands		
3	from Lebanon		
3	from Indonesia		
3	from Poland		
3	from Philippines		
2	from Chile		
2	from Syria		
2	from Afghanistan		
2	from Morocco		
1	from India		
1	from Sri Lanka		
1	from Togo		
1	from Jordan		
1	from China		

Table 6
Distribution of nationalities in Hinschenfelde School, May 1989

489 children from 16 foreign States including the former USSR			Percentage
333	from Germany of which 11 from Poland and 2 from the former USSR		68.4
92	from Turkey		18.9
21	from Yugoslavia		4.3
12	from Iran		2.5
9	from Italy		1.8
4	from Spain	Others	4.5
3	from Portugal		
2	from Afghanistan		
2	from Hong Kong		
2	from Philippines		
2	from Poland		
2	from Thailand		
1	from Czechoslovakia		
1	from Ghana		
1	from United Kingdom		
1	from Indonesia		
1	from Tunisia		

These examples give an impression of linguistic and cultural variety as it exists in the society of the Federal Republic of Germany. According to unofficial estimates there are smaller and larger communities from more than 100 different nationalities to be found in Germany, which together represent considerably more different linguistic communities (cf. Ausländerreport, 1991). Whoever goes through the streets of West German cities with open eyes and ears will easily notice that the public image of this country is given its imprint by many languages and cultures - admittedly they are not equipped with the same rights nor with equal opportunities to express themselves and to develop.

Minority Language Teaching in the Federal Republic of Germany: Legal Position and Organisational Forms[6]

In the Federal Republic of Germany two political groupings have legal consequences with clear effects on the teaching of minority languages. The first is the European Community, of which the FRG is a member and must comply with its regulations in so far as they are binding on national law. Secondly, the FRG is a federal state. The authority to make decisions in all questions of the school system relating to general and professional education resides with the Federal States (the *Länder*). The central government is responsible only for regulating the legal framework of the university system. The *Länder* are obliged to harmonize their regulations in so far as they must ensure that decisions relating to education have to be valid everywhere in Germany and that at any time a change of school between the Federal States must be possible for the pupils.

With regard to the European Community there is only one decree worth mentioning in the context of minority languages teaching, and which has consequences for the legal position of foreign children in the schools of the FRG.[7] This is the EEC directive of 25th July 1977 (77/ 486), regarding the provision of education for migrant workers' children. This directive imposes the following commitments on the member states:

1 to offer the children teaching free of charge;

2 to ensure instruction in the official language of the host country (or in the case of more than one language as in Belgium, in the official language of the region);

3 to offer teaching of the children's mother tongue and the national history of their country of origin and possibly also their religion;

4 to see to the training and further education of those teachers who are to devise and plan the teaching of foreign children, and also those teachers who are responsible for mother tongue teaching.

Regrettably this legal decree of the European Communities has some serious limitations with regard to the language rights which it concedes. Indeed, the directive binds the member states to its regulations, but it does not concede an individual right to teaching of the mother tongue; that means that no child has the possibility to push through a personal claim to teaching of the mother tongue by legal action. Another limitation derives from the fact that the directive was meant to apply only to those children who themselves are members of an EEC state (and some selected others). If a family then does not have the privilege of coming from one of these nations, they cannot in any way, according to the EEC directive, make any claim at all. And finally, the directive commits its member states only to such measures that they wish to, or are able to set up 'in accordance with their national possibilities'. In this way the character of a legally binding instrument gets lost, and every measure remains subject to the discretion of the individual member state (for discussion of the effectiveness of the EEC directive, see Boos-Nünning et al, 1986).

It is not least this latter point which plays a particular part when one considers the precautions taken as regards minority languages teaching in the Federal Republic of Germany. For better understanding of the regulations, a brief retrospective view of conditions follows; these set the framework for activities in the Federal *Länder* until today.

The so-called cultural sovereignty of the Federal *Länder* is, as just mentioned, accompanied by an obligation to co-ordinate their measures with all the other federal governments. The committee set up for this purpose is the Conference of Ministers of Education. The Conference of Ministers of Education (KMK=CME) concerned itself for the first time in 1964 with the teaching of immigrant children. At that time - a decade after the policy of recruiting workers began - it was laid down for the first time that the children of foreign workers who had come into the country on the basis of recruitment contracts, should be given access to state schools. This meant that the 'obligation to attend school' became binding also for them.

This ruling affected only children belonging to those countries with which the FRG had bilateral recruitment agreements until 1973. The principal recruitment countries were Greece, Italy, Yugoslavia, Portugal, Spain and Turkey. These were joined for a short time by Maghreb states, but only very few people from there live in the FRG. This principle is still valid today: fundamentally the rulings on the teaching of minority languages in the Federal Republic affect only these states and those languages which are recognised in them as official or national languages.

With their recommendations of 1971, 1976 and 1979 the Conference of Ministers of Education confirmed and varied their first agreements; since that time no noteworthy changes have taken place.

The recommendations of the Conference of Ministers of Education set out the following framework for measures to be taken in the Federal 'Länder' (see Rixius and Thürmann, 1987).

It is affirmed that immigrant children in the Federal Republic of Germany should receive the same educational opportunities as German children. If it is deemed necessary for the promotion of this aim, teaching of their mother tongue should be provided. The preamble to the 1976 recommendation lays this down: 'It is a question of putting the foreign children in a position to learn the German language and to take German leaving examinations as well as to achieve and broaden knowledge of their mother tongue'.

The measures were meant to make a contribution to the social integration of the foreign pupils 'for the duration of their stay in the Federal Republic of

Germany.' Their second aim is 'to preserve their linguistic and cultural identity.' These intentions show that an implicit 'rotation or assimilation perspective' underlies the provisions made in the Federal Republic of Germany, not only in the field of educational policy. This implicit perspective still holds good even today. It is the aim of the measures either to play a part in the smooth integration into the German school system, or to work for possible return later to the country of origin. In this respect, the German interpretation and view coincide with those in the EEC directive: there, too, later return was given as a reason for granting instruction in the official language of the country of origin.

In addition to the definition of the aims of teaching laid down in the 1976 KMK recommendation, essential organisational forms were advised which the Federal *Länder* should or could provide.

- So-called supplementary teaching of the mother tongue. This was meant as provision for children in reception classes (classes for children of new immigrants with the aim of preparing them to be taught in regular German classes within a limited period). Supplementary teaching of the mother tongue can also be provided for immigrant children in regular classes. This teaching may take place within the 'regular' school hours and should not exceed five hours a week.

- The provision of mother tongue teaching in place of the first or second obligatory foreign language (which is usually English or French). By this a special ruling for immigrant pupils as regards the prescribed foreign language sequence in secondary schools has been created. In practice, making use of this provision can mean a severe limitation of the potential school success of immigrant children. In fact, the possibility of receiving the school leaving examination with the highest qualification (the Abitur) is subject to a fixed schedule of obligatory foreign languages; none of the languages of immigrants in Germany belongs to this schedule. Therefore an immigrant pupil is either excluded from the best qualification if he opts for his mother tongue in place of an obligatory foreign language, or he is forced to make considerable additional efforts in order to learn one of the obligatory foreign languages (see the critical discussion of this regulation in Gogolin, 1988, 60ff).

- Mother tongue teaching as an element of the curriculum of reception classes. In reception classes with pupils of the same nationality, parts of the curriculum can be taught in the pupils' native language by teachers of their nationality. By the way, this is the sole recommendation of the Conference of Ministers of Education as regards the employment of immigrant teachers within the framework of the regular state-school system.

- Mother tongue as the language and subject of instruction in so called bilingual classes for immigrant children of one nationality. Nowadays, this regulation concerns only classes in the *Länder* of Bavaria and Berlin; it became well known in the international debate under the heading 'The Bavarian Model' (see the critical discussion for example in Skutnabb-Kangas, 1981). This model turned out to be a special educational system for immigrants which exists alongside the regular educational system. This parallel system provides the pupil with a formal qualification which, if not on paper, then de facto, is inferior and stigmatizing.

Within this formal framework there have been developed two types of minority language teaching in the FRG.

Under the umbrella of cultural sovereignty of the *Länder* and approved by the obligations which the EEC directive imposes, the provision of minority language teaching lies within the responsibility of the *Land* itself in five of eleven Federal *Länder* (relating to the old FRG). These *Länder* finance the classes for mother tongue teaching, employ the teachers for it in their service, and see that the professional school supervision is in accordance with the customary provision of teaching. The *Länder* concerned are: Bavaria, Hesse, Lower Saxony, North-Rhine Westphalia and Rhineland Palatinate.

The remaining six Federal *Länder* have rejected responsibility for this teaching. They have placed it in the hands of the consulates of the countries of origin, which are responsible both for the financing as well as for the appointment of teachers and are answerable for professional school supervision. These Federal *Länder* meet their obligations under the EEC directive by accepting a share of the costs. Usually, this is a very small amount of money, covering for example part of the rents for rooms for the classes.[8] The *Länder* concerned are: Baden-Württemberg, Berlin, Bremen, Hamburg, Saarland and Schleswig-Holstein.

Conclusion

The regulations for mother tongue teaching in the FRG can briefly be commented on as follows.

Taking the (old) FRG as a whole, less than 50% of immigrant children take part in minority language lessons. It is not surprising that most of those children who do attend such classes live in the *Länder* which have made themselves responsible for mother tongue teaching. In the six *Länder* which leave the responsibility to the countries of origin or to private initiative, less than 25% of the children take the opportunity of these offers (cf. Rixius and Thürmann, 1987; see also Ausländerreport, 1991).

There are many factors that give support to the opinion that minority languages are still inferior in the German school system. To mention only one, mother tongue teaching is only offered to a very small, privileged group of immigrant children. They must fulfil at least two prerequisites:

Firstly, only those children who fortuitously belong to a linguistic community whose language is identical with the official language of their country of origin have the potential chance of being offered lessons in their mother tongue. No child who belongs to a linguistic minority of his or her country of origin has any chance at all; the biggest group which is systematically excluded from mother tongue teaching for this reason in the FRG is the Kurdish speaking group.

Secondly, only those children who are lucky enough to belong to families who emigrated from one of those countries with which the FRG had bilateral recruitment agreements have access to mother tongue teaching. Children whose families come from other regions of the world cannot profit from any official provision for teaching their mother tongues at all.

This is but one of the many circumstantial proofs for the view that minority languages are still marginalized in the German school system. In the official educational policy of the Federal Republic of Germany, even today, the languages of immigrant children do not enjoy the status of a cultural heritage with a value of its own regardless of whether learning them is advantageous either in 'supporting integration' or in 'preparation for a return' of immigrant children. The inferior position of minority languages in the German school system is also indicated by the fact that the teaching addresses only immigrant children. No German child is allowed to take part in Turkish, Greek or Italian lessons for immigrant children, except on the basis of private agreement with a teacher or within a school. This indicates that minority languages today are still not considered to be worthy of recognition in German society - after nearly 40 years of immigration, the teaching of minority languages remains a marginalized provision for a marginal societal group.

Notes

1 I have to draw attention to the fact that as regards the information and reflections that I present, by far the greater part apply only to the territory of the former Federal Republic of Germany. Where the five new 'Bundesländer' that previously made up the German Democratic Republic are to be understood as included, this will be explicitly mentioned. See, for further information on the situation of immigrants and ethnic minorities in the GDR, Krüger-Potratz,1991.

2 In German scientific discourse, the term 'immigrants' is used for all groups of people from abroad who have or intend to have their permanent residence in Germany.

3 Other groups, as members of military forces, managers of international companies, scientists in exchange programs or artists can be disregarded here; for these groups, special regulations are in force.

4 The German (or so-called Eastern) version of the concept of 'Nation' is based on derivation, whereas other versions, e.g. the French, are based on the principle of being born on the territory of a nation. For the different concepts of 'Nation' see Heckmann, 1988; Hobsbawm, 1991.

5 It is only recently, that these regulations have been altered; my description shows the former level of rules still in force in Spring 1992.

6 Which only related to the former, smaller Federal Republic and started out from a basic figure of 4.5 million immigrants in Germany. This prognosis was calculated before the upheaval in eastern Europe started; therefore the estimated increase of immigration is certainly too small.

7 None of the measures taken for immigrant children in Germany - whether these are lessons in the mother language or special coaching - have up to now been carried over into those Federal States belonging to the territory of the former GDR. Until today, it cannot even be said that the discourse about innovative initiatives for teaching and education which has been conducted for a long time in West German schools and universities under the key-words 'intercultural education' or 'anti-racist education' has been taken up in the so-called new Federal States. Therefore, the information given in the following section pertains only to the 11 Federal States of the former FRG. Krüger-Potratz, 1991, discusses the situation of foreigners and ethnic minorities in the former GDR. See also the overviews of the West German debate in the context of European innovative activities in: Gogolin et al. (eds.), 1991; Hohmann and Reich (eds.), 1989.

8 As it is customary in German scientific discussion in this field, I use the terms 'mother tongue teaching' and 'minority languages teaching' synonymously in order to characterize the teaching of immigrant children's languages of origin. I do not refer to German for indigenous children nor to autochtonous minorities' languages in this article. See for information on the latter Kroon and Jaspaert, 1991.

9 In Hamburg for example, the *Land* pays some 600,000 DM per year as subsidies for mother tongue teaching. If the *Land* itself were responsible for the classes, it would have to raise more than ten times this amount of money.

References

Auernheimer, G. 1990. *Einführung in die interkulturelle Erziehung*. Darmstadt: Wissenschaftliche Buchgesellschaft

Ausländerreport 1991, vorgelegt vom Kultusminister des Landes Hessen, Wiesbaden: Hartmut Holzapfel

Beauftragte der Bundesregierung für die Integration der ausländischen Arbeitnehmer und ihrer Familienangehörigen. 1990: *Bericht 99. Zur Situation der ausländischen Arbeitnehmer und ihrer Familien - Bestandsaufnahme und Perspektiven für die 90er Jahre*. Bonn: Bundesministerium für Arbeit und Sozialordnung

Boos-Nünning, U., Hohmann, M., Reich, H. H., and Wittek, F. 1986. *Towards Intercultural Education. A comparative study of the education of migrant children in Belgium, England, France and the Netherlands*. London: CILT

Büchergilde, G. 1987. *Land der begrenzten Möglichkeiten. Einwanderer in der Bundesrepublik*. Frankfurt: Basisbücher der Büchergilde, 12

Castles, S. 1987. *Migration und Rassismus in Westeuropa*. Berlin: Express Verlag

Cohn-Bendit, D., et al (eds.) 1991. *Einwanderbares Deutschland oder Vertreibung aus dem Wohlstandsparadies?* Frankfurt/ Main: Horizonte-Verlag

FABER-Arbeitsgruppe (Gogolin, I., Krüger-Potratz, M., Neumann, U., and Reich, H. H.) 1990. F A B E R. Ein Schwerpunktprogramm zur Erforschung der Folgen der Arbeitsmigration für Bildung und Erziehung. *ISS - Informationsdienst zur Ausländerarbeit*, 1: 12-14

Geiss, B. 1990. Ausländerbeschäftigung und Bevölkerungsentwicklung. *Beauftragte der Bundesregierung* (op.cit.), 139 - 45

Gogolin, I. 1988. *Erziehungsziel Zweisprachigkeit. Konturen eines sprachpädagogischen Konzepts für die multikulturelle Schule*. Hamburg: Bergmann and Helbig

Gogolin, I., Kroon, S., Krüger-Potratz, M., Neumann, U., and Vallen, T., (eds)., 1991. *Kultur- und Sprachenvielfalt in Europa*. Münster: Waxmann-Verlag

Heckmann, F. 1988. Volk, Nation, ethnische Gruppe und ethnische Minderheiten. Zu einigen Grundkategorien von Ethnizität. *Österreichische Zeitschrift für Soziologie*, 3: 16-31

Hobsbawm, E. J. 1991. *Nationen und Nationalismus. Mythos und Realität seit 1780*. Frankfurt: Campus

Hohmann, M., and Reich, H.H., (eds). 1989. *Ein Europa für Mehrheiten und Minderheiten. Diskussion um interkulturelle Erziehung*. Münster/ New York: Waxmann Verlag

Iranbomy, S. S. 1991. Die juristischen Rahmenbedingungen für Ausländer in der gegenwärtigen deutschen Industriegesellschaft. In: D. Cohn-Bendit et al. (op cit.), 77-109

ISS. 1990. *Informationsdienst zur Ausländerarbeit*, 3, ed. by the Institut für Sozialarbeit und Sozialpädagogik, Am Stockborn 5-7, D-6000 Frankfurt/Main

Kroon, S. 1990. Opportunities and constraints of community language teaching. 'IN ed. Hans Reich and Ingrid Gogolin. *Migrantenkinder in den Schulen Europas - Versuche und Erfahrungen*. Münster: Waxmann Verlag

Kroon, S. and Koen, J. (eds.) 1991. *Ethnic Minority Languages and Education*. Amsterdam: Lisse Swets and Zeitlinger

Krüger-Potratz, M. 1991. *Ausländer und Minderheiten in der DDR: Anderssein gab es nicht*. Münster: Waxmann Verlag

Lutz, Dieter S. 1992. Die Wohlstandsinsel Europa - eine stacheldrahtbewehrte Festung? *Frankfurter Rundschau* 9. Januar 1992, 16

Rixius, N., and Thürmann, E. 1987. *Muttersprachlicher Unterricht für ausländische Schüler*. Berlin: Express Edition

Skutnabb-Kangas, T. 1981. *Bilingualism or not? The Education of Minorities*. Clevedon: Multilingual Matters

Wilpert, C. 1991. Demographische Entwicklung und Migration zwischen den Mitgliedsstaaten der europäischen Gemeinschaft und in sie hinein. IN Gogolin et al (eds.) *Kultur- und Sprachenvielfalt in Europa*. Münster: Waxmann-Verlag, pp20-37

THE LANGUAGE SITUATION IN HUNGARY (1990-1991)

S. Radnai *Janus Pannonius University, Pécs*

In this particular part of the world - Central Europe - the problem of language use has always been closely connected to the problems of national identity, and in many cases to those of national independence. Consequently, the concept of anything 'foreign', be it language, culture or any industrial product, used to be received with suspicion and reluctance. This reluctance and sometimes hostility have been overcome - on the surface - by a new kind of behaviour, which is more open, more flexible and more in harmony with the new trend of unification and cooperation in Europe and in the world. Nevertheless, some traces of the old tradition still survive, rooted deeply in a certain type of institution and also in the thinking of the people.

Partly for the same reason, and partly for even more complex and intricate ones, amongst them relationships between Hungary and its neighbouring countries, the problems of the majority and minority language use and rights have also become a battlefield which needs a lot of clarification and problem-solving from a scholarly point of view.

The first important question to pose is whether Hungary is the monolingual country which it has been considered for quite a long time to be. The answer can be given through some statistical data.

The number of Hungarian citizens belonging to 'national' (ethnic and/or linguistic) minorities can be estimated as follows:

Germans	200-300,000
Slovaks	50-200,000
Yugoslavs (Croats, Serbs and Slovenes)	50-100,000
Romanians	10-25,000

Furthermore there is also a large group of Gypsies, an ethnic group comprising 500-600,000 people, of whom a third speaks one of the Romany dialects.

The groups listed above make up approximately 8-11% of the total population of Hungary, which is significant enough for these minorities to have an effect on language policy and language planning.

The second factor to consider is the place and role of Hungarian in the European language situation. In this respect Hungarian is distinct from all the other languages in the region. It does not belong to the Indo-European language family, and is - but distantly - related to Finnish, Estonian and several other less widely spoken languages which together make up the Uralic language family. Hungarian, however, is spoken by millions outside the Republic of Hungary; at the present time a third of all Hungarian speakers live elsewhere, mostly in one of the five countries which border present day Hungary. The redrawing of boundaries in the treaties after the wars and revolutions of the twentieth century as well as the massive movement of refugees, has resulted in the presence of large numbers of Hungarian speakers on territory, which though once Hungarian, now falls within the frontiers of her neighbours. There have also been several waves of migration towards the countries of Western Europe, North America and to virtually every other country of immigration. This is why Hungarian as a language is spread all over the world, despite the fact that it remains one of the European languages least likely to be taught formally.

The third problem which may influence the language situation in a given geographical region is access for the majority of people, not only for a limited elite, to the use of various languages. Here, first of all, one must consider real life communicative situations, secondly the influence of the language input through the mass media plus that of popular culture (eg rock music and fashion), thirdly the chances (and need) for mobility in people's professional career.

The real mass-scale use of a variety of languages can be clearly detected in the regions which are located alongside the borders. Here there is constant direct communication among people of all social strata, with a trend towards bilingualism (even trilingualism), and with the dominance of one of the languages. The 'dominance' is not always very strong with the exception of that of German in the Transdanubian region. The position of German, however, has to be treated separately because of a multiplicity of underlying factors.

Tourism - both inside and outside Hungary - reinforces the need for communicating in the two widely spread languages - German and English - but there is a third language emerging, Italian, which is becoming more and more popular, especially among young people. French maintains its elite character, in that it is more likely to be learned in cities than in the provinces, by women than by men, by people of higher education than by uneducated ones. As to the spread of youth culture, fashion and technical culture, there is absolutely no doubt about the significance and leading role of English, although since most products enter Hungary through German speaking countries, the latter language has also gained importance through this channel of communication.

Last but not least there is the question of mobility to be taken into consideration. This is a relatively new phenomenon in Central Europe, despite a certain mobility in the times of the Austro-Hungarian Empire; and this is the consequence of the social and political changes in the region. Here again, the two widely spread languages take the lead, though several others are and will be included among those of importance.

The learning of foreign languages in general naturally involves such factors as traditions, cultural motives and availability. Thus direct needs and goals are but one facet of the problems, though a powerful one.

After this rapid survey of the present language situation in Hungary, we may consider how this is reflected in language education in the country both at present and in the near future. The real difficulty here is in common with neighbouring countries, namely the abrupt change in language policy practised by the countries of the now defunct socialist block. The core of the problem lies in a shift from the mandatory learning of Russian to an offer of several languages with seemingly equal chances. Equal educational status for languages is a noble intention; there are, however, quite a few obstacles on the road.

Let us digress for a moment into the level of language knowledge in Hungary yesterday. Yesterday, not today, as the rapidly changing circumstances do not allow any solid measurement at present.

In the second half of the 1980s several surveys, conducted through questionnaires and careful estimations were published on the level of knowledge of foreign languages in Hungary. The numbers turned out to be horrifying: although the vast majority of the population between 10 and 35 has been exposed to long years of study, the percentage of admitted speakers of Russian was about 3%. German seemed to be the most effective among the learned foreign languages with approximately 5.5%, supported by the knowledge of the German speaking minority of 2.3%. English, a language which the authorities had not promoted, had 2.2%, and French had almost reached 1%. These were hard facts which prove that the reaction against the long-time dominance of Russian was not merely of political nature, but also a sign of a peaceful revolt against the failure of the given system of mandatory language teaching in general.

The new - democratically elected - Hungarian government introduced a new directive for the learning of foreign languages in Hungarian schools:

(a) in the primary schools (8-14) one foreign language was to become obligatory in the 4th grade (at the age of 9);

(b) in the secondary schools (14-18) two foreign languages would become obligatory;

(c) the number of classroom periods could be increased.

The network of 'bilingual' schools, launched during the last years of the previous regime has been maintained; in these schools the language of instruction is - in most subjects - one of the following six: English, French, German, Italian, Russian and Spanish. Language requirements at college level are now under discussion. Furthermore language learning and teaching for all age groups outside the school as well as on an extra curricular level is mushrooming. Hungary receives help from the 'target countries' in developing both language teaching and teacher education. All these improvements are doubtless positive.

Let us now return to the factors inherent in the present situation which might counteract these positive developments for a while.

Alongside the structural change in the system of language education, the 'market' for language teachers has also been reshaped. As a consequence, a very significant surplus has gathered as regards teachers of Russian, while in teachers of all other languages there is a big shortage. According to official estimates, the numbers on both sides reach 10,000. One solution may be 'retraining' or 'conversion' of Russian teachers into teachers of other languages. The process is under way now, with thousands of Russian teachers studying either German or English, and some hundreds one of the other languages. This is, however, a highly problematic, and in many cases a rather hazardous enterprise, where success depends on a number of factors, from the age of the retrainee teacher, his/her motivation, private circumstances (family, children), the language courses available, to the quality of the teachers educating their colleagues, and many others. The control over the whole system is not conducted by any expert body, and only a small percentage of the candidates will have the chance of continuing their training at college level. As a result, the next generation of children is very likely to start language studies with a partially trained teaching staff.

Another solution could be a radical restructuring of the system of higher education, especially of teacher education in Hungary. Several measures have been taken in order to raise the number of language teachers with the goals and needs in view. This is where the support provided by the World Bank will also be used. This development, however, needs a couple of years' time, as not only is the necessary Faculty missing, but so are the well prepared students leaving secondary schools with a fair knowledge of the target language.

A further problem in this respect is the wish of the parents which in many ways contradicts any effort to establish diversity in language education. The list of motives and goals I mentioned earlier, plus the present prestige of a given language in the country, destroy a 'healthy balance' in the choice of language, and this may turn out to be very harmful as regards the real needs of society, and indeed, of the individual learner. Factors like personality, local traditions, international relations, and many others are not taken into consideration at all. Obviously a lot has to be done in preparing parents, schools and learners for language learning in order to become more successful than it has been up to now.

The school system of 'national minorities' - ie of Germans, Slovaks, Yugoslavs, and Romanians - has been built up from the nursery school to teacher training colleges. Courses, materials, school environments and teacher staff, however, are not on an equal level in all the languages involved. Neither is the motivation of children to carry on the studies, mostly in the language of their home. This largely depends on the prestige of the language and the homeland where the language is spoken. These questions of prestige and motivation are key variables in L1 maintenance or L1 attrition (in a move to assimilation). German is a lucky mixture of a wide-spread European language and a national minority language, where the two facets support each other. From the viewpoint of sociolinguistics, however, there is also a negative result rising from this amalgamation: local dialects rapidly die out, giving way to the standard variety.

Applied linguists have discovered one more shortage in language education: the neglect of two very important aspects, namely the more and more popular programmes with an early start, and secondly the possibilities hidden in students' overall language and communication skills (both in the first language and in the second one). Both fields have significant potential for helping students to develop their foreign language skills and abilities. Utilising these potentials will certainly raise the standard of foreign languages in Hungary.

LANGUAGES IN THE NETHERLANDS: A STUDY OF SUPPLY AND DEMAND

M. Oud-de Glas, E. van Hest, F. Peels, R. Diephuis, and T. van Els, *Institut voor Toegepaste Sociale wetenschappen, University of Nijmegen*

Languages in the Netherlands

The Netherlands have never been a strictly monolingual country. Besides Dutch, there is the Frisian language. The use of the latter is restricted to the province of Friesland, where it is used in public administration and taught in schools. Outside this province few Dutch people are familiar with it.

In recent decades the arrival of great numbers of immigrants from the former colonies and from the Mediterranean countries has brought a touch of cosmopolitanism to the linguistic map of the Netherlands. In primary schools, one out of every 20 students now has a mother tongue other than Dutch. Approximately half a million of the 15 million inhabitants of the country come from abroad.

The Netherlands form a small country depending largely for its economic survival on trade with neighbouring countries. Therefore, the learning of foreign languages has a very strong tradition in the Dutch educational system. The Dutch have a reputation for knowing foreign languages, and deservedly so. Foreign languages occupy an important position in the curriculum of Dutch schools: every fourth or fifth lesson in general secondary education is devoted to them. The vast majority of students learn a second foreign language besides English, while well over 75 per cent even learn a third. Within the EC, the Netherlands and Denmark follow Luxembourg as runners-up in terms of the scope of their foreign language teaching programmes. On the Test of English as a Foreign Language (TOEFL) the Dutch tend to outdo most, if not all, of their fellow Europeans (TOEFL, 1987).

And yet there is concern that the available knowledge may not be sufficient to meet the growing demands of an increasingly international society. Therefore, two years ago, mainly under the spur of the coming single European market, a committee was established to devise a programme of improvements for the teaching and learning of foreign languages (Van Els et al, 1990). To help this committee in the preparation of its programme, preliminary investigations have been carried out. The objective of these research activities was to establish an overview, as complete as possible, of the supply of and demand for foreign languages in the Netherlands. A distinction is made, in considering 'supply' between, on the one hand, all types of educational provision which help to produce foreign language competence, and, on the other hand, the type and range of the resulting foreign language competence itself. 'Demand' was defined as the actual use of foreign languages, the problems people experience when they have to use foreign languages, and the (economic and cultural) opportunities that foreign language competence gives access to.

In thc following paragraphs some results of these studies are presented (Van Hest et al, 1990).

Foreign Language Teaching in the Netherlands

In the Dutch education system, all children up to the age of twelve attend primary education, at which level English was introduced as a compulsory school subject in 1986. In primary schools, each year, approximately 350,000 children are introduced to a foreign language and its culture in the English language classes. They attend 60 to 100 hours of English language classes, some a few more, others somewhat less. Listening and speaking skills are most often stressed. There is a common core of several conversational topics, but there is a lot of variety with respect to grammar and vocabulary.

At present almost 83,000 children of foreign descent attend primary education (5.6% of the total number). Many of them come from Turkish and Moroccan families. For these children ethnic minority language classes are offered. We do not know exactly how many children attend these classes, as they are offered on a voluntary basis. At present, schools may have available facilities for 2.5 to 5 weekly language classes in Turkish, Arabic, Moluccan-Malay and the languages of the member states of the European Community.

Moving on to secondary education, the students split up into two streams; about one quarter go on directly to a four-year junior vocational training programme, while the remaining three quarters go on to either the short form of general secondary education (4 years) or the extended form (5 or 6 years). After four years students may move on to senior vocational training. Having finished this training, or the extended form of general secondary education, they may then move on to higher education. In the remainder of this article we will refer to junior vocational training and the short form of general secondary education as 'short secondary education'. Similarly, the term 'extended secondary education' will be used to refer to senior vocational training and the extended form of general secondary education.

Foreign languages are taught in all types of secondary education, and especially in both the short and extended forms of general secondary education. Apart from English, German and French, they sometimes include Spanish and Russian.

English is a compulsory subject for a number of years for all students, including those in vocational training. German and French are only compulsory in general secondary education; two years in the short form, three or four years in the extended form. For each foreign language on the timetable two to three classes are taught per week. After the period of compulsory foreign language instruction students can choose which language or languages they want to include in their final examinations. Students in general secondary education must take at least one foreign language, but a majority choose two. In the short form of general secondary education, 99% of the students choose English as one of their examination subjects. A much lower proportion of students chooses German; about 60%, so that about 40% attend only two years of German language classes. The percentage of students taking examinations in German has been pretty stable over the last three years. French comes in third. A quarter of the students choose French as an examination subject, a figure which has also been stable for many years. On average, the other 75% have presumably had two years of French. The fourth foreign language in this sector of secondary education is Spanish, which, up till now, has hardly taken root. In 1988 only 180 students took examinations in Spanish. In comparison, in the corresponding sector in adult education about 6,000 people are attending Spanish language classes; in 1988 the number of examinees was 1,150.

In junior vocational training it is not compulsory to take a foreign language as an examination subject, but many students do choose English: about 80%. No more than 15 % choose German. French and Spanish are hardly taught at all.

Foreign language teaching in senior vocational training varies by sector. In most sectors foreign languages are not taught very much. In the sector preparing for administrative jobs foreign language teaching is more important, and students can choose English, French, German and Spanish.

In the extended form of general secondary education the percentages of students choosing German and French as examination subjects are somewhat higher than in the short form: German about 50%, French about 35%. Spanish and Russian are offered in few schools. In adult education there is a growing interest in these languages.

The relative stability of the percentages of students choosing German and French in general secondary education is surprising, certainly in view of the complaints about a continuous decrease in the number of people speaking foreign languages. Critics of the Secondary Education Act introduced in 1968 have constantly referred to the situation before 1970 in which all students of all types of general secondary education attended classes in three foreign languages until final examinations. Looked at from that point of view, an enormous decrease of the scope of foreign language competence seems to have occurred.

However, we have to take into account the fact that the level of education has been rising sharply and that the programmes have changed considerably. The proportion of an age class attending general secondary education has increased very much, and as a consequence many more students than 20 years ago learn, at least for some years, three foreign languages. And however critical one may be of present-day foreign language teaching, its focus on the four skills is much more realistic than the heavy accent on grammar and translation tasks that was characteristic of foreign language classes before 1970.

Also in secondary education ethnic minority language classes are offered, albeit as yet, on a very small scale: 25 schools offer Turkish, 23 Arabic and a few schools offer Portuguese and Spanish. The marginal position of this type of education is, moreover, accentuated by the changing status of the subjects involved: outside school hours, sometimes during school hours; sometimes they are only offered as extra subjects, rarely do they take the place of another language. Although it is permitted to take Arabic and Turkish as an examination subject, very few schools actually offer this possibility to their students. It is striking, though, that syllabuses have been developed for Turkish and Arabic, whereas there are none for the 'major' languages.

In higher education there is little foreign language teaching, except in specialist language programmes. The Netherlands have 24 universities offering about 100 different full-length degree courses and some 60 'post-propaedeutic' courses in some forty different foreign languages. The courses comprise so-called 'specialist studies', in which the foreign language is the main subject, and 'area studies' or 'combination studies', in which the foreign language is an essential element of a wider combination of subjects. In addition, there are foreign language courses functioning as supporting subjects, but they are not widespread: universities traditionally hold the view that students at entrance bring along the necessary foreign language competence. Traditionally the most popular 'specialist studies' were English, French and German language studies. For all three studies enrolments have been decreasing. Especially with respect to German there has been a strong downward trend over the last few years, so that Spanish - which has been attracting more and more attention - has now become third on the list. For each of the other languages, enrolments total a couple of hundred students (roughly between 200 to 500 students per language or group of languages). So generally speaking, only very few people have a high-level command of foreign languages other than English, German, French or Spanish. In some cases this does not seem to be a problem (for example in the case of Korean or Swahili), in others an increase seems to be called for. Take, for example, the growing economic relations with Italy (about 450 students study Italian as a main subject), or the changing situation in Eastern Europe (about 550 students altogether study Slavonic languages as main subjects).

At present there are some 12 'combination-studies' which go by names like European Studies, Business Communication, Japanese Studies, International Management, Technology and Communication, Technology and Linguistics. These studies consist of a combination of foreign language training and elements from other disciplines, e.g. Law, Economics, Business Studies, Computer Science. These studies are increasingly popular: the number of participants is growing, while traditional language studies attract fewer students.

'Specialist studies' comprise, besides language acquisition, predominantly linguistics and literature. Traditionally, the professional perspective is very limited: the teaching profession or an academic career. A considerable number of highly-qualified language specialists are (therefore?) unemployed. The 'combination-studies' are an attempt to amend this situation.

Outside the regular education system there is a very high number of foreign language courses offered by private schools, TV channels, various types of schools for adult education, institutions offering correspondence courses, and so on. Although exact figures on the number of participants are not available for every type of course, a fairly reliable estimate would be that every year at least 100,000 people attend a foreign language course. From this impressive figure it necessarily follows that formal education is not able to meet all foreign language needs. It is striking that there is an enormous demand for courses in the so-called 'school languages' (languages traditionally taught at school), certainly in view of the fact that most of the foreign language training offered concerns beginners and intermediate courses. Apparently many people feel the need to refresh or improve the foreign language competence acquired at school. Unfortunately we do not know the age structure of the participants. If among them we were to find a large proportion of people older than forty, this could shed some new light on the popular hypothesis that, in the old days, foreign language teaching used to be so much better. There is also a remarkably high demand for Spanish, and to a lesser extent also for Italian, considering the relatively large number of courses in these languages.

Foreign Language Education Levels in the Dutch Population

The conclusion that foreign languages occupy an important position in the curriculum of Dutch schools may teach us something about the importance the Dutch give to language learning, but what about the results? What are the outcomes of this 'language competence producing system'? Is it possible to say something about how many people in the Netherlands have learnt which languages, and what level of proficiency they have achieved in these languages?

Not quite, but at least a partial answer to these questions is possible. As part of the research done for the committee mentioned above, a project has been carried out to assess language education levels. It addresses the question as to which education levels have been reached in which languages by a specific age group, or 'cohort', viz. those students who left primary education in 1977.

The original research questions were (a) What foreign language knowledge do the Dutch have? and (b) How is this knowledge distributed over the population? A variety of research methods might be employed to answer these questions. One would be to administer language tests to large samples of the population. Alternatively and rather more simply, *can-do* or self-assessment scales (Oscarson, 1989) might be used to measure foreign language proficiency levels; a practicable but rather expensive and time-consuming method. Since the research had to be completed within a few months, a less time-consuming research method was needed which would allow the maximal use of existing data.

The method that was chosen takes the education levels of the Dutch population as its starting point. The Dutch Central Bureau of Statistics (CBS) keeps accurate accounts of these levels and can indicate precisely how a particular age category is divided over the various levels (CBS, 1987). CBS data indicate that the population's average education level has risen sharply over the past few decades. For example, in 1987 one in three members of the age category 45 - 65 had attended only primary school, while this proportion was reduced to one in six in the 25 - 45 category. And since a higher education level tends to go hand in hand with a better foreign language knowledge, this rise in the average education level suggests that a growing proportion of the Dutch population has gained an increasing amount of foreign language knowledge.

Table 1 shows a breakdown of two age groups of the Dutch population by the highest diploma of education obtained or, in other words, by education level (CBS, 1987).

Table 1
Two age groups of the Dutch population by education level

Education level	Age group	
	25-44	45-64
Primary education	16%	35%
Short secondary education	29%	27%
Extended secondary education	35%	24%
Higher education	17%	10%
Unknown	3%	4%

Unfortunately, however, the link between educational level and the amount of foreign language knowledge is not so direct that the one can automatically be deduced from the other. The reason for this is twofold: firstly, there is the intricate structure of the Dutch education system, which has undergone considerable changes over the years. Thus, one and the same level of education may be reached via a variety of paths, and a greater or lesser amount of foreign language knowledge may be picked up en route. Secondly, students at most schools enjoy a certain freedom to choose their own subjects, so that even within one school, educational levels in foreign languages tend to vary between students.

If we were to make an accurate estimate of the Dutch population's foreign language attainment levels based on its overall educational attainment, we would therefore require an answer to a number of questions. How many people took which education path and when? How much foreign language instruction is supplied on each of these paths? And how much use is made of this supply? To answer these questions for the Dutch population as a whole proved impossible; that is, if we were only to make use of existing data, following the requirements of our short-term research project. What was possible, however, was to draw up a detailed account of the school careers of one specific age category, viz. those students who left primary education in 1977. This group, the so-called CBS 1977 cohort, consists of some 246,000 students whose average age was 24 when the research was carried out in 1989. A random sample of about 28,000 was periodically surveyed by the CBS in order to collect data on their school careers (CBS, 1982). The last survey dates back to 1984, when their average age was about 19. What and how well this group did after 1984 is not described in the CBS cohort study. However, fairly accurate estimates were possible on the basis of additional education statistics, including data on the number of students who move on to higher education (CBS, 1985). Thus, of this cohort we knew not only which levels of education they had reached but also which paths they had taken. This information was then combined with data on the amount of foreign language teaching at the various school types and on the students' choice of foreign languages as school subjects.

For each of the languages (English, French and German) the cohort students have been assigned to 5 categories of foreign language education levels. There are two points in secondary education where foreign language examinations involve centrally developed tests: at the end of short secondary education, and at the end of extended secondary education. For brevity's sake these examinations will henceforth be referred to as C(entral) E(xamination)-short and CE-extended. We have used these two 'completion points' together with the 'zero point' (i.e. no foreign language instruction received) to devise a classification system whereby the cohort students were categorised according to the education levels they have reached in English, German and French. The system comprises the following five levels:

level 0:	assigned to those students who have not received any instruction in a particular foreign language;
level 1:	assigned to those students who have received some instruction, but who have not taken CE-short in the foreign language;
level 2:	assigned to those students who have taken CE-short in the foreign language, and to those who have reached a comparable level in the extended form of general secondary education without taking CE-extended in the language;
level 3:	assigned to those students who have taken CE-extended in the foreign language;
level 4:	assigned to those students who have completed a specialist language training in higher education (language teachers, interpreters, translators, etc).

We know for each student in the cohort what their highest diploma is and what education path they have taken to obtain it. For example, we know how many students with a senior vocational training diploma have first attended the short form of general secondary education, and how many have gone directly to the vocational stream. But this information does not suffice to reconstruct the language education levels of all students with a diploma of vocational training. Further information is required about the amount of foreign language instruction and about the students' participation therein. As a case in point, junior vocational training comprises five separate substreams, each with its own curriculum and exam regulations. For each of these substreams it is necessary to know what languages are taught, how many students receive instruction in which language, and how many of them take an examination in which language. Thus, a large database had to be compiled that would contain the relevant information for each of these substreams. Most of this information was derived from CBS studies, while the rest was taken from previous research (for references, see Van Hest et al., 1990) and from reports by the education inspectorate. On a few occasions educated guesses had to be made based on expert opinions.

Table 2 shows the education levels in English, German and French of all the students in the CBS 1977 cohort.

Table 2
The CBS 1977 cohort by education levels in English, German and French, percentages (N = 246,140)

	English	German	French
level 0	0.0	20.4	39.1
level 1	33.2	32.0	26.6
level 2	31.9	30.0	24.9
level 3	34.4	17.4	9.1
level 4	0.5	0.2	0.3

The average education level in English is clearly the highest by far; two out of every three students have reached at least level 2 (CE-short), while one in three has reached level 3 (CE-extended). Levels in German are clearly lower; one in five students has never learnt any German, while no more than one in six has reached level 3. But the lowest average level is in French, with two in five students having learnt no French at all, and barely one in ten reaching level 3.

These differences in language education levels are of course closely related to education levels in general; a student who spends six or seven years in secondary education will probably acquire more foreign language knowledge than a student who leaves secondary school after four years. And yet, as we have observed earlier on, even where the overall education level is equal there are wide variations in language education levels. This can be demonstrated by looking at table 3, which concerns the group with the highest education level, i.e. a diploma of higher education. At this level students are required to be able to read specialist literature in a foreign language.

Table 3
Students of the CBS 1977 cohort with higher education diplomas by education levels in English, German and French, percentages (N = 40,908)

	English	German	French
level 0	0.0	3.8	6.5
level 1	3.4	8.6	14.4
level 2	8.8	41.2	49.8
level 3	85.0	45.3	27.5
level 4	2.8	1.2	1.8

Here we see the same relation between the languages as in table 2 above. Levels in English are the highest by far, followed by German and French. While less than half of this group have reached level 3 in German, less than 30 per cent have reached this level in French. Since level 3, i.e. CE-extended, may be considered a minimum requirement for reading specialist literature in a foreign language with some ease, it may be concluded that only English specialist literature is fairly easily accessible to large proportions of this group. This contrasts sharply with the situation 20 years ago, when the population of students in higher education, much smaller than nowadays, was far more homogeneous in terms of their foreign language knowledge in that virtually all students reached level 3 in all three languages. It is therefore understandable that complaints about students' limited command of foreign languages have persisted over the past two decades.

Because of its connection with the commonest examination levels, the categorisation used in this study can be said to offer a valid scale for measuring foreign language proficiency levels. The periodic use of this scale in new cohorts could provide an insight into any changes in the output of foreign language teaching.

Foreign Language Needs in the Netherlands

What is the demand for foreign language knowledge in the Netherlands? That was the third question of the committee in charge of formulating recommendations to improve foreign language teaching. In this study, too, we were faced with a number of limitations. Following the extensive 1978 research on the foreign language needs of the country conducted - at the request of the Ministry of Education - by the Institute of Applied Social Sciences (ITS) of the University of Nijmegen, not much further needs research has been carried out in this field (Claessen et al, 1978a, 1978b, 1978c; Oud-de Glas, 1983). In 1987 the ITS conducted a comprehensive survey into the need for foreign language competence among ex-students of senior vocational training (Lucassen et al, 1987). Others have investigated the transition between upper secondary school and higher education (e.g. Van Dijck et al, 1985). And there have been some nation wide inquiries, such as the survey commissioned by the Association of Language Teachers (Bureau Lagendijk, 1987). Besides these research reports there are a number of signals of growing foreign language needs, especially from trade and industry, that have also been taken into account.

On behalf of the committee, a small additional survey has been carried out. Fourteen experts from various social sectors (government and trade and industry) have, by means of structured interviews, been questioned about the need for foreign language competence in their sectors. Among other things, they were asked to reflect on the ITS findings from 10 years back and to indicate to what extent these were still relevant.

The most important results of these various sources of information are summarized here.

The need for foreign language knowledge is increasing in all sectors and the required level of competence is rising. Some examples: while in the past it was mostly large companies that had international trade relations, at present this also goes for an increasing proportion of small and medium-sized companies; the government becomes more and more involved with other member states of the European Community; the number of participants in higher education is growing considerably and as a consequence also the need for foreign languages; and with respect to private needs, tourism abroad is on the increase.

In professional practice the need for German is almost as great as that for English, and in a number of sectors it is even greater. The importance of German seems to be systematically underestimated. French still comes in third, but the use of French is perhaps avoided, because of the big problems which people have in using it and which are reported over and over again. Export companies especially consider a good knowledge of a Romance language (preferably French) of vital importance to further economic growth. Nearly all sectors stress the rapidly increasing importance of Spanish, and this need is especially voiced by trade and industry, which needs more and more employees with knowledge of Spanish. In the case of all other foreign languages there are very specific needs in connection with some relatively small numbers of people and/or relatively limited objectives.

The popular assumption that English helps everywhere, appears to be without sufficient foundation. Almost everyone also needs German and in view of the fast internationalization of a great many jobs it is extremely desirable that an increasing proportion of the inhabitants of the Netherlands also learns French or Spanish. Of course in many cases it is possible to get along with English alone, but there are also many situations in which competence in a language other than Dutch or English is essential.

In 1978, two thirds of Dutch trade and industry used English and German, fifty per cent also used French. Although the number of users and the frequency of use differ strongly for each sector, most experts interviewed think that the use of foreign languages has increased since then, especially the use of English and, to a lesser extent, German. At present the use of French seems to be concentrated in the higher functions. There are five categories in which foreign languages are very often used: in management, commercial functions, secretarial functions, public relations and marketing, and in research. This goes for all sectors of trade and industry. Most experts expect an increase in the use of Spanish.

The situation in public administration is to a large extent comparable to that of trade and industry. In 1978, in general, there were a few more foreign language users here than in trade and industry, but the foreign languages were less frequently used. The categories in which foreign languages are frequently used are more or less the same: management, public relations, and research. In government institutions the position of French is more prominent than in trade and industry.

Fast growing international trade is one of the factors which cause an increasing need for foreign language knowledge. With respect to export, the German-speaking territories are by far thc most important trading partners: 30% of Dutch exports go to these territories. Next, in order of importance, are French-speaking (18%), English-speaking (11%), Italian-speaking (6%), and Spanish-speaking territories. English is often the trading language in countries where English is not the official language.

Foreign languages are not only important for professional purposes, but also for study and development, as an instrument for learning other subjects. This type of need does not play any role in the first phase of secondary education. In senior vocational training its role becomes slightly more important, at school, but also during periods of practical training in companies. However, the focus is on higher education. There foreign language knowledge is important in many disciplines. This holds particularly for the language skills needed to read professional literature, to a lesser extent also for skills to follow lectures in a foreign language and sometimes to have a conversation with foreign colleagues; in view of increasing internationalization higher education will have to offer more lectures in a foreign language - especially English , whether or not given by foreign lecturers. Apart from this a number of 'linguistic' study skills involving foreign language competence are often mentioned: looking up information, summarizing, making notes, and so on.

In 1978, the ITS research project had already reported about this type of foreign language need. Staff members and students were questioned on the subject. More than ten years ago teachers of economic and technical disciplines in higher education considered German and English language knowledge essential. Already in that period people indicated a lack of reading skills in particular. Professional English literature was obligatory for all disciplines; 86% of the teachers interviewed also required German literature and 38% French. It was also put forward that problems with French and German prompted teachers to specify professional literature less frequently in those two languages. The students did not only confirm the picture of a lack of French and German foreign language knowledge, they also added that English reading skills were not always adequate.

Since that time the number of students entering higher education has risen dramatically. In 1985 a survey showed that institutions for higher education which have to prescribe specialist literature in a foreign language (for example when there are no Dutch equivalents) get into trouble, because there are always students who have not taken examinations in the relevant languages in secondary education. Out of necessity they leave out this type of literature or try to translate certain articles. The students indicated that they had particular problems with German (in agricultural and technical studies) and English (in technical and economic studies) (Van Dijck et al, 1985).

In 1989 another survey was carried out among study coordinators and tutors in higher education (Van Dijck et al, 1989). They all thought English important (90%), but they also stressed the important role of German. Fifty per cent of the respondents thought French language knowledge important, especially in the field of arts, economics, agriculture and law. Reading skills were important in all disciplines, but the need for other skills differed considerably according to the discipline .

Another type of need appears only at a later stage. Graduates from higher education often start their careers as specialists, but after a period of time they move on to management functions. Then suddenly the lack of foreign language knowledge required for the new function becomes apparent and can only be compensated for with great difficulty.

People do not use foreign languages only in their jobs or for educational purposes. We mentioned above that tens of thousands of inhabitants of the Netherlands attend foreign language classes in their spare time. Often for professional reasons, but more as a hobby: for vacations, to enjoy books and films, or because of personal contacts (friends or family abroad). The ITS research among ex-students of secondary education showed that foreign language use for private purposes was relatively extensive for all groups (Claessen et al, 1978a). In 1987 the Association of Language Teachers commissioned a public opinion poll (Bureau Lagendijk, 1987). The results show that the use of German and English for private purposes appears to be almost the same: about 60% of the population occasionally uses these languages. For French this is over 25%. Vacations abroad probably account for a large part of foreign language usc in the private sector: a considerable proportion of the Dutch spend their holidays outside the Dutch territory.

The Dutch National Action Programme

The research reported here was carried out on behalf of the committee that has already been mentioned. As a result of its work, the committee published a so-called National Action Programme, comprising a set of measures to improve foreign language teaching provisions in the Netherlands (Van Els et al, 1990). One of the main points of this programme can be summarized as: encouraging a good division of labour between all types of foreign language provision, so that extensive and diverse foreign language needs can be met as completely and as efficiently as possible. This means that different sectors of the educational system, both public and private, each have their own responsibilities in offering foreign language learning. Hence general secondary education should take care of the teaching of languages that are most generally needed, and day and evening classes for adults should develop and stimulate provision for other foreign languages such as Italian, Portuguese and Russian.

A second set of measurements proposed by the committee can be characterized as: encouraging the quality of foreign language teaching, so that qualitative and quantitative output will be improved. An example: the committee advises that, in general, the international orientation of teachers and students be strongly stimulated, especially by means of periods of practical training and study abroad, if possible with the help of the EC programmes that have been set up for this purpose: ERASMUS, LINGUA and COMETT.

Recently the Dutch Ministry of Education has installed a working group in charge of the implementation of the Action Programme, chaired by its first author.

Although in the Netherlands, and probably in other European countries as well, there are clearly growing needs for languages other than English, this certainly must not be understood as a sign of a changing situation with regard to a lingua franca in Europe. Firstly, the position of English as the language of science is very strong. Recently the Dutch Minister of Education even proposed to introduce English as the language of teaching in Dutch universities although the reactions were overwhelmingly negative. Secondly youth culture and television are strongly dominated by Anglo-Saxon influences, and this is true for most European countries. For the younger generation, in the Netherlands at least, English is becoming a sort of second language. Nevertheless in trade and industry the situation seems to be different. Understanding and speaking the language of the customer is a trump card in harsh international economic competition, even if many business transactions and negotiations are conducted in English. That is one of the reasons why the Dutch invest in language teaching, and try to regain or reinforce the advantage they traditionally have in this respect.

References

Bureau Lagendijk. 1987. *Nederlanders en talen*

CBS. 1982. *Schoolloopbaan en herkomst van leerlingen bij het voortgezet onderwijs. Deel 1; bestand 1977*. Den Haag: Staatsuitgeverij

CBS. 1985. *Overgangen binnen het onderwijs en intrede in de maatschappij. Onderwijsmatrix 1985*. Den Haag: Staatsuitgeverij

CBS. 1987. *Arbeidskrachtentelling 1985*. Den Haag: Staatsuitgeverij

Claessen, J.F.M., van Galen, A.M., and Oud-de Glas, M.M.B. 1978a. *De behoeften aan moderne vreemde talen. Een onderzoek onder leerlingen, oud-leerlingen en scholen.* Nijmegen: ITS

Claessen, J.F.M., van Galen, A.M., and Oud-de Glas, M.M.B. 1978b. *De behoeften aan moderne vreemde talen. Een onderzoek onder stafleden en studenten van het wetenschappelijk onderwijs.* Nijmegen: ITS

Claessen, J.F.M., van Galen, A.M., and Oud-de Glas, M.M.B. 1978c. *De behoeften aan moderne vreemde talen. Een onderzoek onder bedrijven en overheidsdiensten.* Nijmegen: ITS

Lucassen, P., Oud-de Glas, M., Petersen, B., and Willems, M. 1987. *De behoeften aan moderne vreemde talen bij oud-leerlingen van het meao, mmo en mto.* Nijmegen: ITS

Oscarson, M. 1989. Self-assessment of language proficiency: rationale and applications. *Language Testing,* 6, 1: 1-13

Oud-de Glas, M. 1983. Foreign Language Needs in the Netherlands. In: T. van Els, M. Oud-de Glas (eds) *Research into foreign language needs.* Augsburg: Universität Augsburg, 151-70

TOEFL. 1987. *Test and Score Manual, 1987-1988 Edition*

Van Dijck, M., van den Elshout, J., and Hoogeveen, K. 1985. *Van voortgezet onderwijs naar HBO: problemen, oorzaken, oplossingen?* Den Haag/Leiden: SVO/LICOR

Van Dijck, M., Schneider, H., and Baks, R. 1989. *Vakkenpakketten en de kwalificatie voor HBO en WO.* Leiden: LICOR

Van Els et al. 1990. *Horizon Taal. Nationaal Actieprogramma Moderne Vreemde Talen.* Zoetermeer: Ministerie van Onderwijs en Wetenschappen

Van Els et al. (forthcoming). *National Action Programme for Foreign Languages*

Van Hest, E., Peels, F., Oud-de Glas, M., Diephuis, R., and van Els, T. 1990. *Vreemde talen in de markt. Onderzoek naar vraag en aanbod in het kader van Horizon Taal, Nationaal Actieprogramma Moderne Vreemde Talen.* Nijmegen/Zoetermeer: Ministerie van Onderwijs en Wetenschappen

FROM USSR TO CIS AND BEYOND: VISCERAL POLITICS VIS-À-VIS ETHNO-LINGUISTIC REALITIES

F. Knowles, *Aston University*

The last few years and the last two in particular have witnessed major changes of a political, geopolitical, economic, ethno-social and sociolinguistic nature throughout the vast Eurasian area[1] which formerly constituted the territory of the Union of Soviet Socialist Republics. The changes which have occurred there are of such dimensions that they could never have been predicted and hence prepared for - whether they were an inescapable logical consequence of the policies pursued, or at least presided over, by the erstwhile Soviet President Mikhail Gorbachov is a matter of debate. What is clear is that the socio-political developments which have continually riveted the attention of outside observers but which have been the continuous and intensifying cause - for all sorts of different and conflicting reasons - of consternation to those directly affected by them demolished all the foundations of political, economic and social life in the Soviet Union. Most of all, the events of 1990-1991 and, notably, the coup attempt in August 1991, showed the fallacy and the bankruptcy of concepts such as 'Soviet society', 'Soviet man', 'the brotherhood of the Soviet peoples', 'the fusion of Soviet ethnic communities' etc. Although rich in natural resources, possessing huge areas of space and having the potential advantage of a well-educated population, 300 million strong, the viability of the Soviet state, at least in terms of genuine economic competitiveness, was compromised by the lack of a freely convertible currency, by the obsolescence of those areas of industry operating outside the so-called military-industrial complex and by repeated failure on the part of national and local opinion-formers and decision-makers alike to address and provide a comprehensive - and highly mechanised - solution to the problem of under-production and under-productivity in Soviet agriculture. Most of all, the sclerotic Soviet state was undermined by its unrealistic ambition to maintain its status as one of the world's two superpowers. In 1979 it rashly undertook a colonial war in Afghanistan which turned out to be such a political, moral and military disaster that the morale and military effectiveness of the Soviet Army were seriously impaired, with much damage seeping back into the Soviet Union itself via ongoing transports of soldiers in coffins and the return home of many physically disabled young ex-servicemen. Much more to the point, initiatives such as the SDI programme launched by the USA in the early 1980's challenged, effectively speaking, the USSR to a financial rather than to a military duel: the Soviet Union lost the duel,[2] fatally enfeebling itself in the process.

The outcome for the Soviet Union of all these factors and events - some at least potentially under its control, many not so - was its demise or transmogrification to the Commonwealth of Independent States (CIS). Put quite simply, the Soviet empire disintegrated, losing in that process all its satellite ‘buffer states’ in Eastern and Central Europe and in the Balkans. The proclamations of independence made by Estonia, Latvia and Lithuania in 1990 were a particularly painful experience for the Kremlin, whose previous political tenants had successfully held these erstwhile independent nations in their thrall since 1940, when they were forcibly incorporated into the Soviet Union as a result of a secret protocol in the 1939 German-Soviet Non-Aggression Pact, the existence of which was denied for almost fifty years by the Soviet government. Over these long years feelings of nationhood remained strong in the Baltic states - in spite of the personal risks run by those who voiced such feelings - and led to the above-mentioned declarations of independence which were initially condemned as unacceptable by the USSR, either in principle or at least in terms of any rapid disengagement time-scale. Deaths inflicted on protesting members of the civilian populations (notably in Lithuania and Latvia) by Soviet troops and ‘irregulars’ naturally exacerbated the situation. Realistic Soviet/Russian politicians and observers had mentally conceded defeat by the middle of 1991 and what had previously been unthinkable for fifty years came to pass on September 6th 1991: three independent countries called Estonia, Latvia and Lithuania, now able to orient themselves westward in a renascent Hanseatic League, less threatened by a Russia whose share of the Baltic littoral had just been reduced by three-quarters or more. It was this development which initiated and catalysed the break-up of the Soviet Union as a unitary state. Independence-minded people elsewhere could see that it was possible to proclaim independence and gain it and that much could be achieved by expression of resentment against the ‘Russian overlord’. Moreover, as a result of the quite rapid dismantling of the censorship system in the mass media and in book-publishing, people were very quick to seek and see proof of the enormity of the official mendacity which had been inflicted on them for so many years, particularly the downright lies and half-truths about the deliberate or wasteful sacrifice of millions of lives, about matters such as the vilification and persecution of dissidents or about the relative standard of living in the USSR compared to ‘bourgeois-capitalist’ countries. These mass insights effectively poured petrol on the smouldering fire of frustration and anger which had been alight for a very long time. Politically and sociologically, so to speak, the hunt began in earnest for the perpetrators of this misery, for scapegoats and also for the victims. Centrifugal forces took over from centripetal ones in the sense that local solutions - or panaceas? - were required before national ones. Of course, the most preferred local solution was - at least in prospect - to 'sanitise' by regrouping along ethnic and linguistic lines. 'Togetherness' was out. The first casualties in this process were, naturally enough, the 'outsiders', the 'immigrants', the 'aliens'. In many cases that meant the Russians themselves, who suddenly acquired the extra epithet of being the 'exploiters and despoilers'. In a complete swing of the pendulum, which hopefully, may yet turn out to be temporary, the Soviet Union's ethnic communities seemed to totally turn their backs on gregariousness and intermingling and espouse tribalism and isolationism. 'Neighbours' were forsaken for 'family', for kith and kin. It was back to basics, to the proverbial square one. Things have not moved much further forward since, and in many respects they have deteriorated as emotional and visceral reactions have, on examination, been found to be psychologically, intellectually and socio-politically acceptable.

The above summary account of political developments is intended to serve as priming material for a review of the various ethnic and hence ethno-linguistic conflagrations which have been either kindled or rekindled in the process. At this stage it is, however, important to briefly rehearse the basic political philosophy underlying the whole question of the various nationalities inhabiting the Soviet Union. The foundation of this political philosophy goes back to Lenin who was well aware, as an astute political analyst and politician, of the virtually total lack of proper consideration of and sensitivity about such matters in the Tsarist empire in which the Russians behaved as and were perceived as pure colonial overlords. This was the single biggest blockage inhibiting socio-political progress in Tsarist times and Lenin's philosophical and pragmatic view was that the non-Russian peoples could be politically mobilised and engaged and committed to Soviet power only if a complete break were made with past practice. Lenin's view in the very early years of the 20th century - whether ingenuous or disingenuous is a matter of speculation: it certainly filled a large lacuna in Marxist thought - was that evolution of a multi-ethnic society in polities larger than mere Nation States was both possible and necessary; a precondition for this in the specific instance of a future socialist/Soviet state was to 'reduce' the status of the numerically and culturally dominant Russian people to that of primus inter pares. Lenin entrusted Stalin to elaborate a policy basis relevant to the peoples of the Tsarist empire but this exemplar required a workable solution to the problem of ethnically self-conscious peoples not necessarily distributed compactly in well-defined geographical areas but, rather, co-existing and intermingled with other similar groups. Stalin's well-known axiom, the precursor of legislative documents, posited that a nation is 'a historically constituted, stable community of people, formed on the basis of a common language, territory, economic life and psychological make-up, manifested in a common culture'. Lenin viewed this formulation as the bedrock on which a multi-ethnic socialist state could be constructed in the politically transformed lands of the Tsarist Empire and his presupposition was that in the course of time the many different peoples involved would draw ever more closely together, finally to merge and emerge as one nation - on the basis of common territory, unified economic life, a collectively transformed psychological make-up, a newly established and integrated culture and Weltanschauung, although - one must assume - this last, albeit one dialectic, would need to be expressed not by one language but by many. Tested in the crucible of the events of the Russian revolutions of 1917 and their aftermath, Lenin's - and hence the Bolshevik - view underwent changes before settling on the formation of a federal state, the Union of Soviet Socialist Republics,[3] consisting of Union Republics, each embodying and representing the political aspirations of its titular nationality. Peoples of lesser numerical strength or with only a nascent politico-cultural infrastructure were given protection in the form of autonomous republics, regions and 'national' areas. Necessarily, this political arrangement required infrastructural support in the shape of a language planning policy. Such policies, of course, are stimulated by *raison d'état* but they must state overtly the terms and conditions of a 'language(s) action plan'. In the Soviet case, there is some basis for the suspicion that the linguistic objectives were merely subordinate to political considerations from the end of the Second World War onwards, when the Soviet state was no longer confronted by internal or external threats to its existence and when the adoption of the Russian language, and perhaps even of a 'Russoid' persona, was embraced by thousands upon thousands as the route to personal upward mobility in Soviet society. This 'career strategy' has worked well for many: see Table 1 in the Appendix for a 1989 analysis of managers in Soviet industry, agriculture, transport, telecommunications, and construction. Part of the phenomenon illustrated there may, of course, be due to quotas and/or a local jobs Mafia, rather than merit. Neither is it possible to glean from the data what level of proficiency and what habitual use of Russian, and in what circumstances, the said managers have.

An 'alternative view' of Soviet language planning adduces the conspiracy theory element in its articulation. In checklist form the argument runs thus:

Soviet Language Planning

Political Purposes

To relieve the logistic problems of the body politic
To counteract demographic pressures
To maximise the impact of Marxist-Leninist values
To consolidate ethnic communities in a socialist framework
To develop Soviet 'patriotism'
To foster 'internationalism' inside the USSR
To develop Soviet cosmopolitanism
To realign the minorities' cultural realia - or to expunge them if necessary
To break up any non-Soviet cultural hegemonies
To connive at the retention of innocuous cultural pluralism
To emphasise super-power achievements and aspirations
To foster the Soviet image outside the USSR

Linguistic Purposes

To establish Russian as a second(ary) native language
To marginalise ethnic languages
To widen the scope for linguistic interaction between Soviet citizens
To establish self-confident, but controlled language 'ecologies'
To standardise as many linguistic subsystems as possible, notably terminologies
To accelerate the controlled development of functionally retarded languages
To maximise the effectiveness of information-handling
To homogenise modes of thought and expression

Nearly all of the linguistic purposes enumerated above relate to what has come to be called 'status planning'. Specific policies, programmes, projects and initiatives proceed logically from the overarching purposes and relate to the two implementational areas of corpus planning and acquisition planning. Examples of the former would be the elaboration and production of dictionaries, grammars and textbooks for L2 learners of Russian who are also Soviet citizens, or -

mutatis mutandis - the generation of similar reference and study materials, conceived and executed in the above mould, for L1 speakers but not usually L2 learners of given ethnic languages. When it comes to acquisition planning then it is almost exclusively a matter of opportunities and incentives for people. Such opportunities and incentives have not been as systematic. The fact that the September 1989 Plenum of the Central Committee of the Soviet Communist Party needed to propose the following package of measures speaks volumes (Lane, 1991, 200ff).

1 the improvement of the Soviet Federation and its infusion with real political and economic content;
2 the expansion of the rights and potential of all types of national autonomous entity;
3 the safeguarding of equal rights for every people and the satisfaction of the specific interests of every nationality;
4 the creation of the preconditions for the free development of national languages and cultures;
5 the strengthening of guarantees to rule out the infringement of citizens' rights on the grounds of nationality;
6 the renewal of all ideological, political, scientific, research and educational work in the sphere of national relations;
7 the affirmation in inter-ethnic communications of mutual respect for the historical traditions and specific national characteristics and consideration for each people's economic and inner (Russian: *duxovnyj*) interests.

Clearly, a legislative and programmatic dispensation in the area of language planning - especially of the sort postulated and striven for by the Soviet government down the years - has to involve some constructive ambiguity, better left undissected and undiscussed. Tacitly, the general understanding was: equal rights do not mean equal significance, much less equivalence or genuinely equal esteem. If Sovietisation was to be pursued, as it was, then one instrument in that process was Russification, whether by design or by necessity. Russians, of course, are the best Russifiers, by definition. It is not sufficient to claim that Russian was merely the medium and the method, Sovietisation the message, the marker and the mark. Russians could so easily think or even claim that their equivalent of the 'white man's burden' relieved them of any personal responsibilities of reciprocity vis-à-vis their protégés. In linguistic terms alone, only about one Russian in twenty-five currently reports any knowledge of any other indigenous language of the erstwhile USSR, whereas half of its non-

Russian population claims knowledge of Russian[4] and another five per cent report knowledge of other languages indigenous to the country.[5]

Mr. Gorbachov, after taking over the post of General Secretary of the Communist party of the Soviet Union (CPSU) in 1985[6], was certainly no innovator in the area of ethnic relations in the USSR and appeared surprised on more than one public occasion at the idea of linkage between socio-economic perestroika and the ethnic question. Those who now find themselves in leading political positions in the CIS are only too well aware that they are dogged in a double sense - vis-à-vis Russia and with respect to their own minorities - by the ethnic issue which needs solutions, effective ones, more urgently than ever before. Firstly, the ethnic problem is now 100% public and to some extent already internationalised and secondly, actors and observers alike are non-plussed about how to apply remedies or even palliatives. One of the biggest issues, of course, is the future of the Russian diaspora in the newly independent Baltic states and in all CIS states apart from the non-autonomous areas of Russia itself.

The list of ethnic trouble-spots in ex-USSR territory is long and frightening. Over the last five or so years television viewers in Western Europe and the USA have had regular pictures and reportages on their TV screens of street demonstrations and/or violence from Abkhazia, Armenia, Azerbaijan, Belarus, Buryatia, Chechnya, Estonia, Georgia, Kazakhstan, Kyrgyzstan, Latvia, Lithuania, Meskhetia, Moldova, Nakhichevan, South Ossetia, Tatarstan, the Ukraine, and Uzbekistan. They have also seen pictures of large numbers of emigrating Soviet Germans, Greeks and Jews. In many of the above instances it would appear that only the physical relocation of the affected communities and/or the re-drawing of borders can provide the radical solution which is required. Yet moves of that scale nearly always create new problems in the stead of the old ones. The emigration of Soviet Germans and of Jews is stimulated by a pull rather than by a push and individual movements are voluntary. Whether the emigratory momentum will exhaust the 'candidate pool' in these two cases is an open question - it is, however, possible. This would be to allow an endemic ethnic problem to cure itself by haemorrhage. It is also on the cards that the Moldovans will wish - would they succeed in such a desire? - to see the international border between the CIS and Rumania re-drawn, with the effect that Moldova, or most of it[7], will revert to Rumania and constitute one of its new provinces. Something along the same lines might occur with respect to Eastern Karelia if a mutually suitable accord can be reached between Russia and Finland, such as the sale price for the 'real estate' and a Finnish investment package to (re)create the area's physical infrastructure. Could analogous moves be made on the CIS southern frontier in the Caucasus? What will happen to the enclave that is now the Kaliningrad Region, the northerly section of the former German province of East Prussia with the major city better known by its previous name of Königsberg? Will pressure from Soviet Germans to be resettled there be successful and what would Polish reactions be to such a move? Will the Kurile Islands be amicably returned to Japan? If any or all of the above changes took place, a cure would have been affected by surgery. This has already happened with regard to the Baltic states. It so happens, however, that citizens of Russian nationality in the new Baltic states may have imposed on them civil rights 'packages' which are inequitable and discriminatory. If this were to happen then the problem would have been internationalised and could possibly benefit from scrutiny and mediation by international agencies. It is to be fervently hoped that a re-run, on CIS soil or in the Baltics, of the Yugoslav experience can be avoided! What, however, about the most difficult cases, those which require therapy rather than intervention? What does Soviet experience hitherto provide in the way of 'do's and don'ts'?

In the ambit of language planning in the former USSR the main 'work-horses', at least in terms of reported effectiveness, for achieving the objectives declared - plus some that were not declared - were the education system (all the way from kindergarten to higher education), the armed forces and the mass media. Compulsory military service was the occasion of and the instrument for 'socialising' the Soviet Union's young men into the use of Russian and the adoption of Soviet mores. The Soviet Army, in studiously eschewing the raising of territorially-bound units, always availed itself of the opportunity to deploy its conscripts in ethnically-mixed units and in areas that were maximally distant from their homes. The Soviet Army is now in a state of disarray as attempts are made to achieve the transformation to a unified command structure for units and formations raised and contributed by the individual governments of the CIS. It remains to be seen whether these attempts will be successful - the auguries are not good. Whether these intentions are carried through to conclusion or not, the Russian language has, to one extent or another, lost its leading role as a means of command over, of communication with, and of the military-cum-Soviet acculturation of young conscripts from all the ethnic minorities living outside the territory of the new Russian Federation. Inside the territory of the new Russian Federation it may be a very different matter for military servicemen from the ethnic minorities - they may receive few concessions under the new dispensation. Russian is bound to be severely eclipsed as the new, non-Russian member-states of the CIS adopt their own languages in their sovereign armed forces. Russian will probably survive, of course, as a purely pragmatic means of communication and interaction between co-operating but independent armies across CIS territory.

The mass media monopoly is now largely broken up in the CIS and in many areas it is under totally new and professional management, in some places waging an internecine war of words with colleagues-turned-rivals! In other words the omens are quite good: the reading, listening and viewing public has more of a choice than ever before. Reading and broadcast material is being purveyed which seeks to put on view all the skeletons in the many dark cupboards. Journalists and broadcasters learnt with amazing rapidity the tricks of the trade so well known to their colleagues in Western Europe and the USA.

The former USSR's education system set great store by its opportunity to socialise children from the non-Russian communities into Soviet ways and behaviour; its dilemma was always to what extent Russian should be used as the vehicle in this process. The state, in 1989, of activity at pre-school level is shown in the Appendix at Table 2[8]. Reliable data about ex-Soviet secondary education is exceedingly hard to come by, especially with respect to ethnic and linguistic matters. No details of this sort are to be found, unfortunately, in the compendium of social statistics already quoted. At the top end of the age spectrum in education is higher education. Details emerging from the 1989 Soviet census show that at least four out of five Estonian, Kazakh, Kyrgyz, Latvian, Lithuanian, Moldavian, Russian, Turkmenian, and Ukrainian students received, in recent years, their higher education within their titular republic, whereas every fourth Azerbaijani, Byelorussian, Georgian, or Tajik student, and every third Armenian student has had to settle temporarily in a different Union Republic in order to study: see Table 3 in the Appendix.

The Soviet education reforms of the late 1950's moved away from the monolithicity which had characterised the educational scene earlier on, by incorporating options which parents could exercise: strict polarity of choice between schooling in Russian or in a 'local' language - almost a personal political barometer for parents - was softened by the institution of mixed-language schools. All of this was reasonable enough in terms of generalities; parents and their offspring, however, do not exercise their choices in a vacuum but only with regard to the given realities in the midst of which they live and having an eye to the pressures they feel themselves subject to. One trade-off they needed to calculate very carefully was the attraction of upward mobility afforded by a secondary education delivered in Russian as opposed to the apprehension that an extra year of secondary schooling might be required in order to attain the 'threshold' standard in Russian required for further education in many subjects. Much more research is needed on this delicate topic - surveys of parental decisions and attitudes over the last thirty or so years are, of course, now possible.

This issue still has lots of mileage in it. Russian settlers, many of long standing, in ethnic regions of the former USSR now seem to be paying for their previous extreme reluctance to learn local languages. It is true that suitable textbooks either never existed or were never made available in the right quantities and the task of making it possible for Russian school-children to learn local languages was side-stepped by the simple administrative mechanism of inducing a permanently short supply of teachers trained for this task. There is, moreover, no doubt that Russians often - perhaps even routinely - behaved insensitively towards their ethnic neighbours, displaying a mixture of ignorance, condescension and haughtiness. In the CIS states and in the Baltics language status must be defined and declared. In most instances this will mean the elevation of the 'autochthonous' languages involved to official languages, and the relegated status of Russian must also be properly codified. Of course, much more is involved than that. We may be the witnesses of attempts at linguistic purification as the nomenclature - and the actuality! - of Soviet realia and of now deprecated and anathematised political and socio-economic concepts are cast aside. Much vocabulary will need to be semantically 'disinfected' and realigned. In those cases where particular terms are compromised beyond redemption, new coinages will naturally be needed for whatever realia or concepts replace them. In this process two competing tendencies are likely to emerge: the rephoneticisation of Anglo-Saxon terminology and calqueing from within the existing word-derivational resources of the languages concerned. Estonians, in particular, will look to Finnish for terminological inspiration.

In today's newly independent Baltic states, however, moves are afoot to curtail civic rights - e.g. by disenfranchisement - and even abrogate residence permits unless Russians can formally demonstrate proficiency in the local languages concerned. Such developments would be regrettable; perhaps rationality, common sense and fair dealing will overcome visceral revanchism in the words and deeds of the new authorities, and the people they represent, in these 'ex-colonies' of the ex-USSR. After all, the problem is no longer 'ongoing'. The Balts need and are undoubtedly planning a totally new strategy for foreign-language education in their countries. The planners will surely be looking westwards, with German and English predominating but also with Scandinavian languages receiving their due. Estonia has an easy linguistic bridge and a narrow strait to cross to its neighbour Finland. Latvia, with its highly industrialised infrastructure, needs to create out of its human and material resources a national economy, minimally dependent on its eastern neighbour. It should be noted, however, that Latvia's population is nothing like as ethnically homogeneous as those of Estonia and Lithuania. The mixed marriage rate in Latvia is high, with approximately one quarter of all weddings involving partners from different ethnic communities[9]. Two out of every five brides or bridegrooms currently contracting ethnically mixed marriages at the present time are Russian. Lithuania may also resuscitate more direct links with Poland, whilst remaining suitably aware of its own former, often troubled, relationship with Poland. Moldovans, on the other hand, do not need a new language-learning policy: all they need to do is to carry on speaking their native language which is Rumanian. A decision has already been taken to revert to the Latin alphabet and this will surely ensure an easy re-entry into the Rumanian ambience of a mode of speech separated from its centre of gravity by hostile political circumstances, not by linguistic evolution. Elsewhere on the western frontier of the CIS, other trends will establish themselves. Ukrainians, especially in Galicia, and Byelorussians will look to and co-operate much more closely with Poland, resurrecting their historical links with that country. The teaching of Polish in Ukrainian and Byelorussian schools is bound to acquire greater importance. A little further south it is to be confidently expected that Hungarians and Slovaks living in the Ukraine will avail themselves of the new and exciting opportunities for cross-border trade, for tourism and for cultural and sporting events in Hungary and (Czecho-)Slovakia. All of these developments, as they occur one by one, relegate Russian by degrees. Of course, Russian cannot be ignored — it can, however, no longer be supreme. Any new supremacy would have to arise organically, in economic terms, and can most certainly no longer be based on a fiat emerging from the Moscow Kremlin.

Analysis of preliminary and summary information from the 1989 Soviet Census permits some tentative inferences to be made about the demographic-cum-sociolinguistic state of play three years ago as 'the clock was about to strike midnight'. It should be noted that census returns ideally represent not only a cross-sectional, 'snapshot' picture but also a 'period statement' in the course of a longitudinal evolution. The Soviet census fell regrettably short here, both in terms of task design and investigatory activity. The latter, longitudinal type of analysis is preferable, if it is attainable, because the evolutionary behaviour of cohorts of people can be traced. It is to be hoped that institutionalised 'glasnost' and open democracy will make it possible for researchers to gain better access to better, multi-faceted census data in the CIS states and in the Baltic republics; perhaps it will also be possible for them to become more involved in the design and implementation of 'socio-linguo-demographic' enquiries. For the moment, however, it must be realised that the 1989 Soviet Census is what might be called a termination statement at the closing of the account. Future developments will have to be studied piecemeal.

The Soviet census returns - self-reports allocated to coarsely defined categories, it is to be emphasised! - show, in the left-hand column of Table 4, the 'loyalty' of the constituent peoples of the then USSR to their own 'ethnos', as judged by their use, as a native language, of that particular ethnos' medium of linguistic and cultural expression. Inspection of this data shows the Russians as the most loyal group vis-à-vis its own ethnic language, Russian. No-one should be surprised by this - after all, Russians do represent about half of the former Soviet population and need no stimulus to use Russian as a first language, having no incentive to adopt a different L1. Inertia may also have something to do with it! Only one Russian out of five hundred is 'deviant' in this respect. The bulk of figures in the left-hand table demonstrate a very high degree of cohesion among the Soviet peoples in terms of allegiance to the native language of their ethnos. Only ten peoples have apparently lost a majority in the sense that at least half of their nominal adherents have either been reared in or have opted for the language of a different ethnos. The main Jewish community in the USSR has seemingly lost the taproots of Yiddish, with almost nine out of ten attesting re-acculturation to other languages, Russian in almost 90% of cases. In the newer conditions of life in the CIS, it is now possible for Jews to revitalise Yiddish and to learn and use Hebrew: it will be interesting to watch developments with regard to any shifts of linguistic loyalty (Gilboa, 1982). The average score, by the way, in the left-hand column of Table 4 is 80.3, with a coefficient of variation of 25.9%.

The central column of Table 4 arrays the data emerging from the census question addressed to non-Russians stating that Russian is their - original or new - 'native' language. The tabulation shows the ethnic differentials with regard to this factor. Those peoples at the top of the list are communities without a strong cultural infrastructure within the Soviet environment. The table also shows that the practice and maybe the concept of deliberately shifting across to Russian is almost unheard of among the numerically strong and culturally robust peoples of Soviet Central Asia. The average score in the centre column is 15.6, with a coefficient of variation of 117.8%. This indicates very high variability and would compel, for proper analysis, the introduction of break-points in the table on qualitative grounds. However, there is a very strong inverse correlation of -0.902 between the language loyalty figures and those appertaining to declarations from members of the non-Russian communities[10] that Russian is their - possibly deliberately adopted - 'native' language or, better, present L1. The associated coefficient of determination, 0.813, shows that over four-fifths of the variability between the set of data pairs is systematic, being explained by the close inverse linear relationship detected by the correlational least squares technique. It might be argued that this relationship is clear by visual inspection of the raw data but quantifying it precisely could well be the stimulus for more microscopic analysis. When it comes to the adoption of first languages other than Russian - the data on this are in the right-hand column in Table 4 - one conclusion that can be drawn is that largish compact communities living outside the Russian Federation gravitate towards the locally dominant language. Examples of this would be Poles adopting Lithuanian, or Czechs turning to Ukrainian. The notion of Rumanians converting to Moldavian is, of course, an artificiality. In general, there is not much movement with respect to this parameter: the figures quoted speak for themselves. The average score in the right-hand column is 4.3, with a coefficient of variation of 205.5%. Once again, this shows variability on an exceedingly high order and very firmly points to a need to disaggregate the table for the purpose of any further in-depth analysis.

Table 5 arrays the 1989 Soviet Census returns with respect to the ability of people in the USSR to speak a second USSR language fluently. The tabulation is dichotomised by the census analysts so as to distinguish between L2 speakers of Russian and L2 speakers of languages other than Russian. The left-hand column treats Russian alone as L2. The average score in the left-hand column is 53.9, with a coefficient of variation of 36.7%. Variability is hence of medium order. The table shows that, in 1989, every other non-Russian in the USSR claimed a knowledge of Russian. Measures of the functionality of such knowledge, however, are not derivable from these findings and the 'Si, Señor' syndrome, so familiar to survey analysts and census-takers, may have also played a part. Nonetheless, the basic result must be acknowledged as an achievement of Soviet citizens, probably, rather than of language-planning efforts. This, then, is the melody line in the USSR's ethno-linguistic swan song. Knowledge of other second languages of the USSR are reported in the right-hand column of Table 5. The average score in the right-hand column is 9.93, with a coefficient of variation of 128.8%. Variability is very high and is clearly not determined by random factors. Micro-analysis of these findings is called for, but they may now be only of academic interest. Figure 1 gives a visual impression of the percentage scores in the five distributions shown in Tables 4 and 5. This graph is in the form of box-and-whisker plots. The bottom and top 'hinges' on the actual boxes represent the 75th and 25th percentiles,[11] respectively, while the boxes themselves are divided into two parts by the medians. The difference between the 75th and 25th percentiles is often termed the inter-quartile range (IQR). The upper whisker symbolises the value represented by the top hinge plus 1.5*IQR. As might be expected, the lower whisker symbolises the value represented by the bottom hinge minus 1.5*IQR. Circles represent values falling between the top hinge and the point represented by the top hinge plus 3.0*IQR, or values falling between the bottom hinge and the point represented by the bottom hinge minus 3.0*IQR. Points falling outside this range are denoted by star-bursts. The box-and-whisker plots give a good impressionistic picture of the underlying figures.

Conclusion

What comments can be made in conclusion about a state of affairs that is highly complex and sui generis? Experience of life in the multi-lingual, multi-ethnic state that was also a superpower has been set down by many individual writers and commentators. What is still needed is a rich stream of detailed, analytical, uncensored and honest studies and accounts of the successes and failures of language planning in the Soviet Union. We need dispassionate analyses from inside and also personal accounts of what it **felt** like to be in that environment. We need clear statements from those now entrusted with planning and monitoring future ethno-socio-linguistic developments in the CIS. We must hope that a modus vivendi et cooperandi can be found in these new societies, one which will render unnecessary large-scale transfers of population such as occurred between Greece and Turkey after the end of World War I or in Eastern and Central Europe during and after World War II. There may be a role for ongoing activity by agencies such as UNRRA and UNESCO in a revitalised UNO. Now that the Soviet Union has moved off stage, India must presumably don the mantle of the world's most-plagued country in terms of its ethno-linguistic make-up. India is not the country it was prior to 1947 and Pakistan is not the country it was prior to 1971. Is it the fate of large and ethno-linguistically complex states to possess viability for only a limited period before tension and strife tear them apart?

Notes

1 No less than one sixth of the globe's land surface.

2 Some would say 'only just', pointing to the USA's totally unprecedented huge budget deficits caused by overspending on defence!
3 Formed in 1922 and consisting, at the beginning of September 1991, of 15 Union Republics, 20 Autonomous Republics, 8 Autonomous Regions and 10 National Areas.
4 Taken together, then, three-quarters of the Soviet population can use Russian.
5 What level of knowledge is involved has never been systematically investigated and tabulated but it seems to have been overestimated in typical hyperbolic fashion; the only real pointers are the outcomes from a disappointingly small number of sporadic enquiries pursued at local or republican level. Above all it must be borne in mind that the census-takers record the self-reports of the people in their enumeration district.
6 And subsequently Soviet President.
7 This depends on the fate of the Gagauz region and of Transdnestria which has declared independence from within the newly independent Moldova.
8 The material for all the Tables has been derived from *Social'noe Razvitie SSR 1989 - Statističeskij Sbornik (Social developments in the USSR 1989 - A statistical handbook)*. This compendium is, as yet, the only source of socio-linguistic data from the 1989 Soviet census returns. Unfortunately, the data released is patchy and, regrettably, suffers from design and coverage faults in the census itself.
9 A sympathetic thought should be spared for mixed-marriage partners and their offspring who are exposed to the real risk, in present circumstances, of trauma and misery caused by the inter-ethnic strife which seems to erupt so easily in the ex-USSR.
10 Technically, this means anyone whose identity card ('passport') designates that person as a member of any Soviet nationality apart from Russian.
11 That is, the lower and upper quartile, respectively.

References

anon. 1991. *Social'noe Razvitie SSSR 1989 - Statističeskij Sbornik* (Social developments in the USSR 1989 - A statistical handbook). Moscow: Finansy i Statistika

Cooper, R. 1989. *Language planning and social change*. Cambridge: Cambridge University Press

Gilboa, Y. 1982. *A language silenced: Hebrew culture in the Soviet Union*. New York: Farleigh Dickinson

Guboglo, M.N. 1984. *Sovremennye ètnojazykovye processy v SSSR*. (Current ethno-linguistic processes in the USSR) Moscow: Nauka

Isayev, M. I. 1977. *National languages in the USSR: Problems and solutions*.Moscow: Progress

Karpenko, M. A. and Semenov, N. A. 1980. *Russkij jazyk v sem'e edinoj*. (The Russian language in a united family). Kiev: Radjans'ka Škola

Kirkwood, M. (ed.) 1989. *Language planning in the Soviet Union*. London: Macmillan

Knowles, F. 1989. *Language planning in the Soviet Baltic Republics: an analysis of demographic and sociological trends.* in: Kirkwood
Lane, D. 1991. *Soviet society under perestroika.* Boston: Unwin Hyman
Lewis, E. 1972. *Multilingualism in the Soviet Union: language policy and its implementation.* The Hague: Mouton
Nahaylo, B. and Swoboda, V. 1990. *Soviet Disunion: a history of the nationalities problem in the USSR.* London: Hamish Hamilton
Smith, G. 1990. *The nationalities question in the Soviet Union.* London: Longman
Zvidrin's, P. et al. 1986. *Naselenie Sovetskoj Latvii* (The population of Soviet Latvia). Riga: Zinatne

Figure and Tables

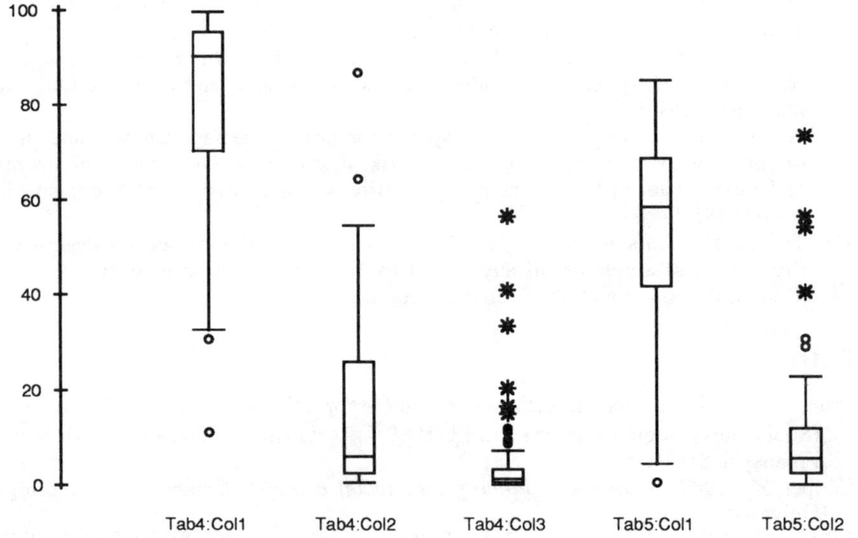

Figure 1
Box and Whisker plots of the responses received in the 1989 Soviet Census to questions about L1 loyalty and L1 competence. Note that Col1, Col2 etc refer to the different sections of Tables 4 and 5.

Table 1

Ethnic origin of managers in industry, agriculture, transport, telecommunications, and building (1989)

		%age of locally ethnic population	%age of locally ethnic population	Com-petitive advan-tage
Buryat ASSR	Buryats	36.7	24.0	1.53
North Ossetian ASSR	Ossetians	75.5	53.0	1.42
Estonian SSR	Estonians	82.2	61.5	1.34
Tatar ASSR	Tatars	64.1	48.5	1.32
Georgian SSR	Georgians	89.3	70.1	1.27
Latvian SSR	Latvians	63.1	52.0	1.21
Kabardinian-Balkari ASSR	Kabardinians/Balkars	69.8	57.6	1.21
Mordovian ASSR	Mordvinians	37.9	32.5	1.17
Lithuanian SSR	Lithuanians	91.5	79.6	1.15
Yakut ASSR	Yakutis	38.2	33.4	1.14
Azerbaijani ASSR	Azeris	93.8	82.7	1.13
Karakalpak ASSR	Karakalpaks	35.5	32.1	1.11
Bashkiri ASSR	Bashkiris	24.2	21.9	1.11
Ukrainian SSR	Ukrainians	79.0	72.7	1.09
Armenian SSR	Armenians	99.4	93.3	1.07
Tajik SSR	Tajiks	66.3	62.3	1.06
Kalmyk ASSR	Kalmyks	48.1	45.4	1.06
Kirghiz SSR	Kirghizians	55.1	52.4	1.05
Chechen-Ingushi ASSR	Chechens/Ingushis	71.5	70.7	1.01
Byelorussian SSR	Byelorussians	77.7	77.9	1.00
Turkmenian SSR	Turkmenis	71.8	72.0	1.00
Udmurt ASSR	Udmurts	30.8	30.9	1.00
Kazakh SSR	Kazakhs	39.5	39.7	0.99
RSFSR	Russians	77.3	81.5	0.95
Uzbek SSR	Uzbeks	67.6	71.4	0.95
Karelian ASSR	Karelians	9.0	10.0	0.90
Chuvash ASSR	Chuvashis	59.2	67.8	0.87
Komi ASSR	Komis	18.3	23.3	0.79
Moldavian SSR	Moldavians	49.8	64.5	0.77
Tuvinian ASSR	Tuvinians	39.6	64.3	0.62
Mari ASSR	Maris	26.4	43.3	0.61

Note: Italicised areas were sub-units of the RSFSR, with the exception of the Karakalpak ASSR which formed part of the Uzbek SSR.

Table 2
Permanent Pre-School Establishments according to languages of instruction and communication (1989)

	Percentage of establishments using			**Establishments in which 'ethnic' children were taught Russian or used Russian**		
	Russian	'Local'	Both	Number of establishments	As percentage of total	No. of children being taught Russian (000's)
RSFSR	95.0	3.1	1.9	4 790	5.6	153.0
Kazakh SSR	81.9	13.7	4.4	1 490	17.6	73.0
Byelorussian SSR	65.8	26.1	8.1	no data	no data	no data
Kirghizian SSR	52.6	40.6	6.8	166	10.0	7.0
Tajik SSR	41.7	43.0	15.3	293	31.2	26.0
Ukrainian SSR	38.1	59.2	2.7	12 601	52.4	588.0
Latvian SSR	37.6	45.2	17.2	234	21.3	8.0
Turkmenian SSR	36.6	61.3	2.1	294	19.2	20.0
Moldavian SSR	29.3	54.5	16.2	1 375	59.8	66.0
Estonian SSR	26.8	67.9	5.3	11	1.5	0.2
Uzbek SSR	25.5	69.4	5.1	2 193	23.6	120.0
Azerbaijani SSR	14.1	66.8	19.1	883	40.4	32.0
Georgian SSR	8.3	81.6	10.1	755	31.3	29.0
Lithuanian SSR	7.7	85.6	6.7	30	1.7	1.0
Armenian SSR	4.4	85.9	9.7	645	57.2	35.0
USSR	**72.1**	**24.3**	**3.6**	**25 760**	**17.4**	**1 158.0**

Table 3
Participation rates for students of different ethnic backgrounds
(per 10,000 of population)

Buryats	354
Abkhazians	327
Kalmyks	304
Georgians	274
Ossetes	272
Khakasis	261
Jews	257
Adygeyans	241
Yakuts	234
Kazakhs	230
Estonians	213
Ingushis	212
Karachais	208
Lithuanians	208
Armenians	207
Kabardinians	206
Circassians	205
Karakalpaks	200
Tuvinians	195
Russians	190
Kirghizians	188
Latvians	182
Byelorussians	176
Azerbaijanis	172
Tatars	171
Bashkiris	170
Altais	164

Ukrainians	163
Uzbeks	157
Chechens	151
Turkmenians	146
Chuvashis	139
Komis	133
Tajiks	129
Moldavians	125
Mordovians	118
Maris	116
Udmurts	115
Karelians	106
Komi-Permeans	88

Table 4
Soviet Census (1989)

'Loyalty' to language of own national group	%
Russians	99.8
Turkmenians	98.5
Tuvinians	98.5
Uzbeks	98.3
Georgians	98.2
Chechens	98.1
Kirghizians	97.8
Azerbaijanis	97.7
Lithuanians	97.7
Tajiks	97.7
Darginians	97.5
Kumyks	97.4
Avars	97.2
Kabardinians	97.2
Ingushis	97.0
Kazakhs	97.0
Belujis	96.9
Karachais	96.8
Tabasaranis	95.9
Estonians	95.5
Tsakhurs	95.2
Aguls	94.9
Adygeyans	94.8
Dunganis	94.8
Latvians	94.8
Rutulis	94.8
Karakalpaks	94.1
Hungarians	93.9
Yakuts	93.8
Balkars	93.6
Lakis	93.6
Abkhazians	93.5
Abazians	93.4
Crimean Tatars	92.6
Armenians	91.7
Lezgins	91.6
Moldavians	91.6
Turks	91.1
Georgian Jews	90.9
Circassians	90.4
Talyshis	90.4
Kalmyks	90.0
Nogayans	89.9
Gagauzis	87.5
Ossetes	87.0
Uigurs	96.6
Buryats	86.3
Altais	84.4
Tatars	83.2
Ukrainians	81.1
Maris	80.8
Kurds	80.5
Gypsies	77.4
Chuvashis	76.5
Khakasis	76.1
Mountain Jews	75.8

Table 4 (continued)
Soviet Census
(1989)

'Loyalty' to language of own national group (continued)	%
Bashkiris	72.3
Tats	71.9
Byelorussians	70.9
Komis	70.4
Komi-Permians	70.1
Udmurts	69.7
Bulgarians	68.2
Mordovians	67.1
Central-Asiatic Jews	65.2
Rumanians	60.9
Assyrians	59.6
Shors	56.7
'Peoples of the North'	52.4
Vepsians	50.9
Koreans	49.4
Germans	48.8
Karelians	47.8
Greeks	44.5
Czechs	35.3
Finns	34.6
Persians	33.2
Chinese	32.9
Poles	30.5
Jews	11.1

Table 4
Soviet Census (1989)

Nomination of Russian as native language	%
Jews	86.6
Chinese	64.3
Finns	54.6
Karelians	51.8
Greeks	51.4
Germans	50.8
Koreans	50.2
Vepsians	48.5
Czechs	44.5
Shors	41.6
'Peoples of the North'	36.4
Central-Asiatic Jews	33.6
Mordovians	32.7
Assyrians	31.8
Udmurts	30.0
Komi-Permians	29.7
Komis	29.5
Bulgarians	28.8
Poles	28.6
Byelorussians	28.5
Khakasis	23.6
Chuvashis	23.3
Tats	21.0
Mountain Jews	19.5
Maris	18.8
Ukrainians	18.8
Tatars	16.1
Altais	15.5
Buryats	13.6
Bashkiris	11.2
Gypsies	10.8
Gagauzis	10.6
Persians	10.2
Georgian Jews	8.3
Armenians	7.6
Kalmyks	7.4
Moldavians	7.4
Ossetes	7.0
Circassians	6.4
Yakuts	6.1
Rumanians	5.6
Balkars	5.4
Crimean Tatars	5.3
Adygeyans	5.1
Lakis	5.1
Latvians	5.0
Abkhazians	4.9
Lezgins	4.8
Abazians	4.7
Kurds	4.5
Estonians	4.4
Uigurs	3.9
Aguls	3.8
Rutulis	3.6
Nogayans	3.4
Hungarians	3.3

Table 4 (continued)
Soviet Census (1989)

Nomination of Russian as native language (continued)	%
Tabasaranis	3.0
Ingushis	2.8
Karachais	2.7
Kabardinians	2.6
Dunganis	2.5
Kazakhs	2.3
Kumyks	2.1
Avars	1.9
Darginians	1.9
Turks	1.9
Lithuanians	1.8
Azerbaijanis	1.7
Chechens	1.7
Georgians	1.7
Tsakhurs	1.5
Tuvinians	1.4
Belujis	1.2
Karakalpaks	1.0
Turkmenians	1.0
Tajiks	0.8
Uzbeks	0.7
Kirghizians	0.6
Talyshis	0.5
Russians	-

Table 4 (continued)
Soviet Census (1989)

Nomination of other Soviet language as native language	%
Persians	56.6
Poles	40.9
Rumanians	33.5
Czechs	20.2
Bashkiris	16.5
Kurds	15.0
Gypsies	11.8
'Peoples of the North'	11.2
Finns	10.8
Uigurs	9.5
Talyshis	9.1
Assyrians	8.6
Tats	7.1
Turks	7.0
Nogayans	6.7
Ossetes	6.0
Karakalpaks	4.9
Mountain Jews	4.7
Greeks	4.1
Lezgins	3.6
Tsakhurs	3.3
Circassians	3.2
Bulgarians	3.0
Khakasis	3.0
Chinese	2.8
Hungarians	2.8
Dunganis	2.7
Kalmyks	2.6
Jews	2.3
Crimean Tatars	2.1
Gagauzis	1.9
Abazians	1.9
Belujis	1.9
Shors	1.7
Kirghizians	1.6
Abkhazians	1.6
Rutulis	1.6
Tajiks	1.5
Aguls	1.3
Lakis	1.3
Central-Asiatic Jews	1.2
Tabasaranis	1.1
Balkars	1.0
Moldavians	1.0
Uzbeks	1.0
Avars	0.9
Georgian Jews	0.8
Armenians	0.7
Kazakhs	0.7
Tatars	0.7
Vepsians	0.6
Azerbaijanis	0.6
Byelorussians	0.6
Darginians	0.6
Karachais	0.5
Kumyks	0.5

Table 4 (continued)
Soviet Census (1989)

Nomination of other Soviet language as native language (continued)	%
Lithuanians	0.5
Turkmenians	0.5
Germans	0.4
Koreans	0.4
Maris	0.4
Karelians	0.4
Udmurts	0.3
Chechens	0.2
Chuvashis	0.2
Ingushis	0.2
Kabardinians	0.2
Latvians	0.2
Mordovians	0.2
Russians	0.2
Komi-Permians	0.2
Buryats	0.1
Ukrainians	0.1
Yakuts	0.1
Adygeyans	0.1
Altais	0.1
Estonians	0.1
Georgians	0.1
Komis	0.1
Tuvinians	0.1

Table 5
Percentage of national group speaking another Soviet national language fluently

	Russian
Kalmyks	85.3
Adygeyans	81.7
Ingushis	80.0
Nogayans	79.3
Karachais	79.2
Abkhazians	78.8
Balkars	78.6
Abazians	78.1
Kabardinians	77.8
Lakis	76.5
Circassians	76.3
Crimean Tatars	76.1
Kumyks	74.5
Chechens	74.0
Buryats	72.1
Bashkiris	71.8
Gagauzis	71.1
Dunganis	70.8
Tatars	70.8
Ossetes	68.9
Maris	68.8
Aguls	68.4
Darginians	68.0
Khakasis	66.8
Altais	65.2
Chuvashis	65.1
Yakutians	64.9
Latvians	64.4
Tats	64.1
Gypsies	63.3
Rutulis	63.1
Mordovians	62.6
Tabasaranis	62.5
Komis	62.2

	Other langs.
Talyshis	73.5
Belujis	56.3
Tsakhurs	54.3
Kurds	40.4
Turks	30.6
Jews	29.2
Czechs	22.8
Assyrians	19.9
Lezgins	19.8
Persians	18.3
Poles	17.3
Central-Asiatic Jews	17.0
Mountain Jews	16.7
Vepsians	16.7
Greeks	16.5
Karelians	14.8
Gypsies	13.8
Tats	13.3
Ossetes	12.2
Tajiks	12.0
Byelorussians	11.7
Hungarians	11.7
Rumanians	11.6
Karakalpaks	11.4
Uigurs	10.8
Finns	10.7
Bulgarians	8.8
Mordovians	8.8
Ukrainians	8.4
Rutulis	8.2
Crimean Tatars	8.0
Komi-Permyakians	8.0
Udmurts	7.1
Shors	7.0

Table 5 (continued)
Percentage of national group speaking another Soviet national language fluently

Komi-Permyakians	61.3	Gagauzis	6.9
Udmurts	61.3	Avars	6.6
Avars	60.8	Aguls	6.4
Kazakhs	60.5	Komis	6.1
Bulgarians	60.3	Chuvashis	5.8
Tuvinians	59.2	Maris	5.8
Uigurs	58.3	Tabasaranis	5.4
Ukrainians	56.2	Tatars	5.3
Mountain Jews	54.8	Chinese	5.1
Byelorussians	54.7	'Peoples of the North'	5.0
Moldavians	53.8	Armenians	5.0
Lezgins	53.4	Georgian Jews	4.6
Shors	52.7	Kirghizians	4.6
Rumanians	50.8	Abazians	4.4
Central-Asiatic Jews	50.6	Moldavians	4.4
'Peoples of the North'	50.4	Russians	4.1
Vepsians	49.0	Uzbeks	3.8
Armenians	47.1	Bashkiris	3.7
Georgian Jews	46.4	Koreans	3.7
Persians	45.9	Khakasis	3.6
Karelians	45.5	Abkhazians	3.4
Germans	45.0	Dunganis	2.8
Poles	43.9	Kazakhs	2.8
Assyrians	43.7	Lakis	2.8
Hungarians	43.3	Buryats	2.7
Koreans	43.3	Latvians	2.5
Turks	40.3	Altais	2.3
Greeks	39.6	Azerbaijanis	2.2
Lithuanians	37.9	Circassians	2.2
Czechs	36.8	Balkars	2.0
Finns	35.4	Turkmenians	2.0
Kirghizians	35.2	Darginians	1.8
Azerbaijanis	34.4	Estonians	1.7
Estonians	33.9	Lithuanians	1.7
Georgians	33.1	Germans	1.6

Table 5 (continued)
Percentage of national group speaking another Soviet national language fluently

Chinese	30.5	Adygeyans	1.5
Kurds	28.7	Yakutians	1.5
Tajiks	27.7	Kalmyks	1.5
Turkmenians	27.7	Nogayans	1.4
Uzbeks	23.8	Georgians	1.0
Tsakhurs	23.5	Ingushis	1.0
Karakalpaks	20.6	Karachais	1.0
Jews	10.1	Kumyks	1.0
Talyshis	5.5	Chechens	0.8
Belujis	4.6	Kabardinians	0.7
Russians	0.2	Tuvinians	0.3

MULTILINGUAL EDUCATION AS A FACTOR OF INTER-ETHNIC RELATIONS: THE CASE OF THE UKRAINE

O. V. Shamshur, *Institute of World Economy and International Relations, Ukrainian Academy of Sciences*
T. I. Izhevskaya, *Institute of Foreign Languages, Kiev*

Linguistic problems are a major component of inter-ethnic relations and inter-cultural communication in practically all multi-ethnic societies. They are relatively independent, and their relation to other components of the system could be termed intricate. On the one hand, the linguistic situation is to a great extent conditioned by the general climate of inter-ethnic relations, which exists in the particular country and which is dependent on the socio-economic, political and cultural peculiarities of its historic development. On the other hand, the linguistic situation itself influences the process of formation and the present status of inter-ethnic relations: it can either lessen or, as happens much more frequently, stimulate, existing tensions. Not surprisingly, in many countries inter-ethnic contradictions take the shape of linguistic conflicts. So the importance of the harmonious development of the linguistic situation and of intensive inter-cultural communication for harmonizing inter-ethnic relations as a whole is evident.

Normally, the variety of linguistic problems, as far as their ethnic dimension is concerned, could be reduced to one, the most significant: To what extent is there equality between the languages which function in any given country or territory; or, to be more exact, are the language rights of ethnic minorities secured, as compared to those of the majority of the population?. Experience acquired by multi-ethnic states testifies to the fact that violation of the principle of equality and free development of languages seriously hampers the normal development of relations between different ethnic organisms on the macro, meso and microlevels, fosters conservation or even stimulates alienation and marginalization of the cultural life of minorities.

The linguistic situation which existed in a number of republics in the former USSR is really paradoxical or even unique, as there existed a real threat to the very existence of the language of the 'majority', or indigenous nation. Ukraine was the most vivid example.

According to the 1989 Census of population (Table 1), Ukrainians make up 72.6% of the residents of the Republic. Russians make up 22%, other ethnic groups - Bielorussians, Poles, Jews, Moldavians, Bulgarians, Romanians, Hungarians, Tatars, etc. - 5.4%. 88.7% of Ukrainians consider Ukrainian their native language, while in Bielorussia 80.2% do so. In all other republics the proportion of the indigenous population which identify their nationality with their native language is much greater and varies from 95.4 to 99.8%.

Moreover, only 13.3% of the other nationalities residing in the Republic can speak Ukrainian fluently. The situation is quite different with the Russian language: almost half of Ukraine's population (45.5%) can speak it fluently, which means that Russian, not Ukrainian, as one might expect, has become the language of inter-ethnic communication and intercultural contacts.

Data obtained in the process of field research gives an even bleaker picture of the current status of the Ukrainian language. One of the projects carried out in 1988 in Kiev revealed a constant and alarming tendency for the numbers of Ukrainian-speakers to diminish from generation to generation. Only 67% of the respondents speak it fluently. In addition, one should bear in mind researchers have to rely upon self-evaluation by the respondents in measuring the degree of command of the Ukrainian language. They cannot, in fact, check the real linguistic abilities and knowledge of the respondents. So it is quite possible that a considerable proportion of the respondents have poor command of the Ukrainian literary language, using not really the Ukrainian language, but a specific Russian - Ukrainian language mix. We can assume that the real number of those who speak the Ukrainian language fluently is smaller than reported.

This research also revealed a big disparity between knowledge of language and its usage. Ukrainian serves as the means of everyday communication in only 16.5% of responding families, while the corresponding figure for Russian is 67.1%. The respondents used Ukrainian even less frequently in communication outside the family circle (4.7%), at work (8.3%), and while socializing (10.3%). These data quite vividly characterise the linguistic environment of the majority of the Ukraine's population, where cultural orientations and the preferences of the younger generation are being formed. The situation is further exacerbated by the fact that only 2.5% of first - grade pupils (one out of forty) were educated in Ukrainian-language kindergartens -14.5% more in the kindergartens of the mixed type; 3.6% of the respondents provide their children with primarily Ukrainian-language books. 72% of the parents would send their children to Russian-language schools, provided all other conditions are equal.

The situation in Kiev is typical of other urban centres in Ukraine, except for the western region.

The first signs of change have appeared only recently due to the process of political and spiritual revival in Ukraine, which culminated in the referendum on independence. For instance, in the course of three years (1988-1990) the number of Kievites who would opt for Russian-language education for their children fell to 28%, while 58% would now prefer the Ukrainian-language education. Equally encouraging is the growing number of Ukrainian kindergartens, which constitute 60.1% of their total number in Ukraine (as compared to 44.2% in 1986).

56.4% and 57.8% of Ukraine's younger people, correspondingly, claimed Ukrainian to be the language of their formal (business) or informal communication in 1992. That is an evident improvement over the similar indices mentioned above, but the share of ethnic Ukrainians in this age cohort is considerably bigger (75%), and about 30% of ethnic Ukrainian youth still speak no Ukrainian language at all.

Under these circumstances the traditional task of ensuring equal development of languages in Ukraine is being transformed, at first glance, radically. It is the language of the majority that calls for protection. The essence of the problem, however, remains, in fact, the same, as the humble status of Ukrainian has been caused by decades of devalorisation of the language and domination by Russian in inter-ethnic relations.

To do justice to the Bolsheviks, we should say that they were not the first to exert pressure on the Ukrainian language and culture. For centuries the Ukranian people had been the object of the assimilationist policies of the powers which owned its lands, imperial Russia first of all. The new rulers of the multi-ethnic superpower were only too quick to abandon the principle of equality and free development of all nations and ethnic groups, which was proclaimed after the fall of the old order. A short period of Ukrainian renaissance in the 1920s gave way to overt repression: growing ethnic self-consciousness was perceived as a threat to the ideological homogeneity and stability of the Soviet society. The officially adopted concept of 'coming together and all-around flourishing of the socialist nations' too often disguised the practice of forced assimilation. The latter has inflicted irredeemable losses on the spiritual life and cultural heritage of the nations which made up the Soviet Union, causing deformations of their ethnic core. Thus new ethnic tensions and hidden knots of contradictions have been created. To comprehend this is essential for understanding why the process of 'ethnic revival' in the former USSR has taken such acute, sometimes violent forms. Society is now experiencing a virtual 'backlash', a reaction to the inter-ethnic contacts and relations which existed before.

The above highlights the importance of working out a balanced linguistic policy. To our minds, it should meet the following requirements:

- it should promote the revival of the language and culture of the indigenous population ('majority nation'), as well as preservation of the languages and cultures of all other ethnic groups;

- it should be realistic and, thus, it should follow the principle of evolutionary change and take into consideration existing regional linguistic and cultural specificity.

The law 'On languages in the Ukrainian SSR' (1989) is basically designed according to these criteria. It does not mean, of course, that the law is devoid of deficiencies. For its critical assessment see Pinchuk, 1990, 75-83. The law stipulates official status for the Ukrainian language. It also guarantees the citizens of Ukraine the right to use any other national language on the territory of the Republic. It includes free choice of the language of communication with government bodies, enterprises and organisations. Special attention has been paid to the problem of the choice of the language of education. Article 22 of the law establishes that every child has an inalienable right to native-language education. This right is ensured by the creation of a network of kindergartens and schools, with the language of education depending on the ethnic composition of the region's population. To this end special classes were set up in which the medium of education was a language other than that used in the mainstream secondary school: for example, Hungarian forms in a Ukrainian school, or vice versa. The study of the state (official) and the Russian languages, the latter as the language of inter-ethnic communication, is compulsory in all secondary schools of the Republic.

The law contains a strikingly liberal mechanism of implementation, so devised in order to minimise possible strains and rule out discrimination: its educational provisions would come into effect by the end of the century.

Sufficiently active steps are, however, being taken in Ukraine in order to implement the provisions of the law. Their main thrust is aimed at the development of the Ukrainian language - in the course of the last two years the number of Ukrainian-language schools has increased by 103 - raising its status. Preservation and development of the languages of other ethnic groups in the Ukraine is recognized as an equally important task. Pursuant to the law, 'the State programme for the development of the Ukrainian and other national languages in the Ukrainian SSR' was adopted in 1990.

We think it essential to mention the existence of the well-developed infrastructure of multicultural education in Ukraine in the 1920s - 1930s (anon, 1991b, 15-37). There functioned a network of schools and institutions of higher education, which provided representatives of ethnic minorities with education in their native languages. In the 1929-1930 academic year there were, for instance, 73 Bulgarian schools and a Bulgarian department in the teacher training institute; 786 schools, 28 colleges, 1 institute and 5 departments in other institutions with Jewish language of education (Yiddish). The same was true of Greeks, Poles, Germans. This ethnic educational system was an important part of the larger system of ethnic self-government on the local level. Both networks were forcibly dismantled by Stalinist authorities at the end of the 1930s and in the postwar period.

Returning to the subject of the law 'On the languages', it is quite evident that adoption of the law cannot alone resolve problems which have not been addressed for years. To enhance the status of the Ukrainian language through its role in social life is likely to be a most arduous task, due to the perverse linguistic environment still existing in the Republic. The latter is at variance with the growing ethnic self-awareness of the Ukrainian people, its striving for real sovereignty. Thus the field of education becomes the critical sphere, where the future of the new Ukraine is being shaped. (See appendix for Table 1).

Current trends in the Ukrainian system of secondary education send contradictory signals (Table 2). At present it comprises 15,316 Ukrainian-language schools, 73.5% of the total number of schools in the Republic. They educate 3,060,000 pupils, or 44.7% of the total. The corresponding numbers for Russian-language schools are 4303, (20.6%) and 2,792,000 (40.7%) (Table 2). In spite of the efforts made at the political and practical levels, the share of the Ukrainian-language schools is decreasing: they made up 74.6% of the total in 1985-1986, 74%, in 1988-1989; 73.6%, in 1989-1990 and 73.5%, in 1990-1991. This can be explained by the general scarcity of resources assigned for education, and by the growth in the number of schools which offer courses both in Russian and Ukrainian (981 schools) or in languages other than Ukrainian and Russian. This third component of the education system is represented by Romanian - 93 schools (0.4%), Moldavian - 14 schools (0.06%), Hungarian - 59 schools (0.3%) and Polish - 2 schools (0.004%). There are also 51 bilingual and even trilinglial schools, in addition to Russian-Ukrainian schools.

Despite the diminishing share of the Ukrainian language schools, their absolute numbers and enrolment are growing, though the rate of increase is rather small. Pupils in the Ukrainian-language schools made up 48.9 % of the total in 1985-1986, 50% in 1988-1989, 50.1% in 1989-1990, and 50.4% in 1990-1991. These figures do not include data for the Crimean Autonomous Republic, where Ukrainian schools are still non-existent. If they are included in calculations, the share of pupils in Ukrainian schools would drop to 47.9% (in 1990-1991).

An important feature of the development of Ukrainian medium education is the preservation of considerable regional differences. While the number of the Ukrainian-language schools in the Western part of the republic exceeds 90%, in the industrial east it falls as low as 8.9% in the Donetsk region.

Another cleavage runs across the urban-rural divide. The Ukrainian medium schools are concentrated more heavily in rural areas (83% of the total number of rural schools), the Russian medium ones in urban centres (66% of all urban schools). This explains the fact that although the number of pupils in the Russian-language schools differs from Ukrainian only by approximately 300,000, the Ukrainian-language schools outnumber the Russian by approximately four to one, since rural schools are smaller in size. Not so long ago, in some big cities Ukrainian medium schools were virtually extinct. Even in Kiev there are only 49 schools out of 307 (15.9%) teaching through Ukrainian.

The choice of the language of secondary education is determined to a great extent by the influence of higher education. In the past it was subject to almost total Russification, this process affecting both Sciences and Humanities. Only now do we witness restoration of the Ukrainian language to its legitimate role in this field. According to the law, education in vocational schools, technical colleges and institutions of higher education is to be conducted in the official language. Special groups using the medium of Russian, or any other language than Ukrainian, can be created as well.

Higher education is to play an exceptionally important role in preparing the next generation of educators, not only in Ukrainian, but in other ethnic languages as well. Hungarian, Moldavian, Greek and Crimean-Tatar departments have been opened in a number of universities.

In 1992-1993 Ukrainian political leaders and educators face the necessity of making critical decisions. The evident need to reverse negative trends that persist, and to speed up the process of 'Ukrainization' in order to undo the wrongs of Russification might oblige a stricter enforcement of the law 'On languages'. Unfortunately, these measures could put at risk the relatively 'smooth' development of inter-ethnic relations in the Republic, especially as certain political forces within and ouside the borders of Ukraine could be only too eager to utilize them for cultivating distrust of the republican government. It is highly probable that in the course of time the government will experience growing pressures from different parties. In spite of the fact that many of the ethnic Russians have resided in Ukraine for decades, this large section of the population is strongly opposed to the very idea of learning the Ukrainian language, still clinging to the spectre of 'Big Brother'. On the other hand a not inconsiderable number of militant Ukrainians would be inclined to interpret 'Ukrainization' in neobolshevist terms. This potential for inter-ethnic conflict is not guesswork, and already inter-confessional strife indicates its gravity.

So there can be several scenarios of the future development of inter-ethnic relations in Ukraine, depending on a variety of internal and external factors. At the moment a 'low-conflict' option seems to be the most plausible. It would be characterised inter alia by a relatively liberal language policy: alongside fostering expansion of Ukrainian as the offical language, it would be based on the assumption that this aim could not be achieved by exclusively administrative methods. Greater discretion would be given to regional and local authorities, especially in resolving problems concerning the cultural demands of ethnic minorities. This turbulent period when the new identity of 'The people of Ukraine' (this term has been promulgated in the Ukrainian 'Declaration of State Sovereignty') and new relations within this entity are being moulded calls for restraint and tolerance.

We regard as extremely significant and encouraging the adoption by the Ukrainian parliament of the special 'Declaration of the rights of the nationalities of Ukraine'. The Ukrainian state guaranteed all peoples and ethnic groups the right to free use of their native languages in all spheres of social life, including education, labour activities and information. In areas where an ethnic group is sufficiently concentrated, its language can function freely alongside the State language. In areas where a number of ethnic groups live closely together they may choose a common language of communication to function on a par with Ukrainian. The right to unrestricted use of the Russian language is guaranteed to anyone (1991a).

We know only too well from history that a chasm could separate the rights proclaimed from the rights ensured in practice. Let us hope the leaders of the newly-born Ukrainian independent state and its people will avoid this common mistake.

References

Panina N. 1991. The problem of bilingualism: individual and social communication. *Philosophical and sociological thought*, 5: 43-6. (in Ukrainian)

Pinchuk S. 1990. The law on the languages: reality and perspectives. *The Bell*, 9: 73-83 (in Ukrainian)

Pribitkova I. 1990. Children of different nations. *Philosophical and sociological thought*, 4: 77-84 (in Ukrainian)

Martyniuk I, Voitovich S. 1989. The prospects of 'Unnecessary' language. *Philosophical and sociological thought*, 5: 22-5

Vishnyak, O. 1992. The Law 'On Languages': Time for Revision. *News from Ukraine*, 11: 3. (in Ukrainian)

Yatsenko, V. 1992. The Society of the Ukrainian Language must Live. *The Governmental Cournier*, 12: 10. (in Ukrainian)

Anon. 1984. *The composition of the population of the USSR. All-Union Census of population of 1979.* Moscow: Central statistical agency of the USSR, 102-7 (in Russian)

Anon. 1989. 11 Nov. *The Gazette of the Supreme Soviet of the Ukrainian SSR*, Nov 11 1989, 45 (Appendix). (in Ukrainian)

Anon. 1990. State Committee for Statistics of the USSR *Bulletin of Statistics*, 10: 76-9 (in Russian)

Anon. 1991a. *The voice of Ukraine.* Nov 2, 214 (in Ukrainian)

Anon. 1991b. *National relations in Ukraine*, 15-37, 61-4 (in Ukrainian)

Anon. 1991c. *Information release of the Ministry of People's Education of Ukraine* - (in Ukrainian)

Table 1
Population of Ukraine, by nationality* and native language: 1989

Nationality	Total Persons	% Change over 1979	Persons who consider as native language: Language of their nationality Total	%	Language of other nationality: Ukrainian Total	%	Russian Total	%	Other Languages Total
Total	51,452,034	3.7	45,202,380	87.9	446,492	0.9	5,725,765	11.1	77,397 (0.15%)
Ukrainians	37,419,053	2.5	32,825,373	87.8	-	-	4,578,390	12.2	15,290
Russians	11,355,582	8.4	11,172,508	98.4	177,534	1.6	-	-	5,540
Jews	486,326	-23.1	34,635	7.1	10,081	2.1	440,747	90.6	863
Bielorussians	440,045	8.4	156,200	35.4	40,761	9.3	242,713	55.2	371
Moldavians	324,525	10.5	253,024	78.0	19,934	6.1	50,429	15.5	1,138
Bulgarians	233,800	-1.9	162,586	69.5	6,293	2.7	63,676	27.2	1,245
Poles	219,179	-15.1	27,500	12.5	146,026	66.6	44,420	20.3	1,233
Hungarians	163,111	-0.8	156,011	95.6	4,233	26.0	2,604	1.6	263
Romanians	134,825	10.7	83,966	62.3	13,203	9.8	4,607	3.4	32,986
Greeks	98,524	-5.3	18,269	18.5	2,308	2.3	77,717	78.9	300
Tatars	86,875	40.2	26,538	49.0	1,549	2.9	25,744	47.5	369
Gypsies	47,917	39.2	28,074	58.6	5,915	12.3	4,928	10.3	9,000
Crimean Tatars	46,807	705.3	43,334	92.3	83	0.2	1,868	4.0	1,522
Germans	37,849	10.9	8,778	23.2	3,466	9.2	25,451	67.2	154
Azerbaijanians	36,961	Not available	26771	72.4	944	2.6	9,019	24.4	227
Gagauz	31,967	8.7	25401	79.5	450	1.4	5,478	17.1	638

Source: State Committee for Statistics of the USSR. *Bulletin of Statistics*, 1990, 10:76-9
* For nationalities, which number not less than 30000 people

Table 2
Structure of the system of secondary education in Ukraine - according to the language of education

Language of education	1989/1990 academic year: schools number	1989/1990 schools percentage	1989/1990 pupils number thousands	1989/1990 pupils percentage	1990-1991 academic year: schools number thousands	1990-1991 schools percentage	1990-1991 pupils number thousands	1990-1991 pupils percentage
Ukrainian	15,213	73.6	3,051.3	44.8	15,316	73.5	3,060.4	44.7
Russian	4,628	22.4	3,169.6	46.5	4,303	20.6	2,791.7	40.7
Moldavian	108	0.5	33.2	0.5	14	0.06	5.3	0.1
Romanian	-	-	-	-	93	0.4	23.4	0.3
Polish	2	0.01	0.3	0.004	2	0.01	0.4	0.005
Hungarian	55	0.2	10.9	0.1	59	0.3	11.5	0.17
Ukranian and Russian	606	2.9	522.9	7.6	981	4.7	935.7	13.6
inc Ukrainian	-	-	176.0	2.6	-	-	212.7	3.1
inc Russian	-	-	346.9	5	-	-	723.0	10.5
Ukrainian and			3.7	0.05			2.4	0.03
Hungarian	19	0.9	3.2	0.05	18	0.08	2.9	0.04
Russian and			1.4				1.2	0.02
Hungarian	10	0.5	2.8	0.06	8	0.03	2.7	0.04
Russian and			2.2				2.2	0.02
Moldavian	13	0.06	4.6	0.1	5	0.02	1.2	0.02
Ukrainian and							3	0.04
Moldavian	-	-	-	-	7	0.03	0.6	0.008
Russian and							1	0.01
Romanian	-	-	-	-	-7	0.03	2.6	0.04
Ukrainian,							0.03	0.0004
Russian	-	-	-	-	1	0.005	1	0.01
and Romanian							0.04	0.0006
Ukrainian,			0.5				0.50	
Russian	2	0.01	0.1	0.001	3	0.01	0.2	0.006
and Hungarian			0.04				0.6	
Ukrainian, Russian and Polish	1	0.005	0.7	0.01	2	0.009	1.4	0.02

Source: Ministry of People's Education of Ukraine

THE LANGUAGE SITUATION AND LANGUAGE EDUCATION IN YUGOSLAVIA

R. Bugarski *University of Belgrade*

This text was written before the disintegration of Yugoslavia. An explanation and an update are provided in the Appendix following it.

Ethnic Composition

Comparable to Great Britain in size (256,000 km^2) but to Canada in population (22.4 million in 1981), Yugoslavia is a multi-ethnic and multilingual federation comprising six republics: Serbia (including the two autonomous provinces of Vojvodina and Kosovo), Croatia, Slovenia, Bosnia/Hercegovina, Macedonia and Montenegro. These are inhabited by six major national groups, officially called 'nations' and defined as peoples whose mother country is Yugoslavia, though some members may live in surrounding countries as national minorities; and numerous minorities, officially described as 'nationalities', ie groups whose ethnic home is in another state. National status is enjoyed by Serbs, Croats, Slovenes, Macedonians, Montenegrins and Moslems - the last being distinct from the religious denomination of the same name; for historical reasons, people of Islamic faith are generally of Moslem nationality in Bosnia/Hercegovina, but may belong to other nationalities elsewhere. The list of over a dozen nationalities shades off into quite small or relatively large but dispersed and low-status ethnic groups. Defying these official classifications is the sizeable and apparently fast growing group who for various reasons (offspring of mixed marriages, territorial displacement, emotional reaction etc) declared themselves Yugoslav by nationality as well as by citizenship, thus suppressing their various ethnic backgrounds in favour of emphasising allegiance to the country as a whole.

The declared national composition of Yugoslavia for 1981, the year of the last census, is given in Table 1, in decreasing order of magnitude and disregarding differences of status (all the figures in this paper are rounded off). The left column lists the nine largest groups, the first figure referring to numbers in millions and the bracketed one to percentage of the entire population of Yugoslavia. The right column continues with the smaller groups, each of which accounts for less than 1% of the total population, and whose numbers are given in thousands. Not listed are groups less than 10,000 strong, those regionally declared, undeclared and unknown.

Table 1
Yugoslavian National Composition

Serbs	8,140,000	(36.3)	Romanies	168,000
Croats	4,420,000	(19.8)	Turks	101,000
Moslems	2,000,000	(8.9)	Slovaks	80,000
Slovenes	1,750,000	(7.8)	Rumanians	55,000
Albanians	1,730,000	(7.7)	Bulgarians	36,000
Macedonians	1,340,000	(6.0)	Wallachians	32,000
Yugoslavs	1,220,000	(5.4)	Ruthenians	23,000
Montenegrins	580,000	(2.6)	Czechs	19,000
Hungarians	420,000	(1.9)	Italians	15,000
			Ukrainians	12,000

Note: Current Slavic and Balkan linguists' usage is Vlach for Wallachian, Rusyn for Ruthenian.

A few brief comments on this table may be helpful here.

1 Nationality in Yugoslavia is declared rather than assigned. It may be changed over time or withheld altogether. This accounts for demographically inexplicable oscillations recorded for some groups (Moslems, Romanies, Turks, Wallachians), between censuses, where various external considerations may have favoured one declaration over another at specific times.

2 No national group constitutes an absolute majority, which makes Yugoslavia a rarity in European terms and has had important implications for national and language policy.

3 Nationalities may be more numerous than some of the nations, which can cause additional tensions in an already complex ethnic and political situation. The next census of 1991 will certainly show the Albanians in the third place on the list, due to a continuing population explosion characterising that group.

4 Nationally declared Yugoslavs increased from 273,000 in 1971 to 1,219,000 in 1981, mainly by a change in affiliation; if continued at a significant rate, this development may begin to affect national policy.

5 The declared figure for Romanies falls far short of ethnic reality. Estimates put their actual number at some 600,000.

The ethnic composition of Yugoslavia as a whole is markedly heterogeneous, though not nearly to the same degree in all its parts. Thus Slovenia is relatively the most homogeneous and Vojvodina the most heterogeneous. While in all other republics one national group clearly predominates, perhaps with another also well represented, Bosnia/Hercegovina alone exhibits three strong groups (Moslems, Serbs, Croats) with no absolute majority. This picture is complemented by the distribution of national groups among the republics and provinces, which shows different degrees of concentration within the 'home' area. It is highest for Slovenes, in an ethnically homogeneous republic, and Macedonians, in a heterogeneous republic, as well as for Hungarians, and lowest for Montenegrins and Romanies. Yugoslavs, who have no single ethnic base and are correspondingly dispersed, divide largely between Serbia, Croatia and Bosnia/Hercegovina. The two largest national groups, Serbs and Croats, are also in relative dispersion, substantial numbers of them residing outside their home republics - especially Serbs, less than 60% of whom are to be found in Serbia proper. It is also noteworthy that under 70% of Montenegrins actually live in Montenegro, a quarter of them residing in Serbia. And so on - unfolding the rich ethnopolitical mosaic of Yugoslavia would reveal further complexities. But it is time to turn our attention to languages.

Language

Some 27 languages are spoken as mother tongues in Yugoslavia today. Of this large number, 14 have a standard form and some official status, while the rest are quite marginal in size or social standing, are dying out, or are merely spoken dialects of rural populations. All these languages display a considerable variety both genetically and typologically, which essentially allows for interference and some degree of mutual comprehensibility among the major South Slavic idioms spoken by the Yugoslav nations, while leaving out the strongest minority languages - Albanian, Hungarian, Turkish, Romany - which show great diversity. There are also great differences in numerical strength, geographical and social distribution, standardisation, communicative power, prestige, ethnic affiliation, etc. The numbers of native speakers range from over 16 million for Serbo-Croat down to a few hundred or even less. The 14 languages with over 10,000 speakers each are listed in Table 2.

Table 2
Main Languages

Serbo-Croat	16,400,000	Turkish	82,000
Slovene	1,760,000	Slovak	74,000
Albanian	1,750,000	Rumanian	60;000
Macedonian	1,370,000	Bulgarian	37,000
Hungarian	410,000	Ruthenian	19,000
Romany	140,000	Italian	19,000
Wallachian	135,000	Czech	16,000

Once again, a few comments on this table.

1 Serbo-Croat accounts for about 73% of Yugoslavia's total population; the first five languages add up to nearly 22 million speakers (97% of the entire population), all the others totalling about 600,000 (3% of the population).

2 Of these five, Slovene, Albanian and Hungarian use the Latin alphabet, Macedonian the Cyrillic, while Serbo-Croat employs both scripts.

3 Comparison with Table 1 reveals some discrepancies between the number of speakers of a given language and the number of corresponding nationals: while some languages roughly correspond to the size of the national group associated with them, there are deviations in both directions. Most strikingly, of the 135,000 declared speakers of Wallachian only 32,000 expressed Wallachian-nationality, the others declaring themselves as Serbs.

4 Such discrepancies are made possible by the fact that in Yugoslav censuses separate questions are asked about nationality and mother tongue.

Matching up nationality and language, we find that, essentially, four of the Yugoslav nations (Serbs, Croats, Moslems and Montenegrins) speak Serbo-Croat as mother tongue, as well as the vast majority of the declared Yugoslavs (1,142,000 out of the 1,219,000) and some members of other national groups. The remaining two nations, Slovenes and Macedonians, speak Slovene and Macedonian respectively. Small segments of national populations speak other languages, in various arrangements - Serbo-Croat-speaking Macedonians, Slovenes, Albanians or Hungarians, Albanian-speaking Moslems, Slovenian or Italian-speaking Croats, Macedonian-speaking Turks, etc. On the whole, however, there is a fairly consistent language - nationality identification among the largest groups. This link tends to weaken considerably as we move down the list; indeed, among the smaller groups even the notion of mother tongue may become somewhat problematic, given the high incidence of active bilingualism. All told, well over half a million Yugoslavs speak a language other than that associated with their national affiliation.

Status

It should be clear from the discussion so far that there is only a partial - indeed, in most cases fairly rough - match between the Yugoslav languages, nations and republics. This plain fact has far-reaching consequences for many aspects of life in the country, including national and language policy and language planning. Given the particular situation of this multi-ethnic and multilingual federation and the declared goals of Yugoslav society, it is only natural that a policy of linguistic equality, seen as a major ingredient of national equality, should have been adopted. Constitutionally, the languages of the Yugoslav nations and nationalities are equal: none may be discriminated against and none are legally dominant or favoured, which clearly precludes anything like a 'state' or 'federal' language. Even Serbo-Croat enjoys no special privileges, even though it is spoken natively by three-quarters of the entire population, widely acquired as a second language by the rest, and frequently used as an unofficial means of inter-ethnic communication throughout the country. Also constitutionally safeguarded are the language rights of all citizens, whatever language, language variety or alphabet they may use.

As regards official use at the federal level, five languages are regularly found in this function (Serbo-Croat, Slovene, Macedonian, Albanian and Hungarian), the list being extendable for some purposes. At the republic level, Slovene and Macedonian are official in Slovenia and Macedonia respectively, while Serbo-Croat is official elsewhere (in somewhat different standard forms and under various official names). In the autonomous provinces within Serbia, several languages are co-official with Serbo-Croat: in Vojvodina, Hungarian, Slovak, Rumanian and Ruthenian, and in Kosovo, Albanian and (in part) Turkish. Furthermore, communal authorities in any ethnolinguistically mixed area may proclaim additional official languages on their territories, depending on the structure of the local population. Constitutional provisions for language equality are for the most part implemented in actual life; however, the distinction between formal and functional equality must be recognised, since it is in practice often impossible to achieve full equality in all respects, in Yugoslavia as in any other multilingual country. On the whole, linguistic minorities everywhere in the country are well protected, their languages being fully represented in local government and administration, legal proceedings, mass media, publishing, cultural life and last but not least, education, to which we turn in the final section of this presentation.

Language Teaching

The teaching of native standard languages is complicated by the dialectal diversity of the linguistic systems underlying them, which introduces a gap of varying dimensions between the native dialect and the target standard - a problem well known to educationalists all over the world. More specific are the variant norms of Serbo-Croat, which are generally taught on their respective territories but present a major educational difficulty when this language is acquired by foreign learners.

Problems posed by language instruction in ethnically mixed communities are, however, more complex and therefore more challenging. The general goal of the educational system in this area can be defined as the promotion of societal multilingualism through individual bilingualism. Since the Yugoslav model of multilingualism rejects the notion of the superiority of some languages and the inferiority of others, and affirms the equal right of all the nations and nationalities to national, cultural and linguistic development, bilingualism is in principle bidirectional as between these two categories.

That is to say, in order to oppose the view that acquiring another language is of vital importance to nationality members but only a matter of good will to nation members, measures are taken to stimulate members of both groups to learn each other's language, and to provide institutional conditions under which this goal could be successfully achieved. From the nationality point of view, this implies moving from a traditional diglossic position, where the native tongue is restricted to informal use within the group but more formal external communication demands utilising a privileged majority language, towards a type of situation which Yugoslav scholars call functional bilingualism, where nationality members can use their native tongue for all formal and informal purposes both within and outside their own groups, owing to the bilingual organisation of the institutional systems and to the at least passive knowledge of their language by the nation members living together with them.

The development in practice of this kind of bilingualism naturally takes on different forms, being subject to a variety of local circumstances, such as number and size of ethnic groups, historical background and present demographic conditions, territorial and social mobility, number of languages in contact, genetic and typological distance between them etc. From the vantage point of language education, three cardinal aspects involve mother tongue instruction, bilingual education, and the learning of non-native languages; these are interrelated in various ways.

Mother tongue instruction, in addition to representing the exercise of a fundamental human right, is invaluable as a means of protecting the nationalities. In Yugoslavia, at any rate, the minorities could not have attained their present status without the linguistic elaboration and social recognition which their languages received by virtue of being made media of education. This function is no doubt also connected with the increasing use of nationality languages at work, especially in proceedings arising from the self-management system.

While it is not uncommon in some parts of the country to find three or more languages in contact in the same commune, the most widespread pattern is two languages existing side by side, one belonging to a nation and the other to a nationality. The education system reflects this and may be briefly described as follows: following the principle that separate education is undesirable, children of different ethnic backgrounds attend the same schools, which have sections where pupils are taught in locally represented nationality languages. This enables the great majority of children across the country to receive primary education in their mother tongue. In secondary education, this percentage is somewhat lower, both because of problems in securing qualified staff, teaching materials and the like, and because nationality pupils not infrequently opt for continuing education in the majority language. As a rule all subjects are taught in the mother tongue, the non-native language being taught as an additional subject. In practice, this means that nationality groups will almost automatically study the locally represented nation language also, be it Serbo-Croat, Slovene or Macedonian. However, in many cases (for example, in Vojvodina and on the Slovenian coast) the reverse is also true - that is, a section with instruction in the nation language will additionally study the nationality language (eg Hungarian or Italian). Where nationalities are found only in small groups, as in Bosnia/Hercegovina, their members usually do not use their mother tongues much and often know Serbo-Croat better. In such cases no special sections are set up, their native languages sometimes being taught as subjects in primary school and cultivated through folklore groups and similar activities. There are also good facilities for higher education in nationality languages, especially the numerically strongest. At the University of Kosovo in Pristina, which is fully bilingual, Albanians can in principle study all subjects in their language, and Hungarian is well represented in higher education in Vojvodina. A practical constraint is the lack of university textbooks for certain subjects in these languages, a problem which is usually remedied by relying on Serbo-Croat texts.

Bilingual education in the strict sense, with the education process taking place in two languages, is not very common in Vojvodina outside of nursery schools, but is fairly well developed in Slovenia in nursery, primary and partly in secondary education. In some cases a balance between mother tongue instruction and bilingual education must be carefully sought and the role of non-native or second language learning carefully defined. If applied schematically in a multi-ethnic setting with structurally distant languages in contact, and under generally unfavourable economic and political conditions, the superficially democratic idea of relying on the native language exclusively can lead to socially dangerous mutual estrangement, potentially culminating in the creation of cultural and linguistic ghettos. This has in fact happened in Kosovo, where the decision many years ago to make learning the non-native language optional rather than obligatory led to a weakening of communication networks and thus contributed to political tensions in the area. Measures are now being taken to remedy this situation, taking into account the predominance in Yugoslavia of the territorial principle of multilingualism, which implies obligatory official use of a given language or variety in a specific part of the country, over the individual principle of free personal choice anywhere in the country.

In a country like Yugoslavia, whose several major languages perform all the functions characterising a modern society but are not used internationally as languages of wider communication, foreign language teaching must also be counted as a significant aspect of language education. Up to the last war, German had a strong tradition in parts of the country previously under Austro-Hungarian rule, French had enjoyed great prestige among the Serbian intellectual elites, Italian had firm roots along the Adriatic coast, while English was only making a beginning as an academic subject. After the war there was a short-lived prevalence of Russian, but subsequent political developments once again made more room for the Western languages. The basic pattern officially adopted was for English, German, French and Russian to be taught according to pupils' wishes and the availability of teaching staff. English, however, soon emerged as the principal foreign language all over the country, so that measures had to be taken to ensure some continued representation for the other three. With much room left to the dictate of practical exigencies, and with considerable local differences, the present overall picture still shows English far ahead, all the way from kindergarten to university education. This is now easily the first foreign language for an overwhelming majority of young Yugoslavs, many of whom learn two and some even three foreign languages in the course of their schooling.

References

Brozović D. 1983. Die soziolinguistische Situation in der jugoslawischen Föderation, *Wiener slavistisches Jahrbuch*, 29: 9-23

Bugarski, R. 1987. Politique et aménagement linguistiques en Yougoslavie. In Maurais, J. (ed.) *Politique et aménagement linguistiques*. Québec: Conseil de la langue française/Paris: Le Robert: 417-52

Bugarski, R. 1987. Language Planning in Yugoslavia. In Laforge, L. (ed) *Actes du colloque international sur l'aménagement linguistique*. Québec: Les Presses de l'Université Laval, 133-41

Bugarski, R., and Hawkesworth, C. (eds.) forthcoming 1992. *Language Planning in Yugoslavia*. Columbus, Ohio: Slavica (in press)

Magner, T.F. (ed.) 1985. Yugoslavia in sociolinguistic perspective. *International Journal of the Sociology of Language*, 52

Mikes, M. 1984. Instruction in the mother tongues in Yugoslavia. *Prospects*, 14, 1: 121-31

Novak-Lukanovič, S. 1986. Some Yugoslav experiences in asserting equality of the nations and nationalities in the field of education. *Razprave in gradivo/Treatises and Documents*, Ljubljana, 18: 32-89. (and other contributions in the same volume)

Radovanović, M. 1988. Yugoslavia. In Ammon, U., Dittmar, N., and Mattheier, K. J. (eds), *Sociolinguistics/Soziolinguistik*. Berlin/New York: Walter de Gruyter, 2: 1303-7

Statistički bilten 1295. 1982. Belgrade: Savezni zavod za statistiku

Škiljan, D. 1988. *Jezična politika*. Zagreb: Naprijed

Appendix

The foregoing contribution was prepared in July 1990 and was meant to be revised and updated for publication in the present book. Since then, however, Yugoslavia has been torn apart and is going up in flames as these lines are added in April 1992. It is difficult to write about the language and educational policy and practice of a country to the tune of that country's death march. Since Yugoslavia no longer exists as a political entity, an update in the usual sense of revision incorporating recent changes is clearly ruled out in this case. A balanced new account must wait until the dust settles and it becomes possible to cast a cold eye on the emerging landscape. But this will take some time, and in any case such a report would have to deal with several new states individually, and preferably be written by different authors.

Under these circumstances, it has seemed appropriate to let the original report stand as it is, reflecting the situation before the outbreak of open hostilities leading to the destruction of its subject. The reader is asked to keep this perspective in mind. All that can be provided now is a short and highly general summary of major current developments as they affect the picture presented in the discussion above.

As is well known by now, political conflicts, supported by an economic crisis, ethnic tensions and other factors, have resulted in great national, social and demographic turmoil, culminating in the tragedy of internal warfare and the breakdown of what used to be the Yugoslav Federation. The stage for these events was set by the downfall of Communist rule, which opened the way to rapid disintegration. Unfortunately, the ensuing political pluralism did not in itself bring about democracy. What has happened instead in all the former Yugoslav republics - naturally, with local variations - is, essentially, that one kind of totalitarianism has been replaced by another: the Communist by the nationalist. Many of the key labels and symbols have changed, Communism has officially disappeared from the scene, the superficially attractive but inefficient self-management system has been abandoned, etc. There have certainly been some further democratic advances here and there. But the old power structures are mainly still strong under a new guise, and the technology of authoritarian government has not really changed. The principal difference is that authority has definitely moved from an original federal level, via that of the constituent republics, to that of the emerging independent states, where it is largely exercised amidst rampant chauvinistic nationalism and mutual accusations.

Against this general background it is possible to gain a perspective on certain trends and processes now affecting the situation as depicted in the main body of this paper. In general terms, one point emerges rather clearly, even painfully so: the chauvinistic nationalism just mentioned, skilfully engineered and manipulated by the various national leaders bodes ill for minorities everywhere. In countries whose ethnic makeup largely resembles the leopard's skin this is particularly ominous: pressure is exerted on citizens to identify with specific 'national causes', ie with the perceived - even if wholly misconstrued - interests of majority populations. What emerges as a result is a kind of 'majority democracy'. Thus, it is good and often advantageous to be 'a good Serb' in Serbia, 'a good Croat' in Croatia and so on, but it may be dangerous to be a Serb in Croatia or Slovenia, or likewise in reverse and other possible combinations, again with local variations.

A major problem here is that on formerly Yugoslav territories majority/minority relations take the form not only of 'nations' versus 'nationalities' as defined in the paper above, but also of 'national' populations residing outside their 'home' republics. In fact, the status of the large Serbian population segments in Croatia, and now also in Bosnia/Hercegovina, has been at the heart of the present conflicts. On the other hand, the 'nationalities', in the usual sense of national minorities, have felt increasingly insecure in most places. For example, the autonomy of Serbia's provinces of Kosovo and Vojvodina has been drastically reduced in newly unified Serbia, and the Italian community in Croatia has also been loud in protest.

What are some of the relevant features and consequences of this state of affairs? Only a few can be mentioned here, and quite briefly.

1 The new population census, taken in 1991, has not yet yielded official figures, but provisional returns show that the number of nationally declared

Yugoslavs, which under more normal circumstances could have been expected to go on rising, has in fact dropped significantly - most dramatically in Croatia, where many previously so declared have now opted for Croatian or Serbian affiliation.

2 The new republic/state constitutions and attendant acts contain some characteristic modifications in the language provisions. In Croatia the language is now officially called simply Croatian, written in the Latin alphabet, with an added stipulation that other languages and alphabets may also be used in local communities, but without explicit mention of the Serbs or their language and alphabet. In Serbia both Serbo-Croat and Serbian may be used as official designations according to the current constitution, but the more recent act on language use mentions only the latter (as does the draft constitution currently in preparation for the new 'Yugoslavia', consisting of Serbia and Montenegro). In all these documents the Cyrillic alphabet takes precedence over the Latin. It will be interesting to see what decisions will be taken in Bosnia/Hercegovina (if indeed it survives as an entity, which seems doubtful at present), where power is now shared among three national parties, Moslem, Serbian and Croatian. Will their common Serbo-Croat language be artificially split up into three varieties, what will these be called, and what consequences will follow for mother tongue education and public use of language?

3 As regards minority language education, some unfavourable trends can already be discerned. For example, there is less insistence on it, and also on observing language rights generally, in Serbia's provinces. The situation in Kosovo is not sufficiently clear and reliable information is hard to come by, but there is little doubt that instruction in Albanian has dropped heavily on all levels and even been discontinued in some cases, possibly as a result of boycott reacting against imposed restrictions. Unmistakable expressions of anxiety have also come from Vojvodina's minorities, including the large Hungarian one. It must be said in fairness, though, that in Yugoslavia minority rights, language and educational ones among them, had achieved a high level with few parallels anywhere in the world, so that a low here may still be quite high in comparative terms. But this in itself is no guarantee that such rights will automatically go on being respected, as the present situation seems to show.

4 Despite some serious breaks and disruptions caused by the war and its aftermath, intercultural communication can on the whole be said to go on, albeit in a more limited fashion. In the area of foreign language education there are no radical changes to report. The same languages are taught in varying proportions, perhaps with some shifts of emphasis but without

major reorientations such as the one involving Russian in some East European countries.

In conclusion, it is most regrettable that such a dark picture of developments under way has had to be sketched out, and it is hard - especially for an inside commentator with a Yugoslav outlook - to suppress a note of bitterness. The previous system, based on 'Leninist' national and language policy, was highly ideologised and made ample use of resounding phrases. However, it also produced a world-renowned democratic language policy and a network of minority and educational planning that actually worked most of the time. It remains to be seen how things will eventually work out, in this area as in others, for the survivors inhabiting segments of what was once Yugoslavia. It has taken considerable international involvements to contain the conflicts and curb the rising nationalist arrogance. Let us hope that the alarmingly endangered civil and minority rights can still be salvaged in the process - if not by enlightenment from within, then at least by outside pressure to write new safeguards into the relevant documents and to observe them. If this succeeds, true democracy might still have a chance.

LANGUAGE EDUCATION FOR INTERCULTURAL COMMUNICATION IN SLOVENIA

A. Nećak Lük *Institute for Ethnic Studies, University of Ljubljana*

Introduction

In the context of changing European sociopolitical reality and relations among nations, Slovenia, too, is facing the process of reconstruction: a new political model, endeavours for independence and statehood and changes of relationship with other nations of the former Yugoslavia have brought about the search for new allies and partnerships and the establishment of new models of communication with old and new neighbours.

The field of cultural and language policy, which is the subject of this contribution, is also undergoing modifications. One of the conditions of the European arbiters for the recognition of Slovenia as an independent state was a demand that Slovenia should guarantee European standards of human rights and minority protection. Along with a common will to fulfill this demand there exists, however, a common consent in public opinion and in the Slovenian parliament that the standards of minority protection should not fall below the currently established level.

In order to make this concern understandable some basic data on the ethnodemographic constitution of Slovenia and on her language policy seem to be appropriate.

Some Ethnodemographic Data

The ethnic composition of the Republic of Slovenia is relatively homogeneous. According to the population census of 1991 there are 1,962,606 inhabitants in Slovenia. Only 12.45% of her population are not Slovenes by origin, but are members of either the Italian (0.16%) or the Hungarian national minority (0.43%), while the remaining portion of the population are members of nations and national groups from other Yugoslav republics (Croats 2.74%, Serbs 2.4%, Muslims 1.36%, Montenegrins 0.22%, Macedonians 0.22%, Albanians 0.8%, individuals without ethnic adherence, declaring themselves as Yugoslavs (0.62%) and members of the Romany ethnic group (0.12%) compactly settled in two areas).

The Italian national minority is located in three coastal communes, in Koper/Capodistria, Izola/Isola, and Piran/Pirano. The Hungarian population is settled in 33 settlements along the Slovenian Hungarian border in the communes of Murska Sobota and Lendava/Lendva (see map). The Romany ethnic group is more compactly settled in two areas, in some villages of the Prekmurje and Dolenjska region. Most of the members of other nations and national groups from other Yugoslav republics have come to settle permanently or temporarily in Slovenia in the last two or three decades. They live dispersed among the Slovenian population throughout the republic. A more substantial concentration of this ethnically and hence linguistically heterogeneous population can be observed in some industrial centres.

From the point of view of interethnic relations and the language contact situation it may be interesting that the dispersion of members of the Slovene nation in other parts of 'Yugoslavia' is a negligible phenomenon, the result of which is the fact that of all Yugoslav nations the Slovene nation reaches the highest level of concentration in its own republic: 97.6% of Slovenes are residents of the Republic of Slovenia.

On the other hand a substantial number, approximately one third of the total Slovene population, of Slovenes live abroad either as national minorities in neighbouring countries - about 50,000 to 60,000 in Austria, about 10,000 in Hungary, about 140,000 to 150,000 in the Trieste region (Italy) (Nećak Lük, 1983) or as emigrant groups in West European countries, in North and South America, Canada and Australia. Recent events connected with the efforts of the Republic of Slovenia to enact the right to self-determination have shown that the ethnic consciousness of the Slovenian emigrant communities in these countries is very much alive. For the geolinguistic situation in the autochtonous Slovenian settlement area see the map (Page 191).

Basic Features of Language Policy

Owing to historical circumstances the development of the Slovene people into a political nation has been somewhat delayed. In the course of striving for national independence much national energy has been invested in the domain of culture and language development as indispensable features of national identity.

The Slovenian language had for centuries been in a state of diglossia. Slovenian had been the low variety, the language of 'plebs', and the languages of the neighbouring dominant nations, Italian, German and Hungarian, in respective areas and in different periods, had been the high variety, the languages of nobles, and latterly of the middle class and intelligentsia. Though the process of standardisation/codification had been in progress since 1550 (Trubar) and Slovenian had gradually gained access to individual formal speech domains - first to religion, to education and later to mass media and public administration - it was a troublesome endeavour owing to the number of Slovenian dialects on one side and to the lack of institutional support on the other.

After the First World War, with the emergence of Yugoslavia, Slovenian was given the status of a language of public communication as well as the necessary institutional background to assure its functioning - although not on the whole of Slovenian ethnic territory, since, on the creation of Yugoslavia, a substantial part of the Slovenian ethnic territory had been granted to Austria, Italy, and Hungary. Here the Slovenian people were subjected to severe pressure to assimilate. In Italy for instance the Slovenian language was expelled from all public domains, for example from schools, where children were severely punished for uttering a Slovenian word, and even from the church. This extreme case of linguicide is excellently described in a novel by a Slovenian writer France Bevk: 'Kaplan Martin Cedrmac', (The Chaplain Martin Cedermac). Slovenian was not used in all speech domains in Yugoslavia either. Serbian functioned as the State language in the army, in the administrative and political bodies at State level and in foreign policy, while in the State owned institutions on the territory of Slovenia (post offices, railways, customs etc) it was the language of public communication along with Slovenian.

In the post Second World War Yugoslav Federation national, and hence, language, equality had been considered achieved by unification. Hence any deliberations about the status of Slovene was regarded as nationalistic resistance. Therefore, it was only in the mid-sixties that the Slovenian language came to occupy an appropriate place in such an important channel of communication as TV news and only with the 1974 Constitution that equal functioning of Slovenian in communication on the federal level, foreign policy included, was agreed upon. Serbo-Croat, however, remained the language of command in the Yugoslav army. Thus, today it is for the first time in the history of the Slovenian nation that Slovenian language policy is totally in the hands of the Slovenian State.

These historical experiences can probably be considered as one of the explanations why, in Slovene policy making, considerable attention has always been paid to language contact situations. Special instruments were developed for the protection of the rights of the Italian and the Hungarian national minority members. In addition to protection of the rights of all her citizens, the Republic of Slovenia is obliged to safeguard the ethnic character, well-being and promotion of members of the Italian and Hungarian minorities.

In the first article of the 1974 Constitution, Slovenia was defined as the State of the Slovene nation and of the Italian and Hungarian national minorities and was therefore obliged to promote the ethnic, cultural and language characteristics of both indigenous minorities, not only by preventing discrimination of any kind, or assimilation, but also by offering material/financial support for activities necessary for the development of minority groups. Thus, through special communal bodies that decide on equal terms with other councils of the communal assembly both national minorities can give unmediated expression to their authentic and specific ethnic interest. At the same time they are actively involved in the realization of their rights and assume their own share of responsibility for preserving and promoting their identity.

Members of other national groups are guaranteed the right to express freely their adherence to their nation or their national community, to develop their culture and to use their language and alphabet. The possibility of cultivating their mother tongue in school or organising classes with their language as the language of instruction at primary and secondary level is foreseen in the relevant Acts on education in Slovenia.

The new Constitution has preserved the already enacted standards of minority rights and foreseen an explicit article on the status and rights of the Romany group that are to be regulated by law.

Slovenia's language policy is based on the territorial principle. The importance of the right to maintain, develop and use one's mother tongue as a feature of group identity is underlined by this principle as well as the right to unhindered expression and development of one's cultural and ethnic characteristics. Slovene, the majority language, and Italian and Hungarian, the minority languages, are equal in public communication in the regions where minorities reside and in interethnic communication (the so called collective or group right, limited to a given area inhabited by the respective group). The territorial principle also means the development of a system of institutional support which enables a specific ethnic group's language to function on equal terms with the majority language in all channels of public communication, ie in both formal and informal speech domains - the system called institutional bilingualism.

The areas where minorities reside have the status of nationally mixed regions, where in economic development policy-making, safeguarding the ethnic characteristics of the population should be taken into consideration. This means that certain 'security' measures are provided in order to at least attenuate, since it is probably impossible to prevent completely, the usually negative consequences of the upward social mobility which minority members most often pay for with a gradual loss of certain features of their identity, their language being the most endangered. In the first place the strategy of creating appropriate employment conditions should be mentioned: both languages have equal status in the work domain, and there exists the obligation that jobs that demand contacts with clients in institutions, banks, post offices, stores, services etc can be accorded only to a person who is competent also in the minority language.

Language equality is safeguarded on two levels: on the one hand, minority languages have the status of official languages along with the Slovenian language in regions where minority populations live together with the majority population. This means also that institutional and financial support is granted from either republic or communal funds for maintenance of minorities' language functions in formal speech domains - in education, mass media, administration, topographical signs, etc. On the other hand, a policy of societal and individual bilingualism is practised in order to bridge the sociocultural gap and to overcome obstacles in social interaction and communication. Education in nationally mixed regions, therefore, has an important function in developing the bilingual communicative competence of young generations.

Language Policy in Education in Slovenia

A closer inspection of the distribution of languages in education in Slovenia enables at least three types of language status to be observed (in this chapter only regular education and public educational institutions are taken into consideration).

1 **Pupils' mother tongue** can function as a teaching language and as an obligatory or optional subject.

1.1 *Pupils' mother tongue as the language of instruction*

- Slovenian, Italian, Hungarian figure as teaching languages throughout the educational system.
- Serbo-croat primary level. The possibility to organize classes in the other languages of Yugoslav nations and national groups on the primary and secondary level is granted by law but parents prefer their children to be educated in Slovenian. Therefore, Serbo-Croat is the teaching language in one primary school only.
- Romany in preschool institutions only.

1.2 *Pupils' mother tongue as an obligatory subject of the curriculum*

- Slovenian, Italian, and Hungarian throughout the educational system.
- Serbo-Croat where it is the language of instruction.
- languages of other Yugoslav nations and national groups if they demand it.

1.3 *Pupils' mother tongue as an optional subject*

- Hungarian on the secondary level outside the nationally mixed region.
- languages of other nations and national groups if they demand it.

2 **Second language (the language of social environment)** can function as a teaching language and as an obligatory or optional subject.

2.1 *Second language as a language of instruction*

- In bilingual educational institutions Slovenian, as the second language of Hungarian children, and Hungarian, as the second language of Slovenia, are used as the teaching languages concurrently with the pupils' mother tongue.
- Slovenian is the language of instruction for children of other Yugoslav nations and national groups that do not opt for classes in their mother tongue, and for Romany children.

2.2 *Second language as an obligatory subject of the curriculum*

- Slovenian as the second language is an obligatory curriculum subject on all levels of education in the nationally mixed regions for Italian and Hungarian children.
- Italian and Hungarian as second languages are obligatory curriculum subjects on all levels of education for Slovenian children in nationally mixed regions.
- Serbo-Croat is an obligatory subject in certain stages of the primary level for all children in Slovenia. However, at the moment an ardent discussion about whether it should retain this status under new circumstances has been opened.

2.3 *Second language as an optional subject*

- At secondary level, outside the nationally mixed region in Prekmurje, Slovenian children can choose Hungarian as an optional curriculum subject. Once they opt for it they are obliged to attend Hungarian classes throughout secondary school.

3 **Foreign language**

3.1 *Foreign language as a language of instruction*

- There exists an intention to organize instruction through foreign languages in some grammar schools.

3.2 *Foreign language as an obligatory subject of curriculum*

- Foreign language teaching starts in the fifth grade of the primary school. There is a tendency to begin it already in the third grade. Experiments evaluating this possibility and that of beginning foreign language acquisition at preschool level are in progress.
- At secondary level the second foreign language is introduced.
- English, German, French, Italian, Spanish, Russian, in this order, are the most frequently taught foreign languages. Distribution differs according to the region and the type of school.

3.3 *Foreign language as an optional subject curriculum*

- A foreign language can be chosen as an optional subject from the third grade of the primary school. Latin figures among the most frequently chosen foreign languages.

Bilingual Education in Slovenia

In the areas where Italian (coastal areas) and Hungarian (Prekmurje) minorities live education is conceived as an integral part of the general system of education of Slovenia. Nevertheless, educational institutions there, regardless of whether minority or majority pupils or both attend them, have some additional tasks and goals besides those set before education in general.

Second language acquisition is one of the elements enabling people to fulfill their communication needs in a multilingual environment. In the course of the second language learning and teaching process a series of important socialization goals can be achieved. Along with the development of communicative competence in two languages, awareness about an additive dimension of the duality of living in an ethnically and culturally diverse society becomes evident. By providing knowledge about the others' history, culture, arts, literature, and way of living, and by developing mutual tolerance and respect, education in nationally mixed areas is an important agent of cultural pluralism.

In Slovenia two models of bilingual education are practised. Both are maintenance/enrichment models (Skutnabb-Kangas, 1981), their social goal being cultural pluralism, while two-way bilingualism - minority and majority members are given an opportunity to develop at least a receptive competence of the other group's language - is a linguistic goal.

Owing to the 1954 international agreement - the London Memorandum, which in a Special Statute established the standards of the minority protection for the Slovene minority living in the in Italy and for the Italian minority in Slovenia - educational institutions in the coastal area, from kindergartens to colleges, are monolingual with either Slovene or Italian as a language of instruction, while the other group's language, the second language, Italian or Slovene respectively, is a compulsory subject. The language of administration in Italian (minority) educational institutions is Italian; so are school textbooks and other material. Teaching and other personnel is, as prescribed by law, Italian by origin.

In the nationally mixed region of Prekmurje children of Slovene and Hungarian origin attend bilingual educational institutions (kindergartens, primary schools and several types of secondary schools). Classes are mixed and the concurrent method of bilingual instruction is practised, with both Slovene and Hungarian used in rotation in each class for each subject of the curriculum. School administration, textbooks and other material are in both languages. Teaching staff and other personnel are bilingual. Both languages as subjects of the curriculum are taught to all pupils regardless of their ethnic provenance, using the mother tongue as a medium of instruction, with slight modifications in literacy instruction of both languages.

Since the area having the status of a nationally mixed region is rather small, and most of the secondary schools are situated outside it, the Hungarian language is an optional subject of the curriculum in all vocational and grammar schools in the region of Prekmurje, either as a mother tongue for the Hungarian children or as a second language for the Slovenian.

Conclusion

It is quite evident that endeavours for the maintenance and development of cultural pluralism and linguistic diversity are one of the features of present Slovenian society which is reflected also in the field of education. One could even argue that the quantity and the quality of the respective legal measures reach far beyond the international standards. It is not the aim of this article to treat the sociopsychological dimension of the problem, but it might be worth mentioning that at the moment there are several research projects in Slovenia investigating interethnic relations in nationally mixed regions and national identity problems, linguistic vitality included.

On the other hand, in a bilingual setting the task of developing adequate language proficiency as a complex skill fulfilling communicative functions in the process of the child's cognitive and academic development seems to be a rather demanding one. In the case of Prekmurje, bilingual communication during lessons with all curriculum subjects can bring results only if a series of linguistic, pedagogical, psycholinguistic and sociopyschological prerequisites is taken into consideration. The child's ability to participate actively in bilingual instruction is closely connected with his language proficiency in his mother tongue and with his second language competence. With language switching within the framework of the class, an adequate knowledge of the second language is indispensable for active participation with all curriculum subjects and for unhindered comprehension of new academic content and domains. A two way process is in action: on the one hand an adequate second language competence is indispensable for effective participation in lessons, and on the other, learning other subjects in a second language promotes a wider vocabulary and linguistic competence in that language.

The importance of the mother tongue or the first language for the emotional and cognitive development of children, especially of minority children, is accepted among scholars. There is no doubt today among serious researchers of bilingualism that academic underachievement of minority children is most often due to sociocultural, sociopsychological and pedagogical factors. When mother tongue and other features of children's group adherence are stigmatized or when their language proficiency is not given due consideration, academic failure does not come as a surprise. The beneficial effects of bilingualism can be expected when optimal mother tongue proficiency has been developed along with communicative skills in the second language.

Several investigations in bilingual schools in Prekmurje showed deficiency in the pupils' second language development. That called for closer inspection into the language teaching process. On the one hand the data showed that the number of lexical items in the mother tongue of Hungarian children lagged behind their competence in the second language, ie Slovene. On the other hand the linguistic competence of Slovene pupils in the second language, ie in Hungarian, after eight years of bilingual school attendance was surprisingly weak (Nećak Lük, 1986). It meant that two important goals of bilingual schooling were not achieved, namely the optimal mother tongue development of Hungarian children which along with other institutional measures should provide for the maintenance and promotion of the Hungarian group identity, on the one hand, and a multicultural and multilingual social environment backed by the majority members' bilingualism, on the other (Nećak Lük, 1986 and the 1982 law).

In order to eliminate these damaging effects a modification of the language teaching approach was introduced in 1986 by means of a longitudinal action research project, which has been found to produce positive results (Nećak Lük, 1989).

Of course the results of the coastal (Italian speaking) model are not ideal either. It is therefore quite natural that in nationally mixed regions as well as in homogeneous Slovenian regions education is subject to evaluation. Some projects introducing different modern approaches to language teaching, based on contemporary psycholinguistic and developmental psychology theories are in progress in the coastal area.

There are of course some serious gaps in the investigation of bilingual education. For instance, a contrastive/comparative study of both language systems (Slovenian/Hungarian, Slovenian/Italian) would contribute substantially to the quality of the programme conception and textbooks preparation. So would access to 'the threshold level' of linguistic competence registers for respective languages.

What seems to be important is the fact that in Slovenia multicultural education is an existing reality. Improving its functioning and results should have promising effects on the quality of life of all citizens.

References

Cummins, J. 1984. *Bilingualism and Special Education: Issues in Assessment and Pedagogy*. Clevedon: Multilingual Matters

Journal of Ethnic Studies - Treatises and Documents, 1/1960 - 25/1991. Ljubljana: Institute for Ethnic Studies

1980. *Minorities: Bridge among Nations. On the Occasion of the XXI Unesco Conference*. Ljubljana

National Composition of Inhabitants by Territory (final results). 1982. *Statistical Bulletin*, 1295, Belgrade

Nećak Lük, A et al. 1983. *The Italian and Hungarian Nationalities in the Socialist Republic of Slovenia*. Ljubljana: Institute for Ethnic Studies

Nećak Lük, A. 1986. *Bilingual Education - the factor of personality development and coexistence among nations. Research Report*. Ljubljana: Institute for Educational Research, University of Ljubljana

Nećak Lük, A. 1989. *Education in multilingual environment - Motivation for the first and the second language learning and use*. Ljubljana: Institute for Educational Research, University of Ljubljana

Offical Gazette of the SR Slovenia. 12/1982, art 16, 27, 28. *Law on the Implementation of Special Rights of the Members of Italian and Hungarian Nationalities in the Field of Education*

Nećak Lük and Strujelj, I (Eds). 1984. *Bilingualism - Individual and Societal Issues.* Ljubljana

Skutnabb-Kangas, T. 1981. *Bilingualism or not: The Education of Minorities.* Clevedon: Multilingual Matters

Trubar, P. 1550. *Abecedarium*

Writers' Journal, Special Edition. 1991. *A Chronology of the Decay of Tito's Yugoslavia 1980 - 1991. The Case of Slovenia.* Ljubljana

MAP OF SLOVENIA

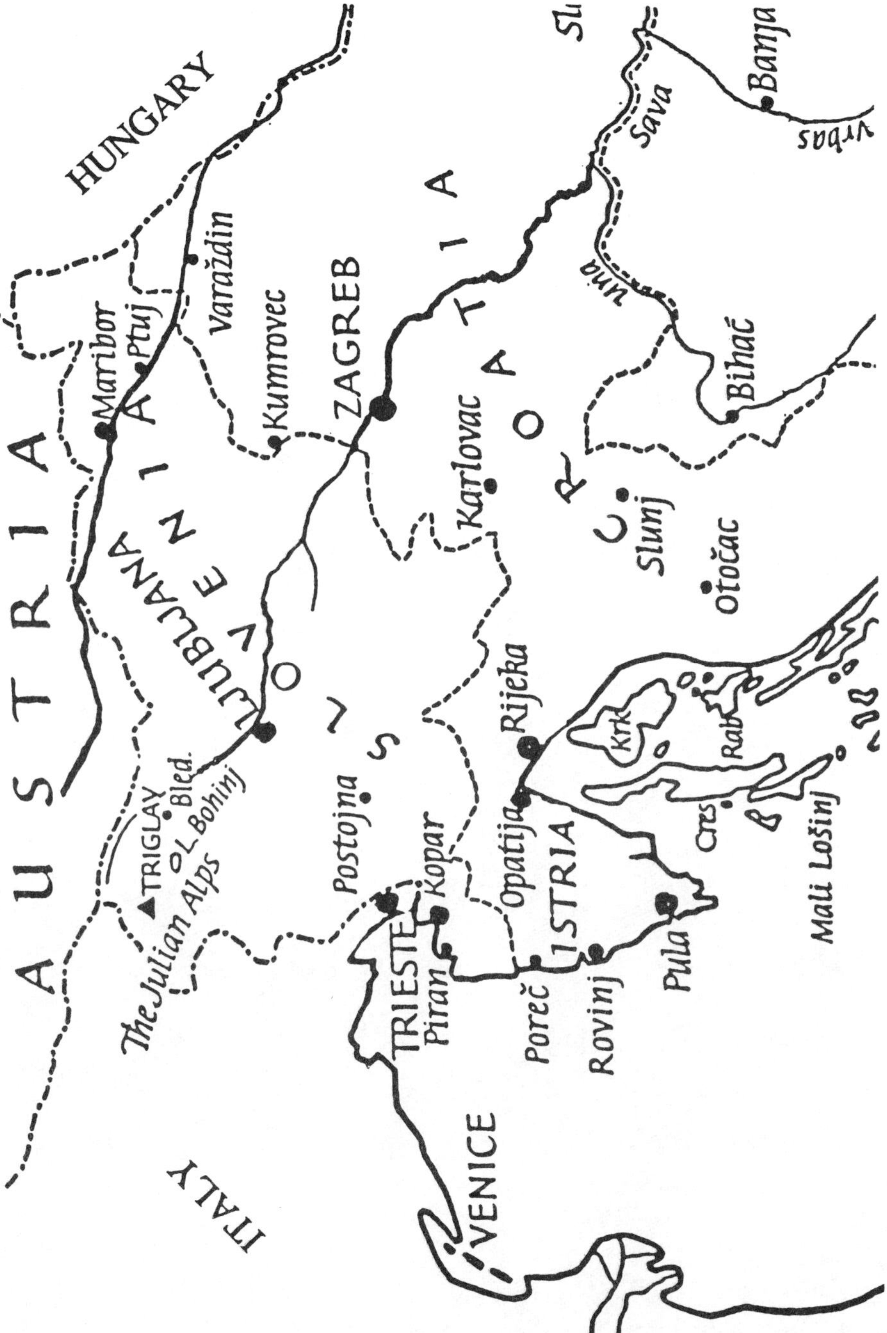

NEW TRENDS IN EDUCATIONAL POLICY IN THE REPUBLIC OF SERBIA, 1990 TO THE PRESENT

S. Savić *Faculty of Philosophy, Novi Sad*
Z. Jukić *Vojvodina Department of Education, Novi Sad*

What kinds of changes have taken place as a result of the new constitution adopted by the Republic of Serbia in 1990 (Figure 1)? In Yugoslavia at present (ie 1991), the Federal Constitution of 1974 is still in force, guaranteeing equality for all languages and peoples. The new Constitution of the Republic of Serbia, enacted in 1990, specifies that in areas of Serbia inhabited by members of minority nationalities, their written and spoken languages will be used for official purposes, along with Serbo-Croat, as confirmed by legislation. The law defining the political status of the Province of Vojvodina (1991) states in Article 13 that the Province is to ensure that individuals belonging to other peoples and nationalities be educated in their own languages, as defined by the law.

The law governing the use of written and spoken languages for official purposes further spells out these rights. This law, passed in 1991, states that the Serbo-Croat language and Cyrillic alphabet are to be used for official purposes in Serbia, while in areas inhabited by minority nationalities (in Vojvodina), the written and spoken languages of these peoples and nationalities are to be in official use, along with Serbo-Croat. The law specifies various forms of official use. Among other things, it describes the manner and position in which a text is to be written when it is in a minority language: 'For official purposes, a text written in a minority language or languages ... is written beneath or to the right of the original, in the same form and in the same size letters, (so that, for example, a shop sign in Hungarian may never be placed above the same sign in Serbo-Croat, or be written in larger letters). There is an obvious tendency in all these documents to make a hierarchical distinction between the language of the majority, Serbo-Croat (or, as it is called in the law governing the use of languages for official purposes, Serbian), and the other languages of Vojvodina. According to the Serbian education laws, members of minority nationalities still have the right to be educated in their native language, but they are required to learn Serbo-Croat as a non-native language (or in the old terminology, language of the local community) - the aim of such instruction is to provide pupils with a productive knowledge of Serbo-Croat within the bounds of prescribed linguistic and lexical material, acquaint them with basic elements of the culture belonging to speakers of that language, and in general allow them to understand, associate, and establish ties with members of other ethnic groups (Serbo-Croat as a non-native language, 1991, 3). If they do decide to be educated in the language of the majority, mother tongue classes with elements of national culture are optionally provided (2 hours per week, provided at least 11 pupils sign up) (see Figure 2).

In September 1991, many districts of Vojvodina decided that this optional instruction would no longer be funded, due to lack of financial resources. This did away with instruction in the four minority languages which were studied as languages of the local community by pupils whose native language was Serbo-Croat, while the language of the ethnic majority was made obligatory. Thus ended a long period of efforts aimed at ensuring that the educational system did not sever ties among pupils who are being educated in their native language, whether they belong to the majority people or one of the minority nationalities; instead, the system aimed at establishing a transitional mode that would encourage reciprocal influences and a sense of community. The absence of an explicitly intercultural concept of education can be understood only by the fact that for years the minority ethnic populations of Vojvodina have lived together with the majority population, so that cultural habits and toleration have evened out and become ingrained. Cultural differences are not so great as between immigrant groups from Asia and Africa now residing in Western Europe, where this form of education originated. A comparison of educational policies in the previous period and the present one can be schematically represented as in Figures 2 and 3.

Almost 100% of minority children being educated in their mother tongue previously voluntarily studied Serbo-Croat, while far smaller percentages of children belonging to the ethnic majority studied minority languages: around 16% at the elementary school level and 10% in secondary school (Table 1). A new educational policy could have more strongly compelled students belonging to the ethnic majority to study minority languages if it had striven to strengthen ties between majority and minority ethnic groups. What the results of a compulsory study of Serbo-Croat will be remains to be seen. It may create a negative attitude towards the study of Serbo-Croat which will in turn be manifested in linguistic and ethnic conflicts. In identifying future ethnic conflicts that might be caused by educational policies, it is not enough to analyse official documents, curricula and instructional plans as we have done here; rather, a detailed examination of instructional materials and textbooks, both native language materials and those for other subjects such as history, geography, etc, must be carried out. For example, the course content for Serbo-Croat as a non-native language at both elementary and secondary level includes little information on the languages of the other peoples (Macedonian, Slovenian, etc), nationalities and ethnic groups of Yugoslavia.

Let us now consider the problem from another angle. The optional subjects (see Table 2) which are to be partially financed (the rest comes from the parents) include foreign languages, starting in the sixth grade. Children from minority nationalities who are educated in the language of the majority will have less and less instruction in their own language (if the economic situation in the country does not change), but will be able to study a foreign language as early as the third grade (with parental co-financing). This will permit an early orientation towards understanding a language and culture that are geographically distant, while destroying a bridge which brought us closer together in improved neighbourly relations.

What consequences can be identified so far? Preschool age children who have spontaneously learned the language of their playmates and had the opportunity to study the language in school at the age of 6 to 7 (Table 1), will no longer have that opportunity even in elementary school. Nor will this opportunity be available to children from bilingual marriages who very early learn two languages within the family. Even for children under 6, this kind of instruction will not be easy to obtain in preschool institutions, for the latter have become very expensive and many parents now prefer to keep their children at home or share childcare responsibilities with other families (of the same ethnic composition). Those children who do remain in preschool institutions will be fewer in number, so that there will be no place for instruction in the native language, since this depends on having a specified number of children.

Even more elementary school pupils will be educated in Serbo-Croat than at present, and the same trend is expected at the secondary school level. In their local communities, minority children in some parts of Vojvodina are exposed to dialects of Serbo-Croat other than the standard form. The language they are exposed to in their general environment therefore does not enable them to learn the standard spoken form nor, more importantly, the standard written form (see Miller, 1992, for data on the English spoken by Scottish children in Scotland). Furthermore, the form of their native language which such children hear in their immediate surroundings is often not the standard form. Thus in a survey conducted in an elementary school in Novi Sad, pupils often answered the question 'Why do you attend classes in your mother tongue?' by saying that generally it was to learn how to read and write the standard spoken and written form of the langugage: 'Because I'd like to learn my own language properly', 'In order to learn how to read and write'. This will create a new view of relations between majority and minority populations (who are smaller not only in numbers but in terms of power), and this will be reflected in the education of children belonging to these groups.

Can such a shift from an ideal conception of equality to one of equality only for members of the majority ethnic group lead to conflicts in multilingual Vojvodina, where for years the population has lived together in mutual dependence on one another? The question can also be formulated differently: did the earlier educational model, which strove for pluralism and linguistic equality for all, contribute anything at all to reducing linguistic conflicts or even avoiding them completely? Certainly the awareness of linguistic and other forms of tolerance which was created in the minds of the people was of inestimable value. Current educational policy on children from minority nationalities is out of step with the data on bilingualism gathered by researchers in Vojvodina (and the world). This new policy does not take advantage of the positive aspects contained in the earlier, pluralistic policy. Furthermore, it is at odds with the new trends in intercultural and interethnic education which are making themselves felt in Europe (see Learning for Life). If ethnic and linguistic tolerance is to be maintained, both majority and minority peoples must make concessions: those in the majority must learn the languages of their countrymen to the same extent that the latter learn the language of the majority.

Conclusion

The question of education is always a question of human survival. As a rule, it is connected with social and political conditions in a given society. In the past, a pluralistic outlook - equality for everyone in all aspects of life - pervaded the value system set up to serve all aspects of Yugoslav society, including education. In Vojvodina, where such attitudes already had a historical foundation, an educational system based on them quickly took root and yielded good results. From preschool all the way to secondary education, mother tongue instruction was provided for both peoples and nationalities, and ties were established by teaching the languages of local communities. A qualified instructional and academic staff was created to guide educational policy in the proper direction. These achievements contributed to intercultural education (though this term was never used in the sense intended by the Council of Europe).

At a moment when the positive results of such an educational policy are being seen (along with some organizational defects), changes were made, not in the direction of further interculturalization and greater linguistic tolerance, but oriented towards nationality, separateness, insularity and distinctness.

Now there is greater emphasis on the study of foreign languages - beginning at an earlier age and later including two languages. Whether this will help develop a sensitivity to differences in peoples who are not immediate neighbours (the English, French, Germans and Russians) remains to be seen. Once created, tolerance and understanding could have been applied in various forms of communication leading to further interethnic ties. National feelings of separateness and self-sufficiency, once created in the younger generation, may not be quickly or easily undone in the future.

References

Bugarski, R. and Mikes, M. 1985. Types and methods of multilingual research in Yugoslavia. IN Nelde, P.H. (ed), *Methoden der Kontaktlinguistik*. Bonn: Dummler, 145-54

Göncz, L. 1981. *Rana dvojezienost i kognitivni razvoj*, Novi Sad

Göncz, L. 1985. Rezultati istrazivanja psiholoskih aspekata dvojezicnosti u Vojvodini. *Psihologija*, Beograd, 1-2: 79-92

Göncz, L. 1991. The psychology of bilingualism: A synthesis of research findings and their educational implications in multilingual communities; II European Congress of Psychology, Budapest, 8-12 July, *Abstracts*, 2: 192

Göncz, L., Kodzopeljic. 1989.

Göncz, L.V. Petrovic, D.R.. Kodzopeljic, J. and Kajstorovic,N. N. 1990. *Zbornik istrazivackih radova 1986-1990*

Miller. 1992.

Mikes, M. 1966.

Mikes, M. 1972.

Mikes, M. 1974.

Mikes, M. 1989.

Mikes, M. and Bulik. 1989.

Mikes, M, Lük and Jung. 1977.

Pizurica and Nedeljkovic. 1987.

Skutnabb-Kangas. 1990.

1981. *Yugoslavia*. Paris. 60

1990. Zakon o Univerzitetu. *Sluzbeni list SR Srbije*. Article 43: 173

1991. Federal Bureau of Statistics. *Reports*. No 015, Year XXXV

1991. *Serbo-Croat as a non-native language.*

Learning for Life

Editors' note

The references are incomplete, as it has proved impossible to contact the authors in the present situation.

Figure 1

Political-Territorial and Legal Basis for Education in the Autonomous Province of Vojvodina

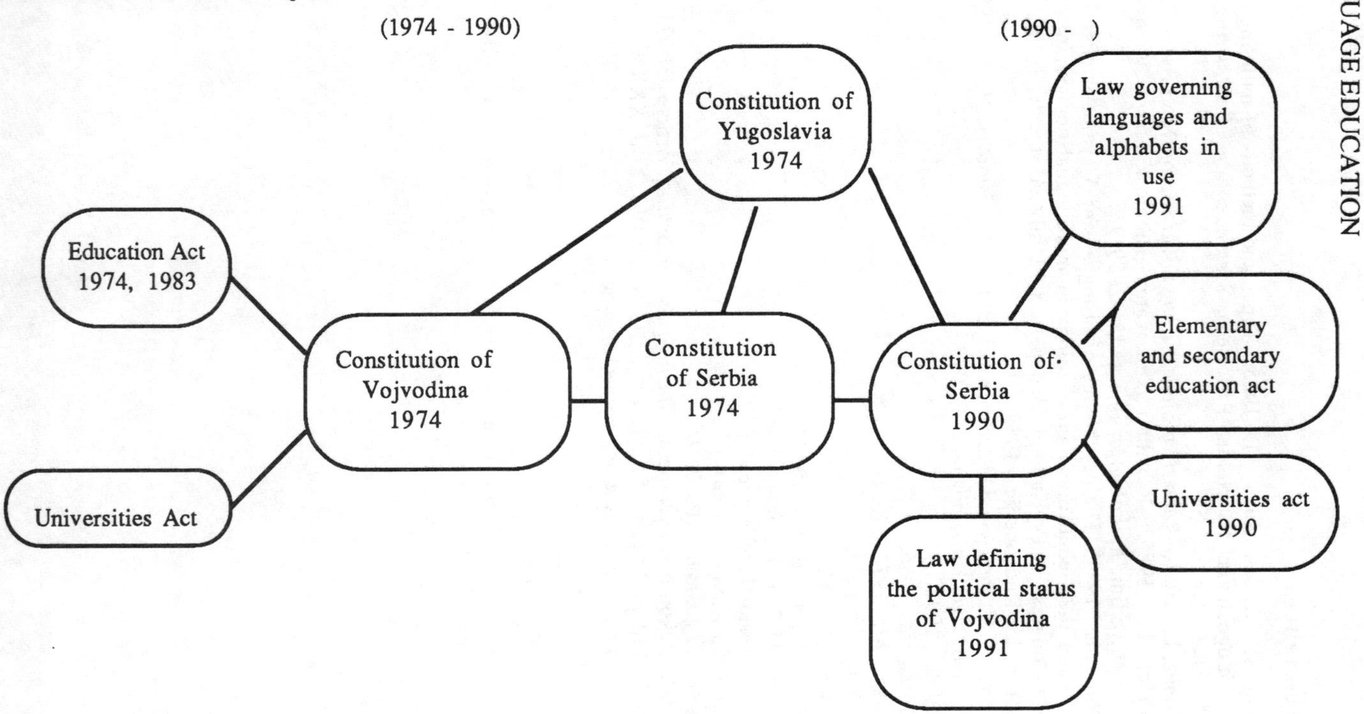

Figure 2
Education System in Vojvodina
(1990 -)

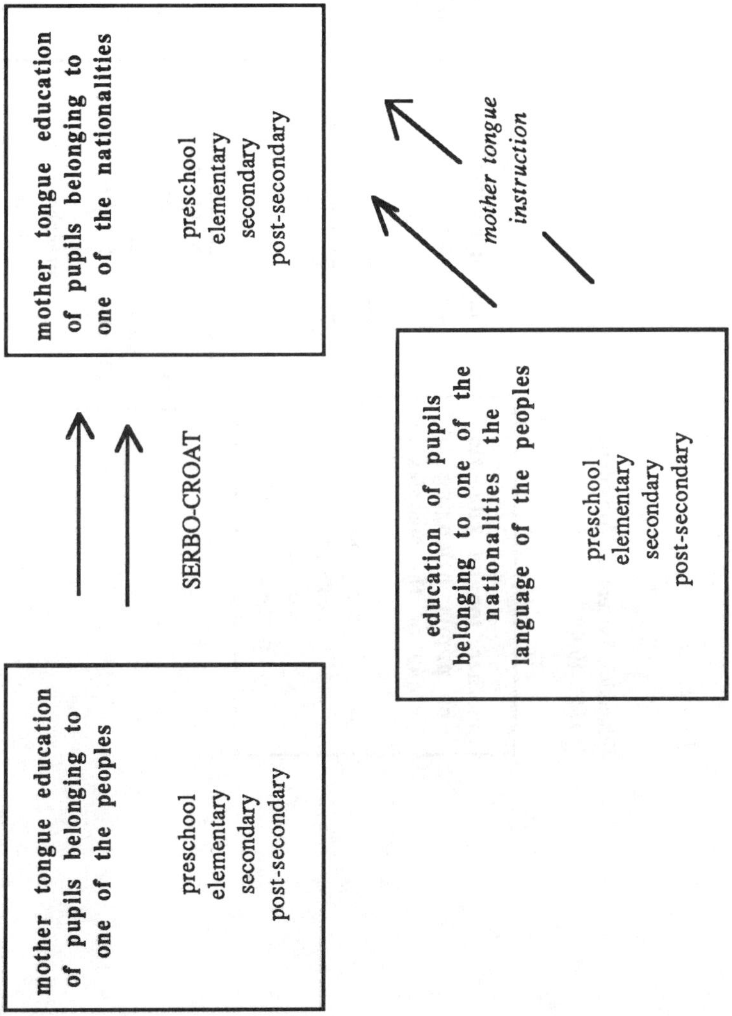

Figure 3

Education System in Vojvodina
(1974 - 1990)

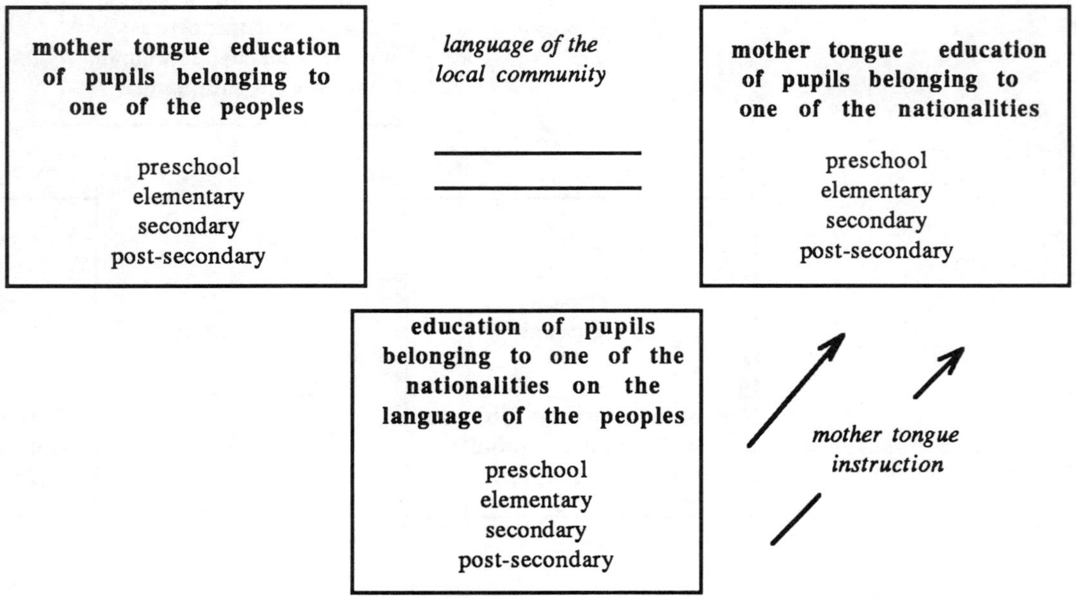

Table 1
Preschool Pupils Studying a Language of the Local Community

Vojvodina 1983		LANGUAGE OF THE LOCAL COMMUNITY									
Total number of:		Serbo-Croat		Hungarian		Slovak		Romanian		Ruthenian	
Classes	Pupils	Classes	Pupils	Classes	Pupils	Classes	Pupils	Classes	Pupils	Classes	Pupils
314	7999	198	5005	88	2434	17	494	9	21	2	45
Vojvodina 1985											
Total number of:		Serbo-Croat		Hungarian		Slovak		Romanian		Ruthenian	
Classes	Pupils	Classes	Pupils	Classes	Pupils	Classes	Pupils	Classes	Pupils	Classes	Pupils
512	12138	279	7039	208	4451	15	425	8	168	2	55

Table 2
Curriculum for Elementary School Education (1990-)

	Name of Subject	I wk	I yr	II wk	II yr	III wk	III yr	IV wk	IV yr	V wk	V yr	VI wk	VI yr	VII wk	VII yr	VIII wk	VIII yr
1	a) Serbo-Croat	5	190	5	190	5	190	5	190	5	190	4	148	4	144	4	136
	b) Serbo-Croat *	2	76	2	76	3	114	3	114	3	114	3	111	3	108	2	68
2	language **	5	190	5	190	5	190	5	190	5	190	4	148	4	144	4	136
3	Foreign Language	-	-	-	-	(2)	(7.6)	(2)	(7.6)	4	152	3	111	2	72	2	68
4	Art	2	76	2	76	2	76	2	76	2	76	1	37	1	36	1	34
5	Music	1	38	1	38	2	76	2	76	2	76	1	37	1	36	1	34
6	Nature & Society	2	76	2	76	2	76			-	-	-	-	-	-	-	-
7	Nature							2	76								-
8	Society							2	76								-
9	History	-	-	-	-	-	-	-	-	1	38	2	74	2	72	2	68
10	Geography	-	-	-	-	-	-	-	-	1	38	2	74	2	72	2	68
11	Physics	-	-	-	-	-	-	-	-	-	-	2	74	2	72	2	68
12	Mathematics	5	190	5	190	5	190	5	190	4	152	4	148	4	144	4	136
13	Biology	-	-	-	-	-	-	-	-	2	76	2	74	2	72	2	68
14	Chemistry	-	-	-	-	-	-	-	-	-	-	-	-	2	72	2	68
15	Technical Training	-	-	-	-	-	-	-	-	2	76	2	74	1+30	66	1+30	64
16	Physical Education	3	114	3	114	3	114	2	76	2	76	2	74	2	72	2	68
17	Home Economics	-	-	-	-	-	-	-	-	-	-	-	30	-	30	-	-
18	First Aid	-	-	-	-	-	-	-	-	-	-	-	-	-	-	-	30
	TOTAL	18	760	18	760	19	836	20	874	26	1036	25	1036	25	1008	25	918

*) For pupils receiving instruction in some other language of a people or nationality

**) Name of language of instruction in schools in which education is offered in one of the languages of the nationalities.

CONCLUSIONS

D. Ager, G. Muskens and S. Wright

The range of language-related situations and topics presented in the preceding chapters inevitably raises questions of power, of intergroup relationships, and of the affective attitudes of individuals, particularly insofar as all three impinge on the policy objectives and practice of governments. In this conclusion we examine some of the main themes arising from the discussions, and review some of the contrasts and similarities in policy, usually at national and governmental level; in practice, most often at regional or local level; and in individual attitudes. The present book clearly has implications for education, language planning, and policies towards ethnic groups; and for research projects and strategies relevant to the range of disciplines represented in these pages - language studies, education and the social sciences.

It is clear, too, that the presentation and discussion of specific national situations demonstrates both how balanced assessment of the data on matters so close to personal identities can be affected by the strength of the researcher's own affective attitude, and also how far the tools of research, in particular the accepted international terminology, are subject to constant reinterpretation in the light of the specific national or regional circumstances. Terms such as 'minority', 'identity', 'nation', 'state', 'republic', 'region' need redefinition in almost every single chapter, while the discrete and often dichotomised categories applied in language learning - such as 'foreign', 'second', 'native', 'mother' tongue - represent, in the reality of most multilingual States, overlapping generalities which need considerable elaboration to be meaningful.

Researchers commonly look for similarities with, and differences from, the situations with which they are most familiar. The juxtaposition of different world views has been very telling. Obviously there are similarities and differences between the national situations described here, but there are also parallels and contrasts in the treatments of the subjects. The contributors' choices and emphases reveal national priorities and preoccupations.

In pursuing contrasts and comparisions, insights from other situations are immensely helpful but at the same time misleading: intercultural education means quite different things in a German secondary school and a Bulgarian adult learners' class. Research methodologies are by now reasonably well established in the field, but it is clear that their implementation in different contexts - for example the interpretation of census data, or the bases for survey work - depends crucially on public debate and scientific exchange. In this context the lack of dialogue between Eastern and Central Europe and the rest of the world until recently means that there is much to do, for example in interpreting the applicability of theoretical approaches developed to aid understanding of immigration from the Third World towards wealthy countries, to situations in which multilingualism is traditional, and the problems lie rather in the desire to create territorial monolingualism and hence smaller political units where previously there were large, supranational and necessarily multilingual empires or federations.

Researchers, too, are inevitably part of their own society. Only two of our authors are not citizens of the area on which they report: Dennis Ager on France and Frank Knowles on the CIS. In both cases they tend to judge the data on which they report from a disciplinary perspective, but also from the perspective of another society. They have been helped in their task by consulting others, but it is inevitable that they may misrepresent - either too kindly or too severely - 'their' area.

Power

Political change

The new nationalisms sweeping Europe underline the breakdown of political organisation as we have known it since 1945, and the extent of the changes which have been brought about since 1989. The relationship between supra-national ideologies such as Communism and its political domination of individual Nations has changed, and with it the East-West dichotomy giving an impression of cross-national unity in organisations such as NATO based, as they were, on ideological opposition. The Nation State itself is under threat, particularly in countries like the former USSR, Yugoslavia or Belgium, where 'regional' aspirations to autonomy override what now seem mere groupings of political convenience. The strength of nationalist and ethnic feelings, of collective identity, has been demonstrated, often tragically. The growth of regionalism throughout Europe and its relationship to community identity markers such as language is indeed one of the major outcomes of the present volume.

Our review of the historical background to present-day national identites, minorities and ethnic conflict in the Introduction to the present volume underlines both how contemporary Europe is subject to its own, in many cases rediscovered, past, and yet how present generations reconceptualise the situations in which they find themselves in terms of uniquely modern pressures. For many commentators outside the relevant communities it is difficult to understand how severe and heart-felt these old and new pressures are: international outrage with what seems to be the senseless destruction of medieval towns and more importantly the seemingly wanton slaughter of whole communities is a natural but perhaps hypocritical reaction as new Nations and political relationships establish themselves. Few of the present European frontiers have been established by peaceful agreement between neighbours: most are the result of conflict. But the reality of socio-linguistic and educational research, and its connection with the underlying questions of identity and attitude, becomes startlingly clear today as communities establish their rights with gun and bomb.

The role of economics

The role of economics in this recreation of regimes and allegiances has been little explored here, except in relation to the UK, where attempts to impose foreign language learning in order to strengthen the European Community might have had deleterious effects on intercultural communication, and particularly in relation to the Netherlands where the techniques of large-scale surveys aimed at establishing real educational achievements throughout the population have identified enormous problems. For the Netherlands, too, the economic problem is crucial: the importance of language use to trade and commerce is underlined several times, and the necessity to ensure economic viability using all available communication techniques is clear to the researchers.

But perhaps less clear to Governments. And economic problems underlie, also, much of the discussion on reverse migration, mainly of Third World citizens to Europe from South to North but also from East to West. Germany, France and the UK are instances, where Government has been apparently happy to make use of immigrant labour to support economic boom, but appears less content to support the costs of the resultant internal diversity and cultural mix.

Territorialism

Prejudice, ideology and lack of contact have played their role differentially, whether in Belgium, Bulgaria, the former Soviet Union, Finland or Hungary, and the political consequences are fundamentally different in each case. While Belgium has moved to territorial solutions for ethno-linguistic conflict, and the continuing conflict in the former Yugoslavia demonstrates the attraction 'ownership' of territory still possesses for politics and politicians, increasing migration of peoples and their relocation across the territory of host communities indicates that simple correlations of territory with political organisation will not always hold good. Hence the continuing tensions between supranationalism, particularly in the development and broadening of the European Community, and regionalism resulting in the creation of ever smaller territorial entities.

Levels of analysis

Our considerations have underlined how necessary it is to keep the macro, meso and micro levels of political analysis separate. The macro level of States, governments, nations; of national policies in education including the curriculum; and of international factors such as cross-border migration or even temporary movement in response to economic pressure, such as prevails in Alsace, requires a different approach from that applicable to the meso level of local and regional authorities, local labour markets, individual schools and educational support systems, or the interpretation of national curricula in the practical circumstances of the school.

And the micro level of political analysis: teacher-pupil interaction, the role of parents in school governance, the motivation of individual learners as outlined in the Netherlands, requires close specification and a clear understanding of its relationship to conclusions drawn about the macro level. The levels come together, as for example in our chapter on Bulgaria, where whole nations are avid for contact and for new understanding of cultural models, and reflect individual aspirations and hopes.

Language and power

The role of language as unifying or boundary symbol in the creation and maintenance of power relationships, whether in the Nation State, or in the creation of new regional loyalties, is strongly evidenced in many of our contributions. The status relationships between 'languages of world-wide diffusion', 'national (or regional) languages', 'neighbour (and hence equal status) languages', 'minority languages', 'minority languages with differing status elsewhere' have consequences for the political structures of some countries and for the access enjoyed by the individual citizen to political rights.

Tosi (1984) points out that bilingualism can have two relationships to political control: language minorities may retain their bilingualism in order to retain control over their own destiny, but also bilingualism may be forced on them precisely because they have no control over their own destiny. Language education policies of Nation States necessarily reflect the distribution of power within the state, and the question of whether a language minority has access to education in and through its language provides a clear measurement of its power relationship with Government. In no country of Europe are Gypsy languages part of the educational scene: how far, and in what circumstances, the languages of immigrants figure within the educational policies of Governments varies with the numerical, and hence political, strength of the relevant group. And the languages of indigenous territorial minorities lie in a range of relationships with their majority governments, from resolute rejection to acceptance to enthusiastic support.

Lingua franca

Such status relationships may have consequences also for the role particular countries will be able to play on the international scene. Access to a new international lingua franca brings with it access to power in international relationships, and although the European situation is by no means clear yet, English, French and German are clearly at the moment in competition for such a new role. The rapid disappearance of Russian in this role, even within the former Soviet Union, indicates very clearly the differential force of push and pull factors - which might affect German, too, in some Eastern European countries. Clearly Russian is suffering from rejection of the ideology associated with it, and from the dominance its users exercised over satellite countries.

But status and ideology are not the only factors affecting the selection of a lingua franca: economic and affective factors also have a role to play. Economics clearly favours English, but also German in Eastern Europe, with French coming last (of the three); whereas affective factors in the area are negative for German and positive for French - and neutral for English. How far European countries are ensuring their language education policies respond to this competition, and the nature of the consequences in both politics and economics, is itself by no means clear. The poverty of some newly autonomous countries, their differential access to resources, means that international contact, exchanges of experts and researchers, and financial assistance are fundamental to enable them to implement rational and reasonable policies towards minorities or to prepare for their world role.

Linguistic insecurity

Linguistic insecurity is a term normally applied to those who use minority languages or dialects, and who consider them to be inferior in relation to a superior form or language: Quebec French in relation to both English and European French in the years before 1960, for example, or the reported attitudes of many dialect users who feel unsure about their own competence in the standard form; or the Finns and the Dutch who know their language is unlikely to be widely used outside their own country. But it may well be that the term should also apply to language users who feel that their language cannot express the full complexity of the life they lead, or that their own language abilities are insufficient to communicate fully their wants and desires, to influence others, or to describe their environment. For some language users, exemplified in the discussion on contemporary Bulgaria, self-esteem may be so low that individuals feel incompetent to learn foreign languages: a reversal of the reasons often proposed, that the learner is unable to learn because he sees little necessity to adopt a foreign language (the native English speaker) or regards foreign languages as uniformly inferior (the Japanese learner?).

Linguistic insecurity may well lead to tentativeness in policy, to uncertainty about which language to learn, which method to adopt, which way to turn. The phenomenon can be seen in other circumstances, too, when former linguistic complacency receives a shock: for example the case of France, where, since the world role of French is under attack from English, policy in language learning in the schools shifts from teaching English as part of general education to teaching it as a communicative necessity, and to asking which language to learn as second foreign language.

Linguistic insecurity may however also lead to very determined policies, to consciously defensive aggressiveness in language laws which exclude the minority, or to language laws which forcibly assimilate the minority. Parts of the former Yugoslavia seem to adopting approaches like these, and of course areas where languages have been in conflict for centuries provide other examples, the foremost among them being Belgium.

Affective Attitude

Underlying the specifics of community relationships are the attitudes, values and beliefs of individuals and groups. In the field we are concerned with here, questions of identity are fundamental and complex, and analysis of the associated affective attitudes is an absolute requirement in understanding specific policies and the type of actions which communities undertake. To take just three of the themes which emerge from the present contributions - racism, dominance and marginalisation, and interculturality - it is clear that any policy proposals, particularly in education, are vitiated if there is a lack of understanding of how the recipients of policy decisions understand and feel their situation.

How we feel about the people whose language we are learning directly affects success in language learning. Particularly in areas of language conflict, emotive attitudes towards languages remote from the immediate environment may dictate the choice of foreign language to study: an example is Finland, where Swedish may be necessary but 'unloved', while success in language learning may be more strongly visible for English, towards which emotive attitudes may be more positive, or even absent. Another example is the Netherlands, where logic dictates that foreign language learning should be more strongly directed towards German, but attitudinal characteristics indicate English.

Attitudes of dominance, and the consequential feelings of marginalisation and exclusion on the part of dominated groups, do not augur well for good inter-community relationships. It is easy to fall into simple dichotomies and to label rather than understand the complexity of such situations: 'racism' is sometimes a convenient shield and UK research on the negative effects of anti-racist policies at school level - which strengthened racism rather than reducing it - has demonstrated some of the dangers here. Similarly attitudes towards marginalised groups, particularly Gypsies, all too frequently descend into simple stereotypes. Furthermore, the example of France, a highly centralised country in every respect, but in which regional languages have survived over two centuries of continued marginalisation, leads to caution in assumptions that exclusion leads to extinction. Recent language policies in newly independent States may however give us pause for thought on this question; unfortunately, the consequences of ignoring research results in bilingualism and education may not be seen for a considerable time.

Another strong factor in language learning success is cultural distance. For most communities in Europe there is sufficient commonality of experience to prevent this being as major a feature of attitudes as it is in contrasts between Africa and Europe, or between Asia and Europe. But, nonetheless, it is of importance in treating community relationships in countries of high immigration from former colonies, such as France and Britain, or in countries where the national language has low international status and yet the nation has ambitions or the need to relate internationally. Whether intercultural education, with its deliberate attempt to understand the other, albeit from a deep understanding of one's own identity, will achieve a better and more coherent approach to acceptance of the multicutural nature of most if not all contemporary societies is open to research and review; on this point the present volume presents little evidence.

Policy and Practice

Educational Policy in foreign and second language learning

Experiences of immersion and submersion in language learning programmes bring in their train the problem of transferring the experiences of societies one to another. Experience derived from the United States, Canada or even one European country cannot easily be transferred to differing socio-economic contexts: this variable is fundamental.

It is a general point that a language chosen for study, whether for international communication or to support national identity, must have value for the individual in his specific circumstances: aspects of human rights, minority policies and respect for the growth of the personality are important in ensuring both that individuals feel committed to both foreign and second language learning and that they are not locked into language ghettoes by inappropriate educational choices. At the present time, and particularly in Eastern Europe, the choice of language for international communication is for example by no means clear. It has until recently been dictated mainly by political allegiance; at the present time considerable investment is being made in favour of English, whether of the UK or USA variety, and in favour of German.

The language chosen for study is also a problem for native English speakers, and for the French, who have a long history of defence of the status and prestige of their language. So the adoption of a new lingua franca for Europe will not be an easy question to resolve.

But language choice is often not a matter of equality. For many languages, even those of international communication, teachers and teaching materials may not be available, or not in sufficient quantities; teacher training may be lacking; the understanding of methods may depend on outmoded ideologies or educational philosophies.

And in education, above all, the 'consumers' should have a voice: parents have rights to influence the education of their children, and the rights of the individual to freedom of thought and to support for his own identity are enshrined in international agreements, not least in the Charter of the United Nations.

Choice of time to study is also important: for many contributors, early foreign and second language education is positively viewed, both from the point of view of effectiveness and also from that of efficiency: early learning should be both cheaper and more successful.

Ethno-national policy

The policy to adopt towards groups and communities, which may or may not be minorities, within the State, is often unclear and unevenly implemented. Policy statements piously promoting equality are not always implemented in practice, and the absence of publicly announced policy does not necessarily imply that practical actions are not coherently pursued. The reports from the former Yugoslavia show how language laws which on paper represent the most enlightened practice may fail to achieve a workable plurality, if the attitudes of groups and individuals are not won over to their support.

It appears right that citizens should be made aware of ethnolinguistic conflicts, particularly in relation to indigenous minorities and to migration. While States must take responsibility for the implementation of minority rights in education, they should also ensure that the majority is conscious of the complexity of its own society. And clearly intercultural education cannot be a one-way affair: it is as inappropriate that minorities should take the strain of understanding the majority without the reverse being the case, as it is that majorities should be pilloried for not making full provision for every minority no matter how small.

The policy choices open to linguistic minorities are always difficult, as are those States make, whether consciously or not, for their minorities. For France, Germany and England, and some other Western European countries, a choice has been made to provide education for the integration of immigrants, and this has in at least one case reversed the previous policy of reinsertion into the country of origin. For most countries represented here, the aim of policy is to create stability: to enable minorities to feel comfortable, but to retain the overriding democratic principle that the majority must decide. But stating a policy is not the same thing as providing the resources - the teachers, the learning materials, the training - to implement it.

There are clear dangers for the stability of the multilingual State in getting these policies wrong: fragmentation, discord and revolt may lead to disintegration, to the creation of ever smaller, but monolingual, political units. Examples of such instability are numerous in the present volume.

Language planning

The opportunities open to newly emergent ex-colonial nations in Africa and the Far East to plan their language policies: to decide which would be their official language, how far they would support rationalisation and codification of one dialect above others, to insist that importers deal in the national language, have not in general been available to newly emergent or newly autonomous European nations or regions. Now, however, such language planning decisions are being made in the Spanish Basque or Catalan provinces, and in a number of the areas discussed in the present volume. How far these policies will develop in the near future is unclear, but the Ukraine, new countries in the former Yugoslavia, and potentially even regions of France, may find themselves able to conduct official business in languages other than those they currently use.

In Belgium the development towards this point has been slow but consistent. In Wales the official use of Welsh is growing, although with little public discussion in the rest of the United Kingdom. In France the battle has been mainly around the use of regional languages and dialects in education.

Research policies and strategies

Some conclusions on research policies and strategies for the future emerge clearly from the contributions. First among these is the growing necessity of a contribution from the point of view of multilingualism, to a range of policy research, whether in education, politics or social questions. Conversely, the political, economic and social dimension cannot be excluded from research into multilingualism. Languages do not exist in a vacuum: their close relationship with their users and with the wider society within which the users exist is evident throughout the present work.

Research and researchers, too, have a duty to assess what really works and to identify the circumstances under which success, whether in education or aspects of policy, becomes possible. Much research in the field of multilingualism is undertaken against a background of received ideas: on the oppressive role of the school, on the primacy of protection of minorities' language use and cultural preferences or vice-versa, or on a misunderstanding of what is possible within the constraints of educational resources. Research based on the real world and devoted to problem-solving in practical contexts is at the moment much needed.

Practical topics and areas in which further research of practical value to the new Europe is clearly required include the nature of underlying educational and language philosophies, and their adaptation to present-day circumstances; curriculum development and assessment; initial teacher education and models of in-service training and support; individual differences in language learning; the development of support systems to encourage greater learner autonomy; and the efficiency and effectiveness of styles of course, school and departmental organisation.

In language studies, the whole question of the norm, of standardised and codified languages, and their relationship with dialectal variety is of major importance. As economic and technical developments gain in importance in countries formerly under the domination of one 'supplier', whether that be the former Soviet Union using Russian or the industrialist using international English, problems of terminology and technical nomenclature rise in importance, and language management becomes an important research topic. So too does the use and value of the norm in education, its role in ensuring educational experience and access to the spiritual and intellectual masterpieces of mankind

In social and political terms, observation of the fragmentation of contemporary Europe should not lead us to consider that nothing can be done, and that supranational or international communication strategies are no longer possible. Intercultural communication, and the education required to achieve it, takes place on a number of levels: those of the community, of the nation, but also internationally. If peace and cohesion are still prized as values, the central role language plays in ensuring them is clear throughout the present volume.

References

Tosi, A. 1984. *Immigration and bilingual education: a case study of movements of population, language change and education within the EEC*. Oxford: Pergamon.